Eccentric Britain

THE BRADT GUIDE TO
BRITAIN'S FOLLIES AND FOIBLES

Acknowledgements

With thanks to all those whom I have interviewed or contacted for help with my assurance that the term eccentric in my mind carries no necessarily pejorative judgment (as in barmy, folly) but almost always a compliment (as in exceptional, fascinating, intriguing); to those surprisingly helpful local officials, tourist information officers, heritage bodies, etc, who have explained the inexplicable with great patience; to my publishers and their hard-working illustrators, map makers, etc, who immediately and enthusiastically saw the potential of a rather unorthodox book; to Jill Donachy and Richard Mcdonald who provided heaps of information as well as excellent pictures of the Burry man; to my family for enduring countless diversions to check on this or that monument or obelisk while supposedly on holiday; and to the Devon author who always intended to write a book perhaps like this (I have recently been told) but never quite got round to it. I hope this book measures up.

FOR KATHRYN MARY

TRAVEL INFORMATION
Practical details of getting to a specific festival or place mentioned in the text, together with relevant phone numbers, are given at the end of each chapter.

Eccentric Britain

THE BRADT GUIDE
TO BRITAIN'S FOLLIES AND FOIBLES

Benedict le Vay

Foreword by Nigel Dempster

Bradt Publications, UK
The Globe Pequot Press Inc, USA

First published in 2000 by Bradt Publications,
19 High Street, Chalfont St Peter, Bucks SL9 9QE, England
www.bradt-travelguides.com
Published in the USA by The Globe Pequot Press Inc, 246 Goose Lane,
PO Box 480, Guilford, Connecticut 06475-0480

British Library Cataloguing in Publication Data
A catalogue record for this book is available from the British Library
ISBN 1 84162 011 4

Library of Congress Cataloging-in-Publication Data
Le Vay, Benedict
Eccentric Britain : the Bradt guide to Britain's follies and foibles
/ Benedict Le Vay ; foreword by Nigel Dempster.
    p. cm.
Includes bibliographical references and index.
ISBN 1-84162-011-4
    1. Eccentrics and eccentricities—Great Britain—Guidebooks.
    2. Curiosities and wonders—Great Britain—Guidebooks. 3.
    Great Britain—Guidebooks. I. Title.
DA650.L394 2000
914.104'859—dc21
                                                        99-088559

Photographs
Front cover: Rob Judges
Back cover: Burry man (Richard Mcdonald)
Text: Ffotograf: Charles Aithie (CA), Patricia Aithie (PA); Alan Lavender/Folly
Fellowship (AL); Benedict le Vay (BL); Richard Mcdonald (RM); Still Moving Pic
Co: G Burns (GB), David Robertson (DR), STB; Phil Vincent (PV)

Illustrations Jo Stearn
Maps Alan Whitaker

Typeset from the author's disc by Wakewing, High Wycombe
Printed and bound in Italy by LegoPrint SpA, Trento

Foreword

Newspaper columnists in other parts of the world may well put a spin on characters and events to make them a better story. Happily I write for a British newspaper and find the people I encounter on a daily basis don't need journalistic embellishment.

In fact the opposite is often the case – if I published everything I knew about some people I would not be believed, such are the eccentricities of certain Britons. It is this strange cocktail of odd people, bizarre customs, almost inexplicable rituals, the follies of rich and poor, extraordinary places and buildings that Ben le Vay has captured in this book, somehow cataloguing people and events who defy categorisation.

One thing is certain: without understanding eccentricity, no one can claim to understand the British.

Nigel Dempster

Contents

'Eccentricity has abounded when and where strength of character has abounded; and the amount of eccentricity in a society has generally been proportional to the amount of genius, mental vigour and moral courage which it contained.'

John Stuart Mill, *On Liberty*, 1859

Preface

How did this book come about? It all started with my job as a sub-editor at the *Daily Mail*, London, where I work on other people's reports of goings-on from around the world. From time to time, thanks to indulgent bosses (or too busy ones, more likely) I would be allowed to slip a paragraph into odd corners of features pages about things that struck me as curious – why vicars preach on horseback to a mounted congregation, the strange castellated house above a railway tunnel, the traffic cone collector, the bizarre cheese-rolling, black pudding throwing, coal-carrying, gate-smashing contests – in short, the eccentricities of Britain, past and present.

It was not part of my job, exasperated bosses would point out – strictly it was someone else's remit – but letters started to pour in offering information, or asking for more, and asking if there was a book of such anecdotes.

There wasn't. There were old books about past eccentrics, but none with a comprehensive guide to present-day oddities in terms of bizarre buildings, unbelievable customs, strange rituals, daft sports, etc that you can visit, witness or endure. Tourist guides sometimes touch on strange festivals, but offer no background or depth in this fascinating field, leaving the reader dissatisfied and of course they exclude Britain's great store of private or past eccentrics. Thus they miss out on much that is fascinating or amusing.

So, five years later, here is the complete guide to both the ongoing eccentricities and history of Britain's oddest eccentrics, and reportage of strange private goings-on and interviews with the peculiar people involved. It is eccentric in that it is neither pure travelogue nor pure description, tackling subjects in themes rather than as a geographical tour. Thus you will find, for example, all Britain's weird pyramids discussed together, not in separate county chapters.

This makes the book far more readable and the breadth of the subject is such that there is something there to fascinate, amuse or intrigue everyone. Many of the eccentric places, things or customs described do not need to be visited to appreciate their peculiarities; but to make the book more useful as a guide to some of the places which can be visited, I have included maps for each chapter, a county-by-county index, itineraries for eccentric days out, and a calendar of strange events in Britain throughout the year.

Did I say complete guide? Of course it is not. There will be some deadly serious strange rituals and follies which need to be added, and others, sadly, may drop out of use. Drop me a line so I can update the book. It'll keep me out of my boss's hair.

Introduction

WHAT IS A GENUINE ECCENTRIC?

To the world-weary traveller, the global village means a McDonald's sameness being inflicted everywhere, the jumbo jet wheel smoothing out the bumps in cultures, making everything universally bland. Today, someone wearing branded American cowboy denims, Korean plastic trainers and an Italian T-shirt could equally be in Düsseldorf, Detroit or Danang. And yet the British – particularly, but not exclusively, the English – eccentric has proved peculiarly resistant to this process, thank God.

True eccentrics don't think of themselves as such. They know they are reasonable and it is the rest of the world which is bizarre. They are usually loners, experts say. The top eccentric academic, Edinburgh's Dr David Weeks, says eccentrics even live longer because they are saner and happier than the rest of us. He has come up with a figure of one in 10,000 Brits being eccentric.

A genuine eccentric does not consciously adopt an odd style or mode of behaviour for effect. Students doing a sponsored pogo-stick over the Andes wouldn't qualify, and neither do young fogies, punks, or others adopting what is merely a different kind of uniform. True eccentrics think it is not at all remarkable to take a plastic lobster for a walk on a string, as Dr Weeks says one Edinburgh lady does – Oscar Wilde, after all, once did the same with a friend and a real lobster in the Strand. Years later, the eccentric millionaire Sir 'Union' Jack Hayward (who saved Lundy Island and the SS *Great Britain* for the nation) took a goat as his guest to a cocktail party.

But what about today's Britain? Is it hard to find the genuine eccentric? Made-for-media figures with eccentric dress, gait, speech or hairdo may not be genuinely eccentric – some sort of vague wackiness is *de rigueur* nowadays to keep the jaded, TV-soaked public tuned in. Equally, entrants for Mr

Loonyverse, members of the Eccentrics' Club, or guests at the Odd Ball, will probably not be the instinctive eccentric. A true eccentric thinks himself entirely normal and wouldn't dream of joining such a group, although one such group, the Idiots' Club which met in recent years at the French House in Soho's Dean Street, was laudable if only because its founder, calling himself Baron Peter de Massenbach, greeted potential members with 'An idiot, I presume'.

The same caveat applies to defining the quintessentially eccentric building, the folly. A rich person such as Lord McAlpine putting up a self-declared folly in recent years is amusing, but not quite pukkah. The truly eccentric landowner must think the structure eminently sensible and useful; it is for others to judge it, preferably universally, a patently useless folly. If it performs a real function, it's not one hundred per cent a folly.

Of course, being rich helps ensure that there will be lasting testimony to your eccentricities – in the form of follies, or whatever – but less concrete manifestations of oddness such as giving your children peculiar names are open to us all. Thus celebrity consort of pop stars Paula Yates may have named her children Fifi Trixibelle, Peaches Honeyblossom, and Pixie, plus, best of the lot, Heavenly Hiraani Tiger Lily; but, to take one example of so many, less well-known Gloucester butterfly buff Matthew Oates and his equally entomologically minded wife Sally named their children Euphrosyne, Lucina, Camilla and Arion (Latin names for their favourite pearl-bordered fritillary, Duke of Burgundy, white admiral and large blue butterflies respectively).

Eccentricity was exported the world over during Britain's imperial heyday. In many a scorching tropical outpost, only mad Englishmen and mad dogs went out in the midday sun, as Noel Coward nearly wrote. The image of Englishmen – dressed in full uniform for dinner in the steaming African jungle – lives on in films of the era. The British went 'troppo' in a big way, as their brains cooked in the heat, with a liberal intake of sundowners and Singapore slings, and the Empire reeked with eccentricity.

In fact the odder you were, the further you were likely to go – in seniority and geographically – because you had less chance of making headway at home in Britain. This is certainly true of oddballs like the extraordinary Gottlieb Leitner, German by birth but British by adoption, who left a puzzling mosque in the middle of middle-class Surrey as his monument, or the explorer Richard Burton, who was laid to rest in a full-scale Arab tent – in suburban London (they are both detailed in Chapter 5).

There was Our Man in Calcutta, Sir Richard Strachey, who lived out his retirement in English suburbia respecting only Indian time. Or the Calcutta judge who built mad Mogul towers in deepest Hampshire retirement (see Chapter 11). Or the general who addressed his troops in Burma stark naked. He may have approached that fine line between delightfully dotty and frankly funny-farm barking, of course, and many a colonial crossed it. And it was also in Burma that the Roedean-educated Ursula Graham Bower, born in 1914, became the 'Queen of the Nagas', a tribe of headhunters whom she fearlessly led into battle to decapitate the invading Japanese during World War II. She

had gone to the area in 1937 to study the tribes – which under previous British influence had almost entirely dropped their interesting habit of presenting a human head to females with whom one wished to mate – when the Japanese invaded. She organised a fearsome army of headhunting Nagas, using looted Japanese arms as well as spears. Their dominance of the mountain passes helped keep the Japanese out of India – a turning point in that war's history. In fact, the Japanese made a point of keeping as clear as possible of the areas she ruled, while she ensured Allied airmen could escape back to India – except on the odd occasion when her men decapitated them by mistake.

British eccentricity in the form of mad inventors and single-minded obsessives was the spring which nourished the industrial revolution and the vast Empire – while the same eccentric ideas provide the drive for today's world-leading music industry, where off-the-wall wackiness is sometimes backed with a hunch that brings in millions after millions of pounds.

It isn't, of course, politically correct to believe there are differences in national character. But while the Japanese and Germans are excellent – yes, often better – engineers and manufacturers, where did the ideas of radar, jet engines, television, hovercraft, radio and steam trains come from, to name a brilliant few? To put it another way, name 20 top German or Japanese pop groups – or 20 great comedians, for that matter, for humour is surely another creative facet of the same flawed gem. Take off-the-wall ideas such as the *Carry On* films, Monty Python, Basil Fawlty, Mr Bean (even the inventions of Edward Lear and Lewis Carroll, to go further back). No sane person would back such concepts with hard cash, yet sometimes, just sometimes, they turn out to be world-beaters.

Talking of Mr Bean, there's a total eccentric in south Wales called Barry Kirk – or Captain Beany from the planet Beanus, as he also likes to be known – who is rather keen on beans. Captain Beany, who spends his leisure time dressed as a baked bean, was fined £140 by Port Talbot magistrates in 1998 after driving for eight months with a Heinz baked bean label on his windscreen instead of a tax disc. 'It looked rather nice. No one noticed the difference for ages', he was reported as saying. When dressing as Captain Beanus he wears a red cape and tights and paints his bald head bean colour. His VW Beetle car is also painted beany orange, and his obsession with the flatulence-generating tomato-sauce covered navy bean started when he had to sit in a bath of them for charity. Since then he's eaten them every day.

Another relevant facet of the British psyche is a kind of bloody-minded, stubborn resistance to change that could be called endearingly daft. For example, in the 1960s it was decided that on Britain's railways the small branch lines would have to go, and steam engines too, with the entire stock being sent to scrapyards by 1968. So what's happened 30 years later? On any summer weekend you can find 100 privately run branch lines with the lovingly restored steam monsters of yesteryear, rescued from scrapyards, South African mines, Greek factories, Javanese sugar plantations or wherever, chuffing along over tracks rebuilt by an army of 100,000 unpaid enthusiasts. Barmy, but splendid.

The same applies to real ale. In the late 1970s the big breweries such as Watneys decided to demolish the small breweries producing live ale made the old-fashioned way, and force drinkers to down the ghastly fake fizzy product produced in places looking like oil refineries. I remember visiting a pub in St Albans, Hertfordshire, which was the only one left in the town still serving the real thing. Then the British people awoke to what was happening. Ten years later we celebrated the last of St Albans' 95 pubs changing back to the real McCoy; the big breweries were so ashamed they had to stop selling beer under their own names and re-open small breweries. This is the admirable bloody-mindedness that keeps so many odd habits and outwardly daft customs alive in the face of Euro-conformity.

Nowhere is this more the case than in local government. Why, half a century after the county of Middlesex was abolished, are there still new 'Welcome to Middlesex' signs, a Middlesex Hospital, University, and Cricket Club? And why do more than a million people still put Middlesex at the end of their addresses? It's the kind of stubbornness which forced the government to reinstate tiny counties such as Rutland after two decades when people refused to admit it had been abolished. It makes no sense, unless you're British.

There are eccentrics at all levels of British society. We even have a suitably eccentric king to come in the new millennium – Prince Charles, for all his other problems, at least talks to plants, meditates in the Kalahari desert, does Goon impersonations, dabbles in alternative medicine and wears Arab dress in Gloucestershire. Good for him.

The late Screaming Lord Sutch

Politically, what other country would field Monster Raving Loony Party candidates at most elections? Three Raving Loony councillors were even elected, although in 1997 one defected to the Tories, whatever that said about his insanity. Even the choice of England's patron saint is downright eccentric – on April 23, the English celebrate St George, an obscure Palestinian, famed for slaying somewhere else an animal that didn't exist.

Britain also retains the myriad odd, very peculiar ceremonies and customs which visitors can still watch with disbelief and which this book sets out to detail. Some are beyond rational explanation and almost all are carried out with the utmost seriousness.

Most official British customs are nonsensical to the outsider, and even sometimes to the insider. For example, outside radio broadcast vans go to great trouble every November 11 to broadcast two minutes' silence (not last year's silence, mind, which they could easily repeat). We have a monarchy which has built the highest order of knights in Britain's chivalry on a humble undergarment – the Order of the Garter. Then there are about 900 plays, 100 of them professional, every winter where the principal boy must be played by a girl, the leading lady must be a man and not one of the stories must ever be at all original. I refer, of course, to the great British pantomime.

So the suggestion that the British reputation for eccentricity is waning might be premature, if hard to define. Perhaps outsiders can identify it best. When the somewhat manic explorer John 'Blashers' Blashford-Snell (see Chapter 2) of the Royal Engineers struggled ashore with his ragged party after descending the White Nile, an American onlooker was heard to intone to her husband: 'Gee, these guys must be crazy.' He responded: 'Hush, dear, they're only British.'

For the true barmy Brit, it's all understood – and understated. In 1997 Miss Debi Reader from Manchester was attempting to beat Briton Ffyona Campbell's record set nine years earlier for walking across Australia, baking empty deserts and all, in 95 days. Just two days before she finished, Miss Reader was astonished to hear that another walker, Craig Brown, had at that moment beaten her to it. Her response was quoted as: 'My first reaction was astonishment that anyone else would be stupid enough to attempt it. But then we realised he was British, so it made more sense.' Or is it less...?

Part One

Eccentric Things We Do

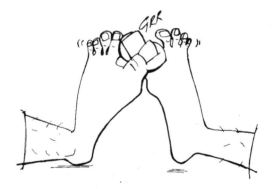

ATLANTIC OCEAN

Orkney Islands

Uppies & Doonies, Kirkwall

Thurso

Orkney & Shetland Is

Shetland Islands

Up Helly Aa, Lerwick

N

Orkney Islands

Uppies & Doonies, Kirkwall

scale as main map

Isle of Lewis

Outer Hebrides

Isle of Skye

Inner Hebrides

Island of Mull

Inverness

Burning the Clavie, Burghead

Aberdeen

Stonehaven Fireball Ceremony

Flambeaux Procession, Comrie

N o r t h   S e a

Burry Man Festival, South Queensferry

Glasgow

Islay

Arran

Edinburgh

Tweedmouth Feast, Berwick-upon-Tweed

Ne'erday Bonfire, Biggar

Selkirk Common Riding

Hoppings, Newcastle upon Tyne

Carlisle

Allendale Guizers

Gurning, Egremont

Middlesbrough

Isle of Man

Great Finborough

Burning of Owd Bartle, West Witton

York

Viking Longboat Races, Peel

Bradford

Kingston-upon-Hull

Irish Sea

Tram Sunday, Fleetwood

Bacup Nutters Dance

Leeds

World Coal Carrying Championship, Ossett

Black Pudding Throwing, Ramsbottom

Manchester

Anglesey

Liverpool

Garland Day, Castleton

Sheffield

Haxey Hood & Sway

Holyhead

Toe Wrestling, Wetton

Well Dressing, Tissington

Royal Shrovetide Football, Ashbourne

Goose Fair, Nottingham

0 ——— 100km
0 ——— 60 miles

Well Dressing, Newborough

Derby

Norwich

Wolverhampton

Conker Championships, Oundle

Cardigan Bay

Birmingham

Cheese Rolling, Stilton

Race of Bogmen,

Bog Snorkelling, Llanwrtyd Wells

Coventry

Hare Pie Scramble, Hallaton

Cambridge

Ipswich

Coracle Racing, Cilgerran

Olney Pancake Race

Fishguard

Cheese Rolling, Brockworth

May Day Frolics & St Giles' Fair, Oxford

Beca Mountain Race

Swansea

LONDON

Oyster Ceremony Whitstable

Cardiff

Bristol Channel

Bristol

Reading

Garter Ceremony, Windsor

Dover

World Marbles Championships, Tinsley Green

Hunting the Earl of Rone, Combe Martin

Chili Fiesta, West Dean

Robertsbridge bonfire

Battle bonfire

Day of Syn & RHD Railway, New Romney

Barnstaple Fair

Southampton

Portsmouth

Lewes bonfire societies

Blessing the Sea, Hastings

Exeter

Blazing barrels, Ottery St Mary

I. of Wight

Bognor Birdman

Garlic Festival

Padstow 'Obby 'Os

Hurling the Silver Ball, St Columb Major

Blessing the Lifeboat, Brixham

Hurling the Silver Ball, St Ives

Worm Charming, Blackawton

Penzance

E n g l i s h   C h a n n e l

Furry Dance, Helston

Tom Bawcock's Eve, Mousehole

ECCENTRIC YEAR

The Eccentric Year

Week by week, the strangest customs of Britain unfold, few of them behind locked doors. This is your guide, the most comprehensive yet produced, to when and where to find the bizarre and inexplicable – to where the unexpected can be expected. As events and venues can change over the years, you should check with tourist information centres in towns concerned before making long journeys.

JANUARY

January 1

Mudathon	200yd dash in often icy conditions through waist-deep oozing mud, Blackwater River, Maldon, Essex.
New Year's Dip	In near-freezing North Sea, Whitley Bay, Tyne & Wear. Often includes over-70s in age, never in temperature.
Uppies and Doonies	Kirkwall, Orkney Islands. A massive 200-a-side communal scrum lasting four hours (see box, page 7). Also December 25.

January 6

Christmas Day	On Fair Isle, between Orkney and Shetlands.

January 6 (or 5 if 6 is Sunday)

Haxey Hood Game	Ancient, oddly chivalrous, colourful village scrum, Haxey, Lincolnshire (see page 4).

January 6 (or nearest Saturday)

Orchard Wassail	Apple trees wassailed with cider by a wassail queen; ancient dances to ensure fertility of apple crop; mummers' play. Evening, outside Victoria & Albert Inn, Stoke Gabriel, near Totnes, Devon.

January 11

Burning the Clavie	Street conflagration, Burghead, Morayshire (see *Biggar Eccentrics*, page 28).

THE CHIVALROUS ORIGINS OF HOODS AND BOGGANS

In Prohibition-era Chicago, the term 'hood' referred to gangs of ruffians who played by their own rules and chased a moll's skirt now and then. In Haxey, Lincolnshire, each January 6 (or 5th if 6th is a Sunday) the term hood refers to a gang of ruffians who play by their own rules and chase an item of lady's clothing – a hood, to be precise.

There the similarity falls down, as do many of the participants in this, another example of ancient inter-village scrummaging.

It's all due to Lady de Mowbray who, riding near Haxey some 700 years ago, lost her hood to a mischievous gust of wind. Thirteen gallant farm workers took part in a muddy race across the ploughed fields to regain the item, the one who caught it being too shy to bring it back and another returning it with exaggerated courtesy. This so amused her ladyship that she donated a piece of land so the drama could be re-enacted annually.

The land – Hoodlands – is 13 half-acres in memory of the 13 farm workers, the characters of those who returned the hood perhaps being recalled by the Fool and the Lord. There are also 13 colourfully dressed Boggans who assemble with the throng at the old village cross near Haxey Church at 15.00 on this, the old calendar's Christmas Day.

The Fool makes a speech urging playing by the unspoken rules but is smoked from his position by a pile of burning straw. (Once in living memory the Fool had to be extinguished.)

The Lord or King Boggan with his wand of 13 willows leads the crowd to the 13 half-acres where 13 sacking hoods are thrown in the air so people can attempt to get them past the Boggans.

Then the real game begins with the Sway Hood, made of rope bound with leather. This is a mass inter-village game with the goals being the pubs in either Westwoodside or Haxey. As in the similar Shrove Tuesday games at Ashbourne, Derbyshire and elsewhere, the Haxey Sway has been known to flatten fences and stone walls, rampage through homes and splinter trees, but unlike the hoods of Chicago, those left on the ground can stand up and cheerfully join in again. Usually.

Friday and Saturday before Plough Monday (first Monday after Twelfth Night, 12 days after Christmas)

Straw Bear Festival
A gruesome figure of straw followed by sword dancers cavorts through the streets, ending with burning the bear on the Saturday night. Whittlesey, Cambridgeshire.

January 14

Hunting the Mallard
Ceremony

Bizarre official hunt across the rooftops, singing
the ancient Mallard song and carrying lanterns, at
All Souls College, Oxford, where a great mallard
duck was found hiding when the college was being
built in 1437. The whole building is searched from
roofs to cellars. The hunt takes place all night,
once every 100 years (2001, 2101 etc).

January 17

Wassailing the Apple
Tree

Traditional singing to apple trees, putting cider-
soaked toast in branches and firing shotguns in
the air over them to ensure a good crop.
Carhampton, Somerset.

Last Tuesday in January

Up Helly Aa

(Includes burning Viking boat) Lerwick, Shetland,
19.30 on (see *Biggar Eccentrics*, page 28).

Late January

Dicing for Maids
Money

Old charity, Guildford Guild Hall, Surrey (see
Chapter 3).

FEBRUARY

February 2

Carlow Bread Dole

Woodbridge, Suffolk (see Chapter 11). First
Monday after February 3 but not February 3. Not
always held.

Hurling the Silver Ball

St Ives, Cornwall, 10.30. An ancient mass rugby
game (see section on Shrove Tuesday).

Shrove Tuesday (variable, according to when Easter falls)

See box page 6–7 for details

Royal Shrovetide Football Ashbourne, Derbyshire, 14.00.

Shrovetide Football   Atherstone, Warwickshire, 15.00.

Hurling the Silver Ball   St Columb Major, Newquay, Cornwall, 16.30;
                           and St Ives, Cornwall (see *February 2*).

Shrovetide Football   Sedgefield, Darlington, 13.00.

Shrovetide Football   Alnwick, Northumberland, 13.00 or later.

Marblers' and   Corfe Castle, Dorset, noon.
Stonecutters' Apprentices'
Conclave and Football

Pancake Bell and Skipping Scarborough, Yorkshire, noon.

The Original Pancake   Olney, Buckinghamshire, Winster, Derbyshire,
Race   and many country villages.

TOSSING PANCAKES? YOU HAVEN'T SEEN THE HURLING

Shrove Tuesday, any schoolchild will tell you, is Pancake Day.

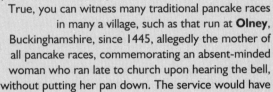

True, you can witness many traditional pancake races in many a village, such as that run at **Olney**, Buckinghamshire, since 1445, allegedly the mother of all pancake races, commemorating an absent-minded woman who ran late to church upon hearing the bell, without putting her pan down. The service would have been a shriving, or blessing to help the faithful through the Lenten fast until Easter: hence Shrove Tuesday. Rich foods would have been used up, hence the pancakes and the name used elsewhere, Mardi Gras, meaning Fat Tuesday.

The Olney Pancake Race starts at the marketplace and still ends at the church, where the winner gets a prayer book and a kiss from a verger. In **Toddington**, Bedfordshire, children climb Conger Hill and lie with their ears to the ground to listen for the witch frying her pancakes as the clock strikes noon (the midday bell itself being a recurrent feature of ancient Shrove Tuesday customs). An equally ancient pancake race runs at **Winster**, Derbyshire, but don't eat any titbits that fall from the pans. These are special racing pancakes made for toughness.

Many more weird and wonderful things happen on Shrove Tuesday than the odd bit of egg on face. Much of it seems to involve spectacular screaming scrums of muddy men instead of women in aprons.

At **Ashbourne** in Derbyshire, for instance, there's the Royal Shrovetide Football game between the Up'ards and Down'ards, defined as people living on opposite sides of Henmore Brook, along whose course the riotous game, starting with the ball being 'turned up' at 14.00 on Shrove Tuesday (and again on Ash Wednesday), runs back and forth until well into the evening. The ball for each day is beautifully made from leather stuffed with cork and painted with scenes relevant to that year's 'turner-up'. Those won on each day become prized family heirlooms. The goals are three miles apart at Sturston and Clifton and the shops are all boarded up against damage as 'the hug', as it is called locally, heaves back and forth. Trees are split, fences flattened, and washing poles uprooted. No one knows what started it all.

In **Atherstone**, near Nuneaton, Warwickshire, another great scrummage of a Shrovetide football game starts with the ball being thrown from the upstairs of Barclays Bank, and the main road is closed for the game. No one knows exactly why, but here the ball can be water-filled, although the water can be let out as darkness falls to speed things up.

The raucous scenes are somewhat similar at **St Columb Major** near

Newquay in Cornwall at 16.30 on Shrove Tuesday, when the game called Hurling the Silver Ball starts. With the Townsmen versus the Countrymen, and up to 300 a side, the fast-running game can degenerate into a huge heaving scrum from which the £200 silver ball can be smuggled out to 'lie luff' under a hedge until the chance arises to go for one of the goals – stone troughs two miles apart.

Again the shops are boarded up – 'You'd think the Hezbollah were coming through,' said enthusiast Ivan Rabey – and with the pitch being the entire parish, the game makes the Guinness Books of Records for having the largest playing area. The game was already old by the reign of Queen Elizabeth I. Its origins? 'No one really knows,' said Rabey. 'Maybe it's from some pagan rite to do with the coming of spring and fertility.' Similarly huge scrummages take place on massive pitches at **Sedgefield** near Darlington at 13.00, and at **Alnwick** in Northumberland where the Duke of Northumberland's piper leads the ball on to the pitch, usually at 14.30. The goals are a quarter-mile apart and each team is 150 strong.

A similar mass football game to the Ashbourne one takes place at **Workington**, Cumbria, on Good Friday, and also shortly after Easter – usually the next Saturday and one other day. Hailing the Ball involves a specially made coloured ball being thrown up at the Cloffocks car park and two huge teams, the Uppies and Downies, heaving up and down to get the ball their side of the River Derwent. At **Jedburgh**, Borders, its Uppies and Doonies is held a couple of weeks earlier, but it's all basically the same game, as is the Orkney Islands' version at **Kirkwall** on Christmas Day and New Year's Day.

Near **St Ives**, Cornwall, another Hurling the Silver Ball takes place on the Monday nearest February 3, but not on February 3. It is thrown by the mayor some time after 09.30 and it is passed, not hurled, from person to person over the whole town; whoever is holding it at noon wins a crown coin. At one time, the sides were selected as simply anyone called John, William or Thomas against the rest of the world.

Very different is the ritual at **Corfe Castle**, Dorset, where at noon on Shrove Tuesday those who have completed quarrying apprenticeships must carry a quart of beer, a penny loaf and the equivalent of 6 shillings and 8 pence to the town hall for the solemn conclave of the Ancient Order of Purbeck Marblers and Stonecutters. They then kick a football all round the town and carry a pound of pepper – why pepper, no one really knows – down to Ower Quay in Poole Harbour to mark their right to carry stone there.

A more elegant form of exercise is undertaken at **Scarborough**, Yorkshire, where, when the Pancake Bell is rung at noon, the town takes to the South Foreshore for skipping in great lines with long ropes, plus a few pancake races. The bell is a remnant of that once-common old shriving bell. But why skipping? A tourism official said: 'Well, it's been going on for at least 200 years, and it helps get an appetite up for pancakes, but the truth is, no one knows.'

Ash Wednesday (day after Shrove Tuesday)
Start of Marbles Season

Late February (Saturday of second weekend of half-term)

Moonraking Festival	Giant paper moon is floated on canal, raked out by a team of women in memory of a smuggling legend (see pub names, chapter 9), then carried round village by 'gnomes' in a procession bearing hundreds of home-made lamps. Canal End, Slaithwaite, near Huddersfield, West Yorkshire, around 18.30.

MARCH
March 1

Whuppity Scourie	Odd race round church, Lanark (see Chapter 6).

Third Thursday

Kiplingcotes Derby	Near Market Weighton, Humberside. Britain's oldest and oddest race (see Chapter 2).

March 21

Druids meet	In Tower Hill, London, to celebrate spring equinox.

March 25 (Lady Day)

Tichborne Dole	Tichborne, Alresford, Hampshire, about 14.00 (see Chapter 3).

APRIL
April 1 (All Fools' Day)
See box opposite

April 5 (approx) every third year (2002, 2005 etc)

Changing of the Quill	Learned address to statue of 16th-century historian John Stow, including changing the pen in his hand by the Lord Mayor of London, Church of St Andrew Undershaft, London EC3.

First Tuesday after 6th (old calendar's Lady Day, see March 25)

Candle Auction	At Tatworth, near Chard, Somerset. Stowell Court meets behind locked doors to hear bids for renting watercress bed, watercress and bread eaten; last bid before candle goes out wins. (For auctions in Berkshire, Lincolnshire and Yorkshire, see Chapter 3)

ALL FOOLS' DAY

The best April Fool ever perpetrated was April 1 1698 and made a laughing stock of the gentry of London, great numbers of whom turned up in their carriages and finery at the Tower of London to 'see the lions being washed' as instructed on their gilt-edged invitation cards. A menagerie of animals were kept here at the time, before being transferred to London Zoo in 1831.

This day, in the North of England originally called April Noddy Day, is the traditional time for sending apprentices to fetch things such as a tin of striped paint, a soft-pointed chisel, a box of straight hooks or a new bubble for the spirit level.

Village signs are waggishly amended (Four Marks in Hampshire gained the official-looking addition 'Out Of Ten' on April 1 a couple of years ago, nearby Liss gained the subtitle 'Twinned With the Outer Limits' and Bedlam, Yorks, gained the equally unkind 'Twinned With L'Unacy').

All such foolery is strictly supposed to end by noon. Hence the rhyme: 'April Fool's gone and past; You're the biggest fool at last', or in the North of England: 'April Noddy's Past and gone, You're the Fool and I am none.'

The concept is ancient, going back the medieval Feast of Fools and the Roman feast of Saturnalia.

In Scotland it is traditionally Huntigowk Day for sending people on a gowk's errand (a gowk is a cuckoo or fool) whereby someone is sent from house to house, everyone being in on the joke except the victim.

Memorable April Fool jokes of more recent times included Richard Dimbleby's *Panorama* programme on the spaghetti harvest in the 1960s, including shots of rows of spaghetti trees, and the declaration of independence of Hay-on-Wye in the 1970s. Whitehall declined to send in the Army after it heard that the town was issuing edible banknotes printed on rice-paper.

April 10 (approx)

Kate Kennedy Procession — Pageant of Scottish worthies, banned as profane for half a century, St Andrews, Fife.

Easter

Date fixed by Golden Numbers, see Pope for explanation

Maundy Thursday

Royal Maundy Money Distribution — Westminster Abbey in even-numbered years, other great cathedrals in odd years. Monarch gives specially minted coins to as many old people as years of reign, travelling by royal train to further cities.

ECCENTRIC EASTER

Are British eccentrics losing their marbles when faced with increasing Euro-conformity? Not if Easter events anyone can witness are anything to go by.

The **World Marbles Championship** on Good Friday is held on special pitches at the Greyhound pub, Tinsley Green, near Crawley, West Sussex. It's a knockout tournament for individuals and teams which goes on for most of the day. Its origins are said to date from when two local lads competed for the hand of a rare beauty in 1600.

On Easter Saturday the town band of Bacup, north of Rochdale, Lancashire, strikes up for the **Bacup Nutters Dance**. The Morris-like team sport blackened faces, black uniforms and white breeches, with wooden clogs. The 'nuts' are wooden discs on their hands, waists and knees, with which they set up a rhythmic clatter. The dance dates from at least 1857, and possibly from an earlier Cornish miners' parody of Moorish (hence 'Morris') pirates. The team is officially called the Britannia Coconut Dancers.

The **World Coal Carrying Championship** sees the nation's coalmen converge on Ossett, West Yorkshire, on Easter Monday (or the following Monday) for a back-breaking event. One hundredweight of coal (51kg) must be carried uphill from the Royal Oak pub in Owl Lane to the maypole in the High Street, a distance of five-sixths of a mile (1.3km). The winner gets a gold medal, and there's also a trophy for the first in the ladies' race carrying

Good Friday

World Marbles Championship	Tinsley Green, Crawley, Sussex.
Hot Cross Bun Ceremony	Widow's Son pub, Devons Rd, Bow, London E3, noon. A sailor or Wren adds a bun to the somewhat stale collection going back at least 150 years, to the time a widow whose only son was at sea put out a hot cross bun on Good Friday expecting his return for Easter. He never came back but each year she laid out another, refusing to take any away.

Easter Saturday

Bacup Nutters Dance	Bacup, Rochdale, Lancashire (see above).

Easter Day

Baron Berners' Folly	Faringdon, Oxfordshire (see chapter 11).

Easter Monday

World Coal Carrying Championships	Ossett, West Yorkshire (see above).
Hare Pie Scramble and Bottle Kicking	Hallaton, Leicestershire (see above).

28lb (13kg) of coal over 100 yards, which usually takes place about noon, followed by the men's event.

Easter Monday sees an outbreak of football rowdiness which one Leicestershire village is rather proud of. The **Hare Pie Scramble and Bottle Kicking** at Hallaton has its origins in the gift of a piece of land in 1770 to the rector of Hallaton, on condition he provided two hare pies, two dozen penny loaves and a quantity of ale to be scrambled for by the poor.

Hare pie is still produced at the church gate at 13.30 and pieces are hurled to the good-natured mob who then make a procession led by a hare on a pole – it used to be a dead one but is now a bronze sculpture – up the hill to a spot where the 'bottles' are blessed, before the start of a rugby-like mass football game between Hallaton and nearby Medbourne. The aim is to get the bottles (three small iron-hooped wooden barrels) across the goals – streams a mile apart – and there is no limit to the numbers on each side.

One recent rector of Hallaton said: 'People take the tradition seriously – there's a village saying – "No pie, no parson". There was a time when the steelworkers and railwaymen from the nearby towns used to come and perhaps too much was drunk, so a few heads got cracked, but now the drinking is more moderate and the game played in a better spirit.'

Egg Rolling	Painted eggs rolled down slope and eaten. Avenham Park, Preston, Lancashire.
Biddenden Dole	Medieval Siamese twins remembered in food hand-out, Kent (see Chapter 11).
Race of the Bogmen and Egg Throwing	Outside the Chesnut Horse, Great Finborough, Suffolk. Originally a race to win contract to plough fields, now for fun.
Running Auction	Bourne, Lincolnshire (see Chapter 6).

Hocktide
Monday and Tuesday of second week after Easter

Tuttimen Collect Tax	Curious customs unfold at Hungerford, Berkshire, all day (see Chapter 6).

Ascension Day (Thursday, 40 days after Easter)

Beating Bounds	Procession to mark parish boundaries, various villages including Cannington, near Bridgwater, Somerset, and Oddington, Otmoor, Oxford; originally choirboys were bumped upside down on boundary stones to make a lasting impression. At Lichfield, Staffordshire, the cathedral choir processes with boughs, stopping at eight places to sing a psalm.

MAY DAY MAY BE PAGAN, BAWDY AND RUDE, BUT NOT OFFICIAL

People sometimes complain that the May Day bank holiday is a socialist-inspired nuisance – brought in by a Labour government in 1978 to celebrate International Labour Day – although governments of various complexions have given up trying to shift it to the autumn.

But the real May Day, May 1, is non-political, non-religious, bizarre, bawdy, ancient and usually pagan.

In **Oxford**, for example, crowds block Magdalen Bridge and the High Street from early morning, and at 06.00 the sweet sound of hymns in Latin floats down from the top of Magdalen College Tower. There are madrigals and a procession of Morris men around the city, waving handkerchiefs, sticks and pig bladders in their ancient dance. City pubs are open from 06.30 for pots of ale or cider and hearty breakfasts. Many an Oxford student has stayed up all night drinking and dancing, and usually some jump from Magdalen Bridge into the somewhat shallow River Cherwell. This has sometimes ended in tragedy but in 1995 a woman student hit the tabloid headlines by jumping in nude.

Oxford May Day celebrant David Martin says: 'The May Day festivities have been recorded in Oxford since 1650 but we believe it goes back far further than that. Forget the official bank holiday on the nearest Monday:

Well Dressing	Tissington, Derbyshire and elsewhere in Peak District. Village wells decorated with elaborate floral pictures of religious scenes, usually with a procession between the different wells (six at Tissington). Also at Bisley, near Stroud, Gloucestershire.

MAY

May 1

'Obby 'Os	Raucous fertility dance, Padstow, Cornwall: similar Hobby Horse, at Minehead, Somerset (see box above).
Magdalen Bridge,	Latin hymn singing, jumping in river and possibly
Oxford	Naked frolicking (see box above).
Garland Ceremony	Charlton-on-Otmoor, Oxfordshire.

May bank holiday (first Monday)

International Festival of Worm Charming	Normandy Arms, Chapel Street, Blackawton, near Totnes, Devon, usually 11.30.
Stilton Cheese Rolling	In teams through village, fancy dress, dancing, Stilton, Peterborough, from 09.30.

no one in Westminster can tell Englishmen on which day to celebrate May Day – or when to stop!'

In London spring festivities going back to pagan times were uninhibited – the street Mayfair is named after a riotous festival of drinking and womanising held there throughout the 18th century.

The more common maypole, innocently copied in primary school dances today, is believed to go back to a pagan fertility symbol, which is why the Puritans in 1644 chopped down an imposing maypole which used to stand in the Strand. May customs in country areas have included maidens gathering the May dew before dawn on May 1 for its alleged healing and beautifying power, and the May Doll dressed in flowers and paraded about by children.

The May Hobby Horse or 'Obby 'Os dances lewdly around places such as **Padstow** and **Minehead** in the West Country and promises fertility to maidens caught in its skirts; there are the more widespread May Garlands, usually carried on sticks, and, of course, school and village May Queens.

All these long predate the workers' holiday beloved of socialists worldwide. Garland Day in Abbotsbury, Dorset, for example, when garlands on poles are carried round the village and money collected by children, dates from long before the calendars were changed in the 17th century – hence it is held on May 13, the 'old' May Day. Either way, it's still not the official government May Day holiday.

Newborough Well Dressing	Staffordshire, 11.00, and general village fair to celebrate retreat of plague of 14th century.

May 8

Furry Dance	Couples dance in ball gowns and morning suits with grey toppers through well-decorated Helston, Cornwall, all day (if the 8th is a Monday, moves to Saturday before the 8th).
World Dock Pudding Championship	Competitive cooking of a bizarre local delicacy made from nettles and dock leaves (not the common docks), Mytholmroyd Community Centre, Elphaborough, Mytholmroyd, Hebden Bridge, West Yorkshire. (Date varies, often Sunday. The address alone is a good mouthful.)

Whit Monday
(late May, or early June, or even on the Spring Bank Holiday)

Corby Pole Fair	Every 20 years (2002, 2022, etc). The town is barricaded off for the fair and travellers are required to pay a toll. Those who won't are carried on a pole (or chair if female) to the three sets of stocks and locked up until someone pays.

WHO SAID FINS AIN'T WHAT THEY USED TO BE?

Some of Britain's oldest, and oddest, ceremonies take place on the ocean wave. Environmentalists warn us that Britain's seas are overfished and we do not take the future of marine life seriously. In fact, Britons never have taken the fruits of the sea for granted, as many ancient ceremonies show.

In late May (usually Rogation Sunday) a lifeboat is used as a pulpit at **Hastings**, Sussex, for the annual **Blessing the Sea**. The thriving fishing community gathers on the shore to say the blessing while three churchmen sail out on the lifeboat and cast a wreath in the shape of a cross into the sea.

At **Brixham**, Devon, fishing boats for many years used to gather together for Blessing the Fleet in late May (again usually Rogation Sunday), the service being held on the quayside with a band playing. However, this is rarely held nowadays because of the catches having declined (or is it the other way round?). Brixham instead has a rather moving Blessing the Lifeboat service in early August, which takes place in the old fishmarket with the lifeboat tied up alongside, the sound of stirring old nautical hymns mixing with the cries of seagulls.

At **Whitstable**, Kent, on the high tide of St James's Day (July 25) the clergy and choir of St Peter's Church gather at Reeves Beach for the Oyster Ceremony service, while fishing boats bob offshore in a watery congregation.

At about the same time of year the **Tweedmouth Feast**, across the river from Berwick-upon-Tweed near the Scottish border with

Cheese Rolling

Various steep hills in Gloucestershire such as Cooper's Hill, Brockworth. Contestants attempt to catch cheese rolled down hills; there are many injuries to runners and spectators hit by flying 8lb Double Gloucesters. This is an ancient and seriously dangerous ceremony and even continued with dummy cheeses during wartime rationing. The master of ceremonies must wear a white coat, ribbons and a top hat and some in the early 20th century were buried still wearing them. The event was cancelled in 1998 (and then resumed) to allow safety to be improved because of a mere 33 injuries the previous year. As one outraged local said: 'This is the Nanny state gone mad. If you can't hurl yourself down a steep hill after a few drinks chasing cheeses, what's the point of bring British?'

Northumberland, sees a week of activities, including the crowning of the Salmon Queen on the Thursday. The Feast Service comes on a Sunday around July 20 and the rituals date back to 1292.

Perhaps the oldest and oddest such ceremony is the Oyster Proclamation at **Colchester**, Essex, on the last Friday in August or the first in September – depending in tides – which sees the spectacle of the mayor and councillors in full regalia setting forth by fishing boat to the oyster beds. These have belonged to the corporation at least since Richard I gave them the town in 1189, and probably longer.

The clerk reads aloud the Proclamation of 1256 which asserts that the rights have belonged to Colchester 'from the time beyond which memory runneth not to the contrary' and the company then toasts the Queen with gin and consumes special gingerbread. The mayor lowers the trawl and eats the first oyster of the season – whatever its condition.

The Oyster Feast is held in the town's Moot Hall in late October and up to 12,000 oysters are consumed with much pomp.

Tetbury Woolsack Races	Racing up and down Gumstool Hill, Tetbury, Gloucestershire (see Chapter 2).

May 29 (Oak Apple Day)

Garland Day	The Garland King rides through on his horse completely covered in a pyramid of flowers, followed by his retinue, Castleton, Derbyshire. Origins uncertain.
Hunting of the Earl of Rone	Combe Martin, Devon (usually spring bank holiday weekend). A hobby horse with huge teeth, used to secure contributions from onlookers, a fool, musicians and villagers dressed as a unit of Grenadier Guards, pursue a masked figure dressed in sackcloth sitting backwards on a donkey. He is regularly 'shot' and is eventually thrown into the sea after calling at various pubs. This commemorates the hunting and killing of a shipwrecked traitor. It was banned because of drunken licentiousness in

1837 (one participant was so drunk that he died after falling down steps) but since revived.

JUNE

Friday after second Monday

Selkirk Common Riding

One of several mass posse-like excursions of hundreds of riders from Scottish border towns, following a standard bearer, asserting rights to what was lawless unmarked bandit territory in the Marches, the scene of cross-border raids. The Selkirk one ends after about four hours with a gallop back into town and a lament for the dead of the battle of Flodden. More recent battles have been about whether women can join in. Also held at Linlithgow, West Lothian, and Lockerbie, Dumfries & Galloway.

Early Saturday

World Toe Wrestling Championships

Ye Olde Royal Oak Inn, Wetton, Ashbourne, Derbyshire. Invented by pub regulars more than 20 years ago, this

sport has not been recognised at Olympic level despite repeated requests.

June 19

Garter Ceremony

St George's Chapel, Windsor Castle. The monarch and knights of the Order of the Garter process with spectacular robes and hats to mark this oldest order of chivalry (from about 1347) and a useful, if humble, garment. A few tickets can be booked.

Third week

Hoppings Fair

Newcastle upon Tyne (see *Fairs*, page 30)

Third Sunday (approx)

Tram Sunday

Fleetwood, Lancashire. Vintage transport affair; it is best to arrive by tram from Blackpool.

June 21

Druid Ceremony, Stonehenge

The Most Ancient (doubtful) Order of Druids mark the summer solstice. Police have entered into the stone age spirit in recent years by clubbing non-violent or even pregnant New Age travellers over the head to stop them partaking or even coming vaguely near (I have seen this). But in 1998 the Druids, who are arguably from completely the wrong era, were allowed in once more to chant their chants, etc. Midnight, dawn and noon.

Saturday before longest day

Bawming the Thorn — Dancing round garlanded and beribboned tree, once said to be descended directly from that which sprung up when Jesus's uncle Joseph of Arimathea's staff was thrust in the ground when he landed at the Isle of Glastonbury. Appleton Thorn, near Warrington, Cheshire, 14.15. (The Glastonbury Thorn itself flowers at the old Christmas, January 5, and a sprig is always given to the monarch for her table. Puritan soldiers cut it down as idolatorous during the Civil War but clergymen secretly saved cuttings.)

Variable date, every leap year

Dunmow Flitch Trials — A flitch of bacon is awarded to a couple who do not repent of their marriage within a year and a day, after a long-winded trial (see Chapter 3).

June 24

Knollys Rose — An odd quit rent, Mansion House, City of London ceremony (see Chapter 3).

JULY
Second Saturday

Black Cherry Fair — Windsor Street, Chertsey, Surrey (see *Fairs*, page 30).

Second Saturday (approx)

World Viking Longboat Races Championship — Peel, Isle of Man. Hairy types in horned helmets re-enact the race of raiding Norsemen to land. Pillage no longer compulsory.

Tuesday before third Wednesday

Lammas Fair — Exeter (see *Fairs*, page 30).

Third Saturday (afternoon)

International Brick and Rolling Pin Throwing Championships — Stratford Park Leisure Centre, Stroud, Gloucestershire. International, that is, if you live in a Stroud. Simultaneous events are held in Stroud, Gloucestershire; Stroud, Oklahoma; Stroud, New South Wales and Stroud, Ontario.

Stroud, Hampshire, isn't big enough. It has to be a British standard brick (men) and an Australian standard rolling pin (women).

Tuesday after July 19
Honiton Fair   Honiton, Devon (see *Fairs*, page 30).

July 25
Knill Ceremony   Virgins prance round pyramid, St Ives, Cornwall, every fifth year: 2001, 2006, etc (see Chapter 12).

Tuesday before third Wednesday (sometimes earlier)
Lammas Fair   Exeter, Devon (see *Fairs*, page 30). Mayoral procession, then craft fair and festival.

AN ALIEN COMES FORTH

Scotland's **South Queensferry** on the Firth of Forth is a fascinating place at any time. The quiet former fishing village and ferry landing for those coming from the kingdom of Fife has the two enormous Forth bridges leaping high over its rooftops across the sky.

But sometimes, as you stand on the waterfront marvelling at science fact, science fiction seems to arrive. An alien stalks round the town – or is it a terrifying Thing From The Swamp? It cannot be human, this puffy figure walking strangely and covered in what looks like rough brown-green fur.

You are lucky, local legend has it, if you meet this creature, the Burry Man, and to mark it you must give a coin to one of his attendants. The Burry Man is central to South Queensferry festival week (the festival starts on the second Saturday in August but he tours the streets the day before), but who, how or why is he?

Why is quickest to answer. Nobody has a clue. Fertility figure, pagan scapegoat, fishing good luck charm – take your pick, the festival is far too old for anyone to remember. There is a mention of the Burry Man as if he were already long established from 1740.

Who and how it is done are remarkable. The volunteer who has the honour of being the year's Burry Man must first spend days scouring the hedgerows for burrs, the bristly hooked balls that are the fruit of the burdock, a common British weed. These burrs with their hundreds of tiny hooks fasten themselves to your clothing as you pass the plant, and Nature would have long ago sued the makers of Velcro for copying the idea, if Nature had a lawyer. Getting them out of a child's hair, or sheepdog's fur, is not amusing.

At 07.00 of the appointed day it all starts at the pub where the volunteer is wrapped in thick clothing including a balaclava helmet and thick woollen tights (often a hot August day!), then layers upon layers of burrs are applied until only his eyes and mouth are showing. The Burry Man cannot put his legs

Last weekend

Marldon Apple Pie Fair   Marldon, Devon (see *Fairs*, page 30).

Towards end of July

Kingsbridge Fair   Kingsbridge, Devon (see *Fairs*, page 30).

AUGUST
Second Saturday

Ferry Fair and   Bizarre, rather frightening figure of a man
Burry Man   totally covered with burdock burrs, who stalks
around the day before leaning on striped poles
collecting money. South Queensferry, at Forth
bridges southside. It is good luck to meet him,
despite his gruesome appearance (see box below).

---

together or his arms by his side all day, lest they stick together, so he sort of wades around, using his two flowery beribboned staffs to support himself.

A flag is tied around his waist like an apron and a hat of flowers on his head. He sets off on his rounds of the town at 09.00, preceded by a bell-ringer and helped by two attendants, collecting money and whisky (sipped through a straw) wherever he calls. He cannot possibly go to the toilet, so he can drink nothing besides the obligatory whisky all day. Somehow he carries this on till returning to the pub at 18.00. The volunteer has to be fit, alcohol and heat tolerant, and keen, as he usually does it once a year for around 25 years before handing on the flowery staves.

No one has yet suggested feminism requires a Burry Woman (sponsored by Velcro, possibly) for the good reason that if they embraced, you could never get them apart. Anyway, the Burry Man appears to have no particular sex, given his shapeless bulk.

An old participant recalled that the Burry Man was so grievously scratched by evening, that he had to be dabbed all over with iodine. Today, thicker materials help to prevent this.

Then it's back to the waterfront to have a beer and watch cars and trains soaring as high as aircraft above you. When the enormous cantilevered arms of the railway bridge were reaching out to meet each other in 1890, they were so huge that they couldn't exactly meet. The reason was that although perfectly made and aligned, they were so big that the effect of the sun on the eastern side in the morning, and the west in the afternoon, could bend the structure enough to prevent perfect alignment. The solution was the send men inside the massive tubes, each large enough to take an express train themselves, to light bonfires to trick the bridge, as it were, into thinking that it was sunny on both sides. The ends aligned perfectly, the bolts were dropped in and the last plates riveted up. But did all the men get out of the smoke-filled tubes?

Third Saturday (approx)

Hengistbury Head Kite Festival	Bournemouth, Dorset. Past highlights have included man-lifting kites and parachuting teddy bears.

August 13

Left-Handers' Day	Covent Garden, London. Right-handers get to try left-hand corkscrews etc and see if they like it.

Mid-August

Chilli Fiesta	West Dean, near Chichester, West Sussex. More types of chillis than are imaginable. Chilli beer, chillis pictures, chilli pottery, chilli lamps, chilli sauces and salsas, chilli growers and chilli seeds.
Lawnmower Grand Prix 12-hour Endurance Race	Brinsbury Agricultural College, Wisborough Green, near Petworth, West Sussex (see page 39). Ride-on and run-behind classes. Advance ticket admission only.

THE UGLY OLD ENEMY

If you happen to meet a hideously ugly giant lurching through the streets with its eyes weirdly lit up and accompanied by strange incantations, don't worry, it's not an alien life-form – at least not if it's on the Saturday nearest Aug 24 in West Witton, in Wensleydale, Yorkshire. The effigy is used in a custom called **Burning of t'Owd Bartle** which involves a march round the village chanting an old verse about Bartle's doom:

'At Pen Hill crags he tore his rags,
At Hunter's Thorn he blew his horn,
At Capplebank Stee he brak his knee,
At Grassgill Beck he brak his neck,
At Waddam's End he couldn't fend,
At Grassgill End he made his end.'

The procession ends with his being hurled onto a massive bonfire stuffed with hidden fireworks. Quite who Bartle was that he still deserves such ire has been forgotten – St Bartholomew did little to offend and the date near the saint's day is thought to be a coincidence. The commonest theory is that he was an evil robber who was chased to his doom, as described in the verse, by a gang of outraged villagers. Either way, it makes an excuse for a weekend of village festivities including a tug-of-war and fancy dress parade.

Garlic Festival	Isle of Wight. Garlic cheese, garlic soup, garlic beer, even garlic ice-cream, and many other goodies for garlic gourmands.

Variable Sunday

Plague Sunday Service	Cucklet Church, Eyam, Derbyshire (see Chapter 6).

August 24 St Bartholomew's Day (on nearest Saturday)

Burning of t'Owd Bartle	An ugly effigy with lit-up eyes is paraded round and burnt for reasons totally forgotten. West Witton, Yorkshire, evening (see box opposite).

Sunday mid/late August

Bognor Birdman	(As successful as that of Alcatraz.) Dozens of hopefuls in various serious or joke one-man gliding outfits try to win a cash prize by jumping a set distance off the end of the pier. Bognor Regis, West Sussex.

Late August (date varies)

Beca Mountain Race	Men dress up as women, run up hills and chop down gates. Near Fishguard, Wales (see Chapter 3).
Coracle Racing	Cilgerran, near Cardigan, Pembrokeshire. Pre-Roman form of transport thrives on a Welsh river.
Bog Snorkelling World Championships	Swimming 60 yards through stinking black water, outside Neuadd Arms Hotel,

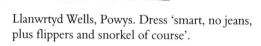

Llanwrtyd Wells, Powys. Dress 'smart, no jeans, plus flippers and snorkel of course'.

Last Monday

Sussex Bonfire Society Marching Season starts	Rotherfield. Procession of dramatic figures in horned helmets, Roman armour, topical enemies built in effigy etc, first of many until November 21 (see box, page 26).

THE VICAR AND THE LEWD

Unbridled lust may have been expunged from many a ritual, but in Abbots Bromley, Staffordshire, they have a good old fertility dance on the first Monday after September 4. The dancers collect the horns from St Nicholas Church at 07.30 in the morning. The Horn Dance involves six men with reindeer horns, plus Maid Marion (a man in drag), a Hobby Horse (as at Padstow and Minehead), a jester and a musician with an accordion. The vicar blesses them, then they dance lewdly all round the village until 20.00 when they return to be blessed again, just to be on the safe side.

The king's fling

Another horn ceremony based on lustiness is the Charlton Horn Fair in the London SE7 suburb, held on the second Sunday in June. It dates from when King John had his wicked way with the local miller's wife, and in desperation at facing the cuckolded husband, said he could hold an annual fair, which locals naturally called the Horn Fair. It's an ordinary sort of fair today, with stalls and so on, but there's a procession involving King John, the miller and some horn decorations.

Syn of the times

The **Day of Syn** which completely overcomes the Kent village of Dymchurch, down on Romney Marsh, is little to do with sins of the flesh, but is named after Dr Syn, the smuggling rector of Dymchurch. The event, held every second August Bank Holiday Monday, returns the village to the days of 1780 when smugglers with their contraband outwitted the beach patrols of dragoons. All this is re-enacted in costume with a fleet of smuggling boats under the command of the Scarecrow (as Dr Syn was known off duty). There is street theatre all morning and a fair in the afternoon in this village otherwise best known for the splendid miniature steam railway right along the coast, the **Romney, Hythe and Dymchurch Railway** (the quickest engine being called, of course, Dr Syn).

SEPTEMBER

First weekend

World Black Pudding
Throwing
Championships

The Corner Pin pub, Stubbins, Ramsbottom, Bury, Lancashire. Contestants bowl three black puddings each at 21 Yorkshire puddings on a platform 20ft high, attempting to knock down the most.

Monday and Tuesday after the first Sunday

St Giles Fair   Oxford (see *Fairs*, page 30).

First or second Tuesday

Cheese and Onion Fair   Newton Abbott, Devon (see *Fairs*, page 30).

Monday after first Sunday after September 4

Horn Dance   Abbots Bromley, Staffordshire (said to be oldest in Europe). Old reindeer horns mounted on dancers' wooden heads prance round the parish, to celebrate hunting rights in Needwood Forest (see box opposite).

Rushbearing Festival   Sowerby Bridge, Calderdale, Yorkshire. The rush cart travels ten miles through villages accompanied by dancers and street entertainment, calling, of course, at all the pubs. Celebrates ancient bearing of fresh rushes for church floor every autumn; takes place in about 40 other villages at various dates but with less razzmatazz.

Second Tuesday

Widecombe Fair   Widecombe, Devon (see *Fairs*, page 30).

Wednesday nearest September 17

Barnstaple Fair   Barnstaple, Devon (see *Fairs*, page 30).

Saturday nearest September 18

Gurning Championships   These involve pulling vile and frankly unbelievable faces, at Egremont Crab Fair, Cumbria – an event which has neither crabs nor fairs, but includes the Applecart Parade, where children vie for apples thrown from a cart, and sports such as Cumbrian wrestling. Legal only since 1267 charter. In the early 21st century, grown men were having all their teeth removed, to compete better.

Around September 22

Charter Fair   Baldock and Stevenage, Hertfordshire (see *Fairs*, page 30).

Third Sunday (usually)

Clipping the Church | Embracing the church, Painswick, Gloucestershire (see Chapter 6).

˙Horseman's Sunday | Service on horseback, St John's, Hyde Park, London W1 (see Chapter 6).

Saturday before and after Michaelmas (September 29)

Mop Fair | Marlborough, Wiltshire (see *Fairs*, page 30).

OCTOBER
Variable

Horseshoe and Faggot Cutting Ceremony | Bizarre quit rent, High Court, London (see Chapter 3).

First Thursday

Goose Fair | Nottingham. It's huge. (see *Fairs*, page 30).

First week

Honey Fair | Callington, Cornwall (see *Fairs*, page 30).

Second Wednesday

Goosey Fair | Tavistock, Devon (see *Fairs*, page 30).

Second weekend

World Conker Championships | Village Green, Ashton, near Oundle, Peterborough, Cambridgeshire.

First Monday after October 10

Pack Monday Fair | Sherborne, Dorset (see *Fairs*, page 30)

October 12 (unless a Sunday in which case October 13)

Mop Fair | Stratford-upon-Avon (see *Fairs*, page 30) and Runaway Mop Fair on the following Friday week.

Mid-October

Mop Fair and Ox Roast | Warwick (see *Fairs*, page 30).

Mid-October weekend

The Big Apple in Much Marcle | Celebration of apple orchards, rare varieties, cider making and much marcling in general, at Much Marcle, on A449 between Ross-on-Wye and Ledbury, Herefordshire. Similar events at Binstead, Isle of Wight; Sandling, near Maidstone, Kent; Sulgrave, Oxfordshire and Blackmoor, near Petersfield, Hampshire at about same time.

NOVEMBER
November 5
See box, page 26, for:

Sticklepath Fireshow	Play enacted by 10ft puppets ending with villain consigned to flames. Finch Foundry Field, Sticklepath, nr Okehampton, Devon, 19.30. Numbers limited.
Bonfire Societies and Spectacular Processions	Lewes, Battle and throughout Sussex (all Sussex); Ottery St Mary, Honiton, Devon.
Turning the Devil's Boulder	Shebbear, near Holsworthy, Devon.

First Wednesday after November 5
Hatherleigh Fire Festival Devon.

November 11 (Martinmas)

Firing the Fenny Poppers	Vicar firing weird cannons, Fenny Stratford, Bedfordshire (see Chapter 6).
Wroth Silver Rent Paid	Knightlow, Derbyshire (see Chapter 3).

Mondays before and after Martinmas (November 11) or three Mondays if that day is a Monday
Mop Fair Cirencester, Gloucestershire (see *Fairs*, page 30).

November 17 (approx)
Biggest Liar in the World Competition The Bridge Inn, Santon Bridge, Holmrook, Cumbria, evening; includes 'tatie pot' supper.

Probably third Saturday
Sussex Bonfire marching season closes Robertsbridge (see box, page 26).

Last Saturday in November
Blacksmith's Procession To celebrate St Clement, patron saint of blacksmiths, an anvil is dragged around the village and fired with gunpowder at various points, with an effigy of 'Old Clem'. Then in the church a re-enactment of the temptation of St Dunstan by the Devil dressed as a woman, who is grabbed by the blacksmith's tongs on the nose and leaps all the way to Tunbridge Wells, making a hole to start the famous spring of sulphurous waters. Mayfield, near Crowborough, East Sussex, 18.30, free.

THE BURNING PASSIONS THAT COME OUT AT NIGHT

Remember, remember the Fifth of November? Citizens of several English towns where Guy Fawkes Night is celebrated with more than usual blazing ferocity have not had much chance to forget it since the old conspirator was caught in 1605.

Lewes, East Sussex, normally one of Britain's sleepiest county towns but once the scene of fiery executions, literally explodes into action with five very serious bonfire societies parading in armour or full costume and carrying flaming torches. They take various routes, race blazing tar barrels into the river, have a mass procession at 19.45 then split off for rival and spectacularly sculptural bonfire creations and salvoes of fireworks.

Religious zealotry, perhaps more often associated with Ulster, surfaces: 'No Popery' banners are carried and until recently an effigy of the Pope was burnt along with Fawkes. Here, however, the slogans are echoes of historical rather than present enmity – after all, the Catholic Gunpowder Plot was discovered just a few years after 17 Protestant martyrs were burnt at the stake in Lewes during the brief, Catholic reign of Mary I. Their names are proudly hung from banners across the streets.

Be in town early and leave late to avoid road closures and traffic congestion, and, to fit in with the rowdy locals as the pubs close, it's best to learn the words of Sussex by the Sea which is sung lustily as the bonfires die down. In recent years the town has been so crowded that some pubs haven't opened at all on the night. Shops are boarded up against the scrum.

Topical hate figures have often been burnt in effigy, such as Hitler or Napoleon at various dates, or even the editor of a local paper who was foolish enough to criticise the whole bonfire society shennanigans.

Not that Lewes is unique. Thirty Sussex villages share this ritual, based on a distant pagan past with fantastical sculptures, untraceable symbols and costumes better than the Mardi Gras. The Sussex bonfire season is ignited at Rotherfield on the last Monday in August, and burns through Uckfield in September, Fletching on the third Saturday in October, before exploding at Littlehampton on the last Saturday.

The anti-Catholicism is little evident outside Lewes, and at Littlehampton Guy Fawkes isn't much mentioned – but then the event takes place on land donated by the Duke of Norfolk who owns the nearby splendid Arundel Castle. The duke is traditionally England's premier Roman Catholic and landlord of many of those taking part in the celebrations.

At **Battle** near Hastings an amazing and politically topical sculpture, built over at least a month, is blown to smithereens in a piece of noisy street theatre outside Battle Abbey on a Saturday near November 5. Other towns, such as Guildford, Surrey, had their celebrations banned after 19th-century rioting between bonfire societies and troops, but in Battle they proudly tell of how the authorities were outwitted in the 1920s. They tried to stop the fire being lit, so decoy rubbish fires were started at the other end of the town; while police were dealing with those, the bonfire supporters threaded through the alleyways and footpaths with great bundles of wood and barrels of tar and set a proper blaze going. It was too late for the authorities, who wisely gave up.

Robertsbridge has the last of Sussex's spectacular celebrations on the third Saturday of November, with a typical procession comprising 1,000 costumed people from 23 bonfire societies.

Topical enemies are set ablaze – recently it was the fat cat bosses of privatised utility companies and the National Lottery which came in for satirical effigies. As a member of the Robertsbridge Bonfire Society explained: 'It hasn't got all that much to do with Guy Fawkes but, as I understand it, goes back to a pagan festival. It was just lucky that Fawkes made his attempt to blow up parliament within three weeks of the old celebration.'

A Sussex fire festival with a dramatic difference is held at Rye, usually on a mid-November Saturday, where a boat is burnt on the Saltings, in memory of burning the boats of captured French raiders.

Blazing tar barrels are also much in evidence at the culmination of a day of celebrations at **Ottery St Mary**, Devon, near Honiton, on November 5, or 4th if 5th is a Sunday. Nine are carried through the village on prescribed routes, men with their hands and arms swathed in sacking carrying each until the heat becomes unbearable. This goes on until around 23.45 and ends in a huge bonfire. Hatherleigh, near Okehampton, Devon, has another fire festival, usually on the first Wednesday after November 5.

Britain's oddest November 5 ceremony can also be found in Devon – at Shebbear near Holsworthy. Turning the Devil's Boulder dates back to well before Guy Fawkes. The massive stone lying outside the churchyard is said to have been dropped by the Devil on his way to harm the village, and it is turned by the villagers each November 5 after a deliberately discordant peal of bells is rung to drive Old Nick away – making a clamour to drive out devils is an almost worldwide folk custom. The Turning has gone on for centuries, but during World War II it was felt that it might be inappropriate and was dropped in 1940. The desperate war news only got worse, so the custom went ahead after all, a week late. It was felt no stone should be left unturned to help Britain's fortunes. The fortunes of war slowly improved.

BIGGAR ECCENTRICS ON NEW YEAR'S EVE

The Scots' Hogmanay has always beaten plain old New Year's Eve as such peaceful festivities go. But many English would be surprised to know that the year end sees Britain's most violent, dramatic and colourful ceremonies literally setting things ablaze in many a northern town.

Most are in Scotland, but in **Allendale**, Northumberland, at about 23.45 the brightly dressed 'guizers' go marching through the town, led by a band. Each bears a blazing half barrel on his head, filled with tar and wood shavings, and these are eventually hurled on a huge bonfire in the marketplace, the ancient ritual being linked to the rebirth of light in the coming year.

Similarly, in **Comrie**, Perthshire, the flambeaux procession starts from the square on the last stroke of midnight. Every corner of the village is visited 'to drive out evil spirits' and the procession ends with the flaming torches being thrown from a bridge into the River Earn and all dancing round.

The **Biggar Ne'erday Bonfire** at the South Lanarkshire town sees a marching band and an enormous bonfire in the High Street (21.00–midnight). Sparks also fly at **Stonehaven** near Aberdeen in the fireball ceremony, which starts at about 23.30 and involves a couple of dozen men marching down the High Street whirling round their heads balls of fire, made of flammable material in wire netting, on the end of wire ropes. As the men march down to the harbour, the circles of fire make a startling sight.

Not far away, in **Burghead, Burning the Clavie** takes place on the old calendar's New Year's Eve – January 11. An old whisky barrel is filled with tar and wood chips and set ablaze, then run up and down the street, bringing good luck to anyone who can seize a firebrand. It is set on a special stone pillar to burn, then brought to earth and smashed to pieces by hundreds of spectators.

Lerwick, Shetland, must take the prize for the most spectacular New Year pyromania, although Up Helly Aa doesn't take place until the last Tuesday in January. Again, guizers in gaudy dress parade through the town with blazing torches, but in keeping with the Shetlands' Norse heritage, they draw a replica Viking galley with them, complete with dragon's head on the prow and dozens of beefy Vikings in horned helmets.

The procession, which starts at 19.30, ends at the King George V playing field where, after certain rituals, the guizers hurl their flaming torches high in the air to rain down on the Viking galley, which blazes fiercely, to the cheers of the crowds. The night is then spent dancing, dining and partying.

Travel information at end of chapter.

DECEMBER
December 23

Tom Bawcock's Eve

Mousehole, Cornwall. Locals celebrate when their hero set forth in a storm to save the fishing village from starvation just before Christmas, and returned with a huge catch of fish. Includes children proceeding with huge fish lanterns, Starry Gazy Pie in which the fish heads poke through the pastry crust, and singing the Tom Bawcock Song about his feat.

TALL, DARK LUMPS OF COAL: NEW YEAR CUSTOMS

No, Liz Hurley, Liz Taylor or even Elizabeth Windsor simply wouldn't do, according to the somewhat sexist First Footing tradition at New Year, which insists that, for a household to have good luck in the coming 12 months, the first person over the threshhold after the chimes at midnight should be a tall, dark man, if possible bearing tokens of warmth and wealth such as a lump of coal. Preferably, the man should be a stranger, and – even harder to arrange – ideally should have been born foot first. Meanwhile women should use the back door.

Women are not barred, however, from another New Year custom – sipping the Cream of the Well, the first water drawn after midnight, said to bestow wealth and happiness. Indeed, in the north of England and Scotland its qualities were thought to be magical and that a lonely maid would be wed within a twelvemonth if she tasted it.

A third, West Country custom not yet quite snuffed out is to prevent evil and diseases from entering the house all year by making a globe of thorn briars and mistletoe, dousing it in cider and hanging it near the door. After the midnight chimes the old one must be burnt outdoors while a new one is hung up. On some farms it was considered essential to carry the burning globe over the first-sown furrows.

At the old water mill at Putley, west of Ledbury, Herefordshire, this Burning the Bush ceremony is still carried out with a ring of 13 bonfires, a crowd growling 'auld cider' nine times, and of course a new globe which is doused with the drink, scorched a little in the fire and then hung up for the coming year.

December 25 (also January 1)

Uppies and Doonies	Kirkwall, Orkney Islands. A massive 200-a-side communal scrum lasting four hours (see box, page 7).

December 26

Walrus Dip	Cefn Sidan Beach, Pembrey Country Park, Llanelli, Wales. About 100 people in fancy dress go for a swim.

December 31

Spectacular year-ending ceremonies include:

Blazing Tar Barrels	Allendale, Northumberland 23.45.
Flambeaux Procession	Comrie, Perthshire, midnight.
Ne'erday Bonfire	Biggar, Strathclyde, 21.00.
Stonehaven Fireball Ceremony	Stonehaven near Aberdeen, 23.30
(for all see box, page 28).	
Nos Galan Midnight Race	Mountain Ash, Mid-Glamorgan (see page 46).

DAILY EVENTS

Wayfarer's Dole	Hospital of St Cross, Winchester, Hampshire (see Chapter 3)
Yelling of News	By Town Crier, 11.00, Coppergate, York.
Wakeman's Curfew	21.00, for at least the last 1,000 years: City Hornblower in Ripon, Yorkhire, wearing his tricorn hat, blows the Wakeman's curfew horn at each corner of the Market Place obelisk.
Blowing of the Forest Horn	Bainbridge, North Yorkshire, to help people on foot up on the moors in the dark (winter only).
Ceremony of the Queen's (or King's) Keys	21.53, Tower of London (see Chapter 3).

FAIRS
Gloves off at lawless fairs

Whether it was Simple Simon going to the fair or Uncle Tom Cobbley and all off to Widecombe Fair, the great fairs of Britain go back in folk memory to the dawn of time, or at least to medieval charters granting the right to hold them.

For those used to common country fairgrounds, the older fairs have downright peculiar customs – such as the lawless, mop and runaway mop or fairs named after foods – while others are just huge and spectacular.

Britain's biggest is **Nottingham's** three-day **Goose Fair** starting on the first Thursday in October. This has its origins in a centuries-old tradition of up to 20,000 geese being driven to the city in great flocks, coming from as far

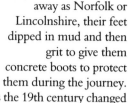

away as Norfolk or Lincolnshire, their feet dipped in mud and then grit to give them concrete boots to protect them during the journey. As the 19th century changed society, so the entertainment section of the Goose Fair became more important, with freak shows such as the Fattest Lady in the World or the Ugliest Dwarf or the Three-headed Chicken giving way to spectacular steam-powered rides with fantastic organs, wall-of-death motorbikes and modern white-knuckle rides of every kind.

Traders still offer all kinds of goods on stalls, and the whole fairground sprawls for a mile or two of riotous colour and cacophony. There are plenty of Goose Fair folksongs and justice on the fairground at Forest Recreation Ground was once dispensed by Pie Powder courts (the term coming from the French pied poudre, dusty feet, meaning the people at the fair).

If you miss the geese there are sheep not so far away, usually the following Monday (in fact the first Monday after the 4th), at the Corby Glen Sheep Fair in Grantham, Lincolnshire. This is more of a real sheep-trading affair but has fairground fun, albeit in much smaller quantities.

Another truly massive fair is the **Hoppings** at **Newcastle upon Tyne**, in the third week in June. The Hoppings is said to be the biggest travelling fair in Europe as a coming together of various showmen; but don't go just for the beer. It was started by the North of England Temperance Society in 1882 to show that the working man can have fun without booze, and it's still dry and still fun.

If, on the other hand, you prefer lawless fairs, with the gloves off so to speak, then Devon might seem the place. On the Tuesday after July 19, Honiton Fair opens with the town crier proceeding up the High Street, followed by a gaggle of excited children, and then ringing his bell and making this proclamation:

'Oyez, oyez, the Glove is up, the Fair has begun, no man shall be arrested until the Glove is taken down, God save the Queen',

with the children repeating every word as in a church. The gilded leather glove is held up for all to see on the end of the crier's garlanded and beribboned pole which is displayed on the balcony of the Kings Arms pub. Then hot coppers are thrown for the children to scramble for in an unseemly mêlée (as in Hungerford and Lanark); but a sense of sadistic humour assures that there are no fancy gloves for them as they burn hands and scrape knees. Some wrap rags around their palms. (The fair takes place on the Wednesday and Thursday.)

A similar amnesty for minor crimes is promised in Exeter at the Lammas Fair – on the Tuesday before the third Wednesday in July or sometimes earlier. The mayor proclaims a charter and the gilded glove is hoisted, then a procession to the Cathedral Green opens a craft fair and festival.

Kingsbridge, also in Devon, has a four-day fair towards the end of July, complete with white glove hoisted to indicate that petty crime is OK (it isn't), plus a picturesque Floral Dance through the main street. It's all laid down in the 1461 charter.

Fair game for every kind of food

On the food theme, the Marldon Apple Pie Fair takes place at the Devon village on the last weekend in July, with said confections for sale and an Apple Pie Princess to be crowned; there's a Goosey Fair at Tavistock, Devon on the second Wednesday in October; and nearby, across the Tamar in Cornwall, the much smaller Honey Fair at Callington in the first week of October (beekeeping does come into it, but it's mainly a funfair); the Cheese and Onion Fair – again in Devon at Newton Abbott – is on the first or second Tuesday in September (this dates back to Edward II and deals in enormous cheeses and onions, but today is more of a funfair).

Barnstaple isn't left out of the comestible celebrations: its four-day fair starts on the Wednesday nearest to September 17 with a Guildhall toasting of a special ale brewed by the Senior Beadle from a secret Elizabethan recipe, and toast, cheese and gingerbread. The white glove is hoisted in the window, as above; and still in Devon, there's the Widecombe Fair as in the song, held on the second Tuesday in September and featuring traditional games such the slippery pole.

One more food festivity is the Black Cherry Fair in Windsor Street, Chertsey, Surrey, on the second Saturday in July. This is ancient, dating from a charter granted by Henry VI to John de Harmondesworth, abbot of Chertsey Abbey; and although it originally celebrated St Anne's Day in August, it now coincides with the supposed cherry harvest. And, being Surrey, there's no white glove indicating freedom to misbehave.

Hiring and firing, and runaway mops

The reason so many of the ancient and more spectacular fairs fall in the autumn is simple. It was the time of the harvest, so the farmworkers received their annual pay and went to hiring fairs to bargain with farmers for the next year's work.

Workers, including servants, would have attended hiring or mop fairs with a few pence in their pockets, so the tradition of providing sweetmeats and entertainment grew up. Each type of worker would gather at a particular corner bearing the sign of his or her job – a crook for a shepherd, a whip for a carter, perhaps even a mop for a domestic servant – and if taken on by a farmer would receive a fastenpenny to keep him loyal to the employer. Nevertheless, this could soon be spent at the fair, and a Runaway Mop fair was held a week or two later for those who changed their minds.

Mop Fairs – now more for fun than for seeking work – are still held at

Marlborough, Wiltshire, on the Saturday before and after Michaelmas; at Cirencester, Gloucestershire, on the Mondays before and after St Martin's Day (November 11) or three Mondays if that day is a Monday; and at Warwick (the Mop Fair and Ox Roast) in mid-October.

Similarly, Pack Monday Fair at Sherborne, Dorset (first Monday after October 10) was once the Pact, or hiring, fair for the whole region. Stratford-upon-Avon has had not only a Mop Fair (October 12 unless a Sunday in which case October 13) for 600 years, but also the Runaway Mop Fair on the Friday week.

Among other autumn fairs are charter fairs such as those which throng the streets in North Hertfordshire at Baldock and Stevenage (around 22 September), and the great **St Giles Fair** at Oxford. This goes back at least 400 years and takes place on the Monday and Tuesday after the first Sunday in September (or after the second Sunday if Sunday is 1 September), in the specially wide thoroughfare north of the city centre.

TRAVEL INFORMATION

Allendale Guizers, Northumberland
Road From A1 near Newcastle, or M6 J43 at Carlisle, take A69 across country to Haydon Bridge, then south on A686 and B6295.
Rail Nearest station: Haydon Bridge.
Tourist information ✆ 01434 605215.

Bacup Nutters Dance, Bacup, Lancashire
Road From M6 J29, take M65 east to J5, B6232 to A690, turn right and onto A681 to Bacup.
Rail Nearest station Burnley or Rawtenstall (East Lancashire steam railway, change at Bolton).
Tourist information ✆ 01282 664421.

Barnstaple Fair, Devon
Road From M5 J27 then A361.
Rail/bus Own branch line from Exeter (from London Paddington and other centres).
Tourist information ✆ 0870 6085531.

Battle bonfire, East Sussex
Road From London or M25, take A21 south and it is signed on right just before Hastings.
Rail Direct from London Charing Cross.
Tourist information ✆ 01424 773721.

Blazing barrels, Ottery St Mary, Devon
Road From M5 J29 at Exeter, take A30 east towards Honiton, look for turn off.
Rail/bus Nearest station Honiton (London Waterloo–Exeter line), then bus 398.
Tourist information ✆ 01404 813964.

Blessing the Lifeboat, Brixham, Devon
Road M5 to Exeter, then A38 for 5 miles, A80 towards Torbay and A3022.
Rail Nearest station Paignton, bus 12 to Brixham.
Tourist information ✆ 01803 852861

Blessing the Sea Ceremony, Hastings, Sussex
Road A21 from London and M25.
Rail From London Charing Cross.
Tourist information ✆ 01424 781111

Burning of t'Owd Bartle, West Witton, Yorkshire
Road Turn off A1 at Leeming, take A684 west 15 miles.
Train/bus: Northallerton station, on London King's Cross–Edinburgh line, bus to Bedale, then bus 156 or 157 to West Witton.
Tourist information ✆ 01969 623069.

Burning the Clavie, Burghead, Moray Firth
Road From south, A9 to Inverness, then A96.
Rail Nearest station Forres.
Tourist information ✆ 01463 234353.

Comrie flambeaux, Perthshire
Road From Edinburgh, Forth Bridge and M90 to Perth, then A85 west.
Rail Nearest station: Perth.
Tourist information ✆ 01738 450600.

Day of Syn and Romney, Hythe and Dymchurch Railway, Kent
Road From M20 J11, turn south to Hythe.
Rail/bus London Charing Cross to Folkestone Central then bus 10, 11, or 12, or get off at Sandling for a downhill walk of just over a mile.
Tourist information ✆ 01303 267799; RHDR: ✆ 01797 362353.

Goose Fair, Nottingham
Also visit castle, and don't miss the Trip To Jerusalem pub underneath it. Lace market and Yates's Wine Lodge worth a visit.
Road Off M1 (J24–26).
Rail From St Pancras, London, and many other centres.
Tourist information ✆ 0115 9155330.

Hare Pie Scramble and Bottle Kicking, Hallaton, near Market Harborough
Road From Leicester (M1 J21) ring road, A47 towards Peterborugh. Hallaton is signed on right at East Norton.
Rail Nearest station: Market Harborough (London St Pancras).
Tourist information ✆ 01858 821270.

Haxey Hood and Sway, Haxey, near Gainsborough, Nottinghamshire
Road From A1(M) south of Doncaster at J34 take A614 to Bantry, A631 east towards Gainsborough, A161 north to Haxey.
Rail Nearest station Gainsborough, from London King's Cross. Change at Retford.
Tourist information ✆ 01427 615411.

Hoppings, Newcastle upon Tyne
Road Off A1 London–Edinburgh road, on A189 to Town Moor. (If coming from south, look out for extraordinary Angel of North sculpture beside A1 near Gateshead. Parking nearby.)

Rail On London King's Cross–Edinburgh line, also from many regional centres. Then bus 10 to Town Moor.
Tourist information ↘ 0191 230 0030.

Hurling the Silver Ball, St Columb Major, Cornwall
Road From end of M5, A30 to Indian Queens, A392 right to St Columb Rd, then A39 right (north).
Rail/bus St Columb Road, on Newquay branch. Change at Par from trains from London Paddington or other centres to Penzance.
Tourist information ↘ 01208 76616.

Hurling the Silver Ball, St Ives, Cornwall
Road End of M5 to Exeter, A30 through north Cornwall, then, before Penzance, A3074 to St Ives.
Rail Short branch line off London Paddington and other centres–Penzance main line.
Tourist information ↘ 01736 796297.

Lewes bonfire societies, East Sussex
Be in town early and expect jams.
Road From London or M25, take M23 and A23 towards Brighton, then just before Brighton A27 to Lewes
Rail From London Victoria, or from Brighton.
Tourist information ↘ 01273 483448; web: www.lewes.gov.uk/visit/htm

Ne'erday Bonfire, Biggar, South Lanarkshire
Road From A74 (M) J13, or Edinburgh ring road, take A702.
Rail Nearest station, Carstairs.
Tourist information ↘ 01899 221066.

Olney Pancake Race, Bedfordshire
Road From M1 J14, take A509 north.
Rail Nearest station Bedford, from London St Pancras.
Tourist information ↘ 01234 215226.

Oxford May Day
Road From London/M25 or Birmingham, M40.
Rail/bus Trains from London Paddington and other centres. Frequent coaches.
Tourist information ↘ 01865 726871.

Padstow 'Obby 'Os, Cornwall
Road M5 to end, A38 to Bodmin, then A389 via Wadebridge.
Rail/bus Nearest station Bodmin Parkway, from London Paddington and other centres.
Tourist information ↘ 01841 533449.

Robertsbridge bonfire, Sussex
Same as Battle but 4 miles closer to London.

Royal Shrovetide Football, Ashbourne, Derbyshire
Road From M1 J24 or J25, enter Derby, go round ring road and leave on A52 for 13 miles to Ashbourne.

Rail/bus Nearest station Derby (London St Pancras), then bus 107.
Tourist information ✆ 01335 343666.

South Queensferry Festival
Road From Edinburgh on A90 take Dalmeny turning before reaching the bridge. From M9 and M8 heading towards bridge, turn right before joining A90 otherwise you might end up crossing the toll bridge.
Rail From Edinburgh to Dalmeny station, which is in South Queensferry.
Tourist information ✆ 0131 473 3800.

St Giles Fair, Oxford
Among many points of interest, don't miss the great gargoyles (see page 208).
Road Off M40 from London and M25, or from Birmingham (J8/9).
Rail From London Paddington, Birmingham and many centres.
Coach Frequent cheap services.
Tourist information ✆ 01865 726871.

Stonehaven Fireball Ceremony, Aberdeen
Road 15 miles south of Aberdeen on A90 which comes north from Edinburgh as M90 at times.
Rail On London's King's Cross–Aberdeen via Edinburgh line.
Tourist information ✆ 01569 762801.

Tweedmouth Feast, Berwick-upon-Tweed
Road The A1 London–Edinburgh road bypasses the town.
Rail Berwick-upon-Tweed is on the London King's Cross–Edinburgh line.
Tourist information ✆ 01289 330733.

Up Helly Aa, Lerwick, Shetland
Ferry From Aberdeen.
Tourist information ✆ 01595 693434.

Whitstable Oyster Ceremony, Kent
Road From London/M25, M2 to J7, then A299.
Rail From London Victoria.
Tourist information ✆ 01227 275482.

World Coal Carrying Championship, Ossett, West Yorkshire
Road Just west of M1 J40 south of Leeds.
Rail Nearest stations Wakefield or Dewsbury.
Tourist information ✆ 0113 242 5242.

World Marbles Championship, Greyhound pub, Tinsley Green, near Crawley, West Sussex
Road From London/M25, M23 to J10, then turn right and right to double back north on B2036; Tinsley Green is on the left.
Rail Gatwick Airport station, from London Victoria and other centres.
Tourist information ✆ 01403 211661.

Eccentric Pastimes

COLLECTIONS OF ECCENTRICS
A cone-shaped world

Collecting is a slightly introverted hobby, even obsessive, solitary or self-absorbed, which seriously cool and street-cred trendy fashion victims would perhaps dub 'sad'. That puts me firmly on the side of collectors, who at least have an original thought in their heads, at least if they collect odder things than coins, stamps, matchboxes or beer mats. And believe me, they do.

Take David Morgan of Burford, Oxfordshire, who collects cones – parking cones, those much-loathed plastic objects which have multiplied endlessly up and down the nation's highways, perhaps contributing to safety but appearing merely to deprive drivers of mile after mile of lanes devoid of any visible repair work.

Mr Morgan, on the other hand, venerates cones. His garage holds 530 or so variations. There are metre-high jobs for the fast lane, small ones, black ones for undertakers, blue ones for water companies, flashing ones, barber-pole swirling striped ones, wooden ones, midget Italian ones, recycled ones, and five-sided ones.

His interest is understandable, perhaps, when you realise that his company, Inotech, based in nearby Broughton Poggs, manufactures perhaps 25,000 cones a week for use around the world. He tends to see a cone-dominated world: 'The really exciting bit of the Gulf War coverage was, when they were filming how the cruise missiles attacked Baghdad, there was one of my cones standing in the street!'

His obsession is more than simply commercial. He keeps standard cones in his car boot to trade for any interesting ones he may encounter and won't let pressing family matters get in the way of his interest: he found the rare rubber Lindvale model, which has pride of place in his collection, being used by funeral directors at his uncle's burial. Perhaps understandably, he says he didn't go on about cones to his fiancée until he was married, but on his honeymoon he left his wife at baggage reclaim to nab the 'fascinating' Adaptaform model at Corsica airport.

His four children have grown up in a beconed environment. 'It saved a lot of money on toys really,' he says. 'The kids can always cycle round cones in the garden.'

Actually, he is the history of the British traffic cone. He believes he made the first experimental plastic one when working at ICI in 1961, so he's got a

ECCENTRIC PASTIMES

KEY
Active pastime
Pastime displa

ATLANTIC OCEAN

Orkney Islands

Thurso

Isle of Lewis

Outer Hebrides

Isle of Skye

Inner

Hebrides

Inverness

Island of Mull

Islay

Aberdeen

Arran

North Sea

Glasgow **Edinburgh**

Carlisle

Newcastle upon Tyne

Middlesbrough

Pencil Museum, Keswick

Isle of Man

y

Tramp Museum, Ripon

York

Stan Laurel Museum, Ulverston

Kingston-upon-Hull

Irish Sea

Bradford

Leeds

Grimsby

Lawnmower Museum, Southport

Liverpool

Manchester

Anglesey

Sheffield

Holyhead

Stoke-on-Trent

100 km

60 miles

Lavatory Museum, Armitage

Derby

Nottingham

Cardigan Bay

Wolverhampton

Gas Museum, Leicester

Mustard & Teapot Museums, Norwich

Birmingham

Coventry

Needle Museum, Redditch

Cambridge

Ipswich

Fishguard

Coracle racing, Cilgerran

National Teddybear Museum, Stratford-upon-Avon

Cinema Organ Museum, St Albans

Advertising & Packaging Museum, Gloucester

Jenner Museum, Berkeley

Oxford

Clog Race, Kew

Dental, Tea & Operating Theatre Museums, London

Swansea

Woolsack Race, Tetbury

Reading

Cardiff

London Fan Museum

Bristol Channel

Bristol

Dover

Shoe Museum, Street

Mechanical Music Museum, Chichester

Southampton

Brighton

National Motor Museum, Beaulieu

Portsmouth

Corkscrew & Wine Museum, Alfriston

Exeter

National Wireless Museum, Ryde

Shock Machine, Overbecks, Salcombe

English Channel

Penzance

Pilchard Museum, Newlyn

lot to answer for. There were wooden ones before that, but strictly speaking they were usually pyramids, not cones. But where do all the cones go? Why do police forces have to re-order hundreds? Are they abducted by cone-headed aliens?

> 'It's a strange thing but if a road repair involves laying 400 cones, only about 390 come back. Students wear them as hats. They screw police ones upside down on ceilings as lightshades so they can read ECILOP on the wall. People use rows of them as flowerpots. They lie under hedges for a bit then end up propping open the village hall door. Hippies even burn them in braziers at West Country pop festivals.'

This may be cone sacrilege but it's all good business replacing them. Still, Mr Morgan's collection continues to grow. He found a lonely deserted cone in the middle of Exmoor once, miles from a road. And ask him where he found the Malaysian police number … would you believe on a Scilly Isles beach?

Cutting edge of old technology

He's not barmy, but he's often on the verge. Brian Radam of Southport, Lancashire, loves lawnmowers and is quite happy to come out of the closet, or rather garden shed, about his obsession. But then he has 400 of the things, including 150 fully restored in the museum he and his wife Sue run above their garden machinery business in Shakespeare Street, Southport (for details see page 51).

He says: 'I'm someone who can't let bygones be bygones. I saw these beautiful examples of old British engineering being thrown away by people who couldn't get spares or wanted new models and I thought it was a shame.' He bought his first veteran mower for 2 shillings (10p) as a teenager and did it up. Now, particularly when the seasonal mower business is quiet, Brian and Sue lovingly restore machines – making unobtainable spare parts and faithfully following original paint styles – not just for the museum but for customers who have come to appreciate fine examples of great names such as Ransome's, Atco, Royal Enfield, Perkins or Hawker Siddeley.

There are horse-drawn Shanks models, water-cooled jobs one can boil an egg in, specialist graveyard models, even the early hover numbers. Brian and Sue also have a Rolls-Royce mower, or rather a JP, which was the brandname Rolls used for a while. It gives a different edge to 'getting out the lawn Roller'. Like-minded members of the Old Lawnmower Society hold rallies around the country where models are as proudly displayed as vintage cars, and aficionados can tell a mower's make just by the sound.

Lawnmower racing and endurance grands prix are no joke either. There's an annual 12-hour event at Brinsbury Agricultural College, Wisborough Green, West Sussex, each August and speeds can reach 70mph in the ride-on class, the walk-behind models travelling at a more sedate 4–8mph. Blades are removed for the duration and admission is by ticket. (Incidentally, when I pointed out to a local mower fan that the Wisborough Green Mower Grand Prix was actually some way from that village, he

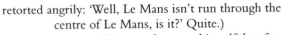

retorted angrily: 'Well, Le Mans isn't run through the centre of Le Mans, is it?' Quite.)

Brian used to race himself, but fate cruelly intervened when he developed hay fever. But as with Beethoven going deaf, Brian wasn't going to let this obstruct his great passion. 'I've even found abandoned mowers with trees growing through them and rescued them.'

People who have donated venerable mowers come and visit them in the museum. Brian and Sue's museum features celebrity mowers such as one from Prince Charles and another from Hilda Ogden of Coronation Street (the actress Jean Alexander). Sue says: 'We have tourists from America calling in because they can't believe we have such a museum. We also had a chap from the empty desert of Saudi Arabia – we had to explain to him about grass cutting and lawns first.'

Crate expectations

There is little outwardly odd about Mike and Naomi Hull's house and garden overlooking the beautiful Golden Valley near Stroud, Gloucestershire, until you notice the flagpole is topped with a milk bottle. And you may spot an oil painting of a milk bottle as you enter the stone-built house. A few ancient-looking milk bottles hove into view, but it is not until you enter their sanctum holding 1,300 different milk bottles that their passion for dairy glassware becomes transparent. One thousand three hundred different milk bottles? Aren't they all the same?

They are not, and this is where the fascination soon begins. For one thing there are different types, from 19th-century ones with wire spring and ceramic stopper closures like some Continental beer bottles have today, to the wide-necked pint bottle with the recessed waxed-cardboard disc which dominated the first half of the 20th century, to the aluminium foil covered tall bottles of my own childhood, to the dumpy glass bottles of today's few dairies which haven't surrendered to cartons, plastic bottles or, horror of horrors, plastic bags.

As Naomi says: 'In the process of development less and less glass was used to make the bottle, from a 29oz quart bottle of before the First World War to about 8oz of glass in the modern dumpy pint ones.'

Milk bottles, one can soon see, were relatively elegant and made far more interesting by the embossed name of the dairy which owned them (plus the usual warning to rinse and return, and sometimes even threats to other milkmen who might use them with STOLEN in huge type). From the early 1920s the addition of colour printing gave dairymen the opportunity for garish artwork, rough doggerel and slogans and even advertisements for completely different products.

It wasn't so bad when pictures of cows or ads for breakfast cereal appeared, but pink sausages on milk bottles seemed wrong somehow. As for the slogans, one W J Pickford's dairy of Downend, Bristol, had a picture of Mickey Mouse plus the somewhat dated:

'Mickey Mouse is always gay,
He drinks two pints of milk a day.'

For Clyde Higgs of Leamington Spa, corny puns were a speciality: 'No milk for seven days makes one WEAK.' Or try this rival's rhyme:

'Old Pat Russell has a farm Ee-aye-ee-aye-oh
At Yerbeston Farm he keeps good cows Ee-aye-ee-aye-oh
Friesians here, Jerseys there
Red top, gold top
You should drink a good drop
Have your milk from Russell's Farm Ee-aye-ee-aye-oh.'

Naomi explains that she and Mike began collecting in 1975 when they were living in Highgate, London, but had a bottle delivered embossed with the name Cricket Malherbie. 'This aroused my curiosity because *malherbie* was obviously Norman French for bad grass, so what was it doing on a milk bottle?' Actually, these kind of thoughts puzzled millions of people in the returnable bottle era, when they wondered how far bottles could stray from home and how they were ever returned. However, Naomi was motivated to find out that Cricket Malherbie was a dairy in Somerset taken over by the Express Dairy and their bottle stocks had been mixed. 'A couple of days later another bottle from a different part of the country turned up on our doorstep and I was hooked,' says Naomi.

Mike says: 'Initially, I said not to clutter up our cupboards with such stuff but eventually I became as interested as Naomi.' Soon students and colleagues of English teacher Naomi were turning up more examples. The Hulls had to know more and set about the task with Sherlock Holmes efficiency.

'We looked at older, pre-motorway maps, and calculated where people would be likely to stop for a picnic or snack on a long journey. A woodland layby with a bit of a view, usually.' The Hulls struck glass as frequently as the best prospectors strike oil. 'We picked a wood on the A303 road to the West Country and there within chucking distance was a treasure trove barely concealed. Bottles from all over the country – Cornwall, Scotland even, so you could tell which towns people came from and when and where they were going not just by the obvious direction but the resort dairy bottles they chucked there on their way home. Social history, really.'

There were so many in this one find that four car trips were needed to ferry them home. Other finds were made by checking under hedges at a likely cycling distance from major towns. The bottles, built for recycling whole, were virtually everlasting if dumped intact. And so the collection grew. There are Kosher bottles from north London with the Star of David; Hindi scripts from northern immigrant areas; an anagramatic 'Liropalfo Dairy' bottle for use on April 1; beautiful French ones with delightful script printed on them; and Pukkah colonial ones from Hong Kong, Rhodesia, and elsewhere.

Then there are the cardboard tops, which being disposable were far more topical and are ranged like stamps in the Hulls' albums. They loyally celebrate Their Majesties' Coronation of 1937, Dig For Victory in the 1940s, or other easily datable events. There is more social history in all the health claims on the bottles of the 1920s and 1930s, when thousands of children died of TB and brucellosis caught from milk, yet dairies proclaimed how safe and tested their milk was.

The death-knell for the cardboard capped bottles – 'such an elegant shape,' enthuses Naomi – came from hygiene requirements. Dust and dirt settled on the recessed top, which was far from tamperproof, with frequent evidence of watering milk or unhygienic practices. Equally, cleanliness has nearly killed off the colour printed bottles. 'The devices now used in bottling plants to detect dirt in the bottles cannot cope with printed slogans, so advertising has nearly come to an end,' says Mike. A rare survivor, luckily, is the Cotteswold Dairy at Tewkesbury near the Hulls' home.

The Hulls are not alone in their hobby. They run a newsletter, *Milk Bottle News*, for the perhaps 750 fans, who indulge in bottle rallies to swap and sell rare examples, and the Hulls' collection is far from the largest. 'There's a chap on the Isle of Wight with 7,000 different ones,' says Mike. 'Then if you start on American milk bottles, they had hundreds of thousands of different dairies. Then there's the cream bottles …'

Giveaway signs

There are as many peculiar collectors as things to collect, but some of the things collected are decidedly odd, whether it be the road signs collected by a Bromsgrove man or the world-beating collection of airline sickbags (unused, thankfully) amassed by Dr David Bradford of Richmond, Yorkshire. He had 1,112 at the last count. Then there is the Cast Iron Implement Seat Society who collect those elaborate iron seats featuring manufacturers' names which used to adorn farm equipment. The chairman, called Dennis, wants a DENNIS seat bolted to his coffin. Crackers? Absolutely, as his wife collects nutcrackers. Certainly, there are more truly odd collectors out there than anyone could believe. Perhaps someone should start a collection of them …

ECCENTRIC INTERESTS
The eccentric explorer

John Blashford-Snell is a man who has been explosively eccentric from an early age. Literally.

The great explorer and former Royal Engineers Lieutenant-Colonel (a rank particularly attractive to eccentrics, it seems), 'Blashers' ('the bloody *Daily Mail* made up that name') started off in the style in which he has carried on.

His father, a Hertfordshire country parson, thought it quite reasonable to clear the church gutters of rooks with rifle fire, gradually destroying the roof in the process. A visiting master of foxhounds, after a glass port too many at the vicarage, thought he was dying when he woke up and saw the family's pet foxes come in and curl up round the hearth. 'Oh my God, Vicar,' he said, 'damn foxes everywhere!' The young Blashers took after his father by carrying out his chore of ringing the early morning communion bell at a distance – with a .303 rifle. At 11, John shot himself in the thumb, trying to force a cartridge into his gun in his bedroom. 'Fortunately, I didn't feel a thing because it blew out my nerve, but bits of nail, bone and blood covered the wall my mother had just painted and she was furious.'

An army commission and a publicly funded supply of explosives set up the young eccentric. Take the way he dealt with a guardsman who kept using his field lavatory in Cyprus, for example. He boobytrapped the 'thunderbox' and the next guardsman who sat down was met by a deafening blast. The guardsman and plastic loo seat were hurled one way, the loo paper another, but there were no injuries.

In 1977 the Fleet Street papers were full of stories about a giant perch – nicknamed Jaws – terrorising a Kentish village pond. The army, unwisely, chose Blashers to deal with it. He took an armoured car and plenty of explosives. The resulting bang was so loud that a duck flying overhead laid an egg in fright. An old lady who had been near-deaf for years said: 'I think I heard something.' One of Blashers' men bellowed helpfully: 'That's only the atom bomb they've dropped on London.' 'Oh dear,' said the old lady in concern. 'Does that mean I won't get my paper in the morning?'

Another time, when Blashers was asked to clear a rubbish dump of rats, the explosives he used landed the rubbish up to 1,000 yards away and a chapel roof was covered in dead rats. Some explosions were unprompted but came nevertheless – like the time Blashers lost his eyebrows and some of his hair when a stove exploded in a remote Himalayan camp. 'Luckily my 24-year-old daughter Emma was there and threw me into a snow drift to put out the flames.'

For several years Blashers was the director-general of the youth expedition charity Operation Raleigh. One night he was lecturing some recruits on the banks of the Zambesi river when a bloodcurdling animal roaring started up close by. Blashers wasn't sure if this was as dangerous as it sounded. He asked for an image intensifier and peered into the night. 'To my amazement there were two hippos copulating a few yards away. They let out a huge roar and made off. God knows what the youngsters made of it, but it shook me up, I can tell you.'

Not that it's all been light-hearted stuff. The Colonel has widened scientific knowledge with his numerous expeditions, and saved at least one life – that of a British climber in Mongolia. It was an extraordinary saga of hopping across country, a borrowed helicopter, bribery for fuel and improvised surgery using the operating table for splints. Blashers' whole life has been one extraordinary saga after another, as his autobiography *Something Lost Behind the Ranges* (HarperCollins, £18) can testify.

One fling led to another

Many a small boy confronted by those history book drawings of medieval siege weapons must have thought: 'That'd be fun.' And contemplating the impractical-looking sling-like trebuchet, a sort of giant tripod the size of a house with an ungainly see-saw and sling, they night wonder: 'But did it really work?'

For a long time no one knew because the things hadn't existed for hundreds of years. The question also intrigued former cavalry officer and Shropshire landowner Hew Kennedy, so he set about building a trebuchet with his friend Richard Barr. First there was a small Meccano model. 'Bloody hopeless,' he said. The next small trebuchet worked and was used to fire blazing lavatory bowls. Then came the monster full-sized version fashioned out of pine trunks and using a 60ft beam and a heavy counterweight. In the Middle Ages, vast boulders were said to have been fired into besieged castles, and alternative missiles were rotting carcasses, blazing objects, heads of prisoners, or plague-ridden corpses – the usual stuff of medieval neighbourly disputes.

'I'm interested in ancient weapons,' Mr Kennedy said, 'and some historians said these machines could only fire small stones and wouldn't be able to batter down walls and gates in a siege. We had to test this out.' Now Mr Kennedy and Mr Barr have proved it that the trebuchet was indeed the heavy artillery of its day. They happily fired an exploding piano, which landed with a satisfying Peyoing!!!, a dead pig – 'very aerodynamic' – and the *tour de force*, an exploding Yugo car stuffed with petrol cans, which flew 150 yards before exploding satisfactorily on impact. 'Well, it worked,' said a satisfied Mr Kennedy afterwards. 'Pity about the car, it went quite well, I drove it up here.'

THIS RATHER ECCENTRIC RACE

The eccentric British race could well describe the decidedly odd sports indulged in annually around the country. These include men who don women's clothing and take axes to smash down gates; a horse race without a course that crosses a busy trunk road; Londoners running in clogs and aprons or rowing for a full-skirted coat; paddling Iron Age craft through rapids; or running up hills carrying heavy sacks of wool or coal. And then, for good measure, there is the re-running of an arduous race where the original entrant dropped dead.

The **Beca Mountain Race** held in Mynachlog-ddu in the Preseli Hills near Fishguard, Pembrokeshire, recalls the Rebecca riots of 1843 when local bands of men, dressed as women with leaders called 'Rebeccas', smashed down hated toll gates that were making life expensive after the roads were handed to fee-charging turnpike trusts to improve them for stagecoaches. The military had to be called out to quell the rioters, who took their name from the biblical Rebecca, who was sent by her father and brother to become Isaac's wife with the words: 'Let thy seed possess the gates of those that hate thee.'

Late in August, the modern race involves climbing steep hills and then, on return, donning women's clothing and smashing down a gate. Another annual race with a dressing up tradition is the **Clog and Apron Race** at the Royal Botanic Gardens, Kew, London, where late in September dozens of horticultural students thus garbed have to clatter their way down the 373-yard Broad Walk.

The third Thursday in March sees one of the world's oddest and oldest horse races, the **Kiplingcotes Derby**, take place on a peculiar uphill route – there is no proper course, although many old maps show the route – along lanes and across fields off A163 near Market Weighton, Yorkshire. The road is closed by police as the riders cross it at full tilt. The start and finish of the race, first held in 1519, are out of sight of each other, so the only spectator ever to see the whole race was a man who once had a helicopter waiting.

Until recently, the second prize was worth considerably more than the first, due to the income from a poor investment in 1618 paying the winner and the second taking the entry money, which once led to an unseemly 'you go first' tussle at the finish. 'This has now been put right,' said the clerk of the course, Mrs Susan Hillaby, 'the first past the post really does get more.' Her duties, handed down from her father and grandfather, include reading the few rules at 11.30 before sending the riders downhill to the start at around noon.

Riders who do not weigh the prescribed ten stone can carry stones or pieces of metal in their pockets to even the odds. Mrs Hillaby is proud that the race has never been stopped, neither by war, plague, famines nor storms. 'There were dreadful snow drifts in 1948 and to keep the tradition alive, a lone farmer fought his way through on foot, leading his horse.' (Another uphill struggle is the **World Coal Carrying Championship**, which sees the nation's coalmen converge on Ossett, West Yorkshire, on Easter Monday for a back-breaking event – see *Easter*, Chapter 1).

Similarly lung-busting endeavours take place at Tetbury, Gloucestershire, on the spring bank holiday Monday when **Woolsack Day** commemorates the town's prosperous role in the medieval wool trade. The Woolsack races entail runners carrying 65lb sacks of wool up and down the 280 yards between two pubs on the fearsome 1 in 4 gradient of Gumstool Hill. It all started back in the

Middle Ages with local lads in the wealthy woollen town trying, as ever, to impress the maidens. There is also a medieval market and street entertainment, featuring a jester and a witch (gumstool means ducking stool for testing witches – if they drowned they were innocent) as the town goes back in time hundreds of years for the day. There's a Gumstool pub a couple of miles away.

Someone who did drop dead after a race was Guto, a local hero born in 1700 who lived at Nyth Bran farmhouse in mid-Glamorgan. Local people said Guto could outrun a horse, but when he took on an Englishman named Price over a 12-mile course, Guto won handsomely, only to drop dead. His memory is kept alive by a torchlit midnight road race on New Year's Eve at **Mountain Ash**, mid-Glamorgan.

A much older Welsh sport is **coracle racing**, which still takes place in Cilgerran, near Cardigan. These Iron Age oval boats made from animal skins, light enough to be carried on a man's back, are still used for fishing on several Welsh rivers. The course runs over a rocky stretch of the River Teifi every August. The National Coracle Centre is nearby at Cenarth, a few miles upstream on the Teifi.

A river race of precisely datable origins is the **Doggett's Coat and Badge Race**, held every July (the date depends on tides) between London Bridge and Chelsea on the Thames. Comedian Thomas Doggett launched the race in 1716 to celebrate the accession of George I to the throne. Prizes from money left by Doggett include a splendid full-length red coat with a tight waist and a silver badge for the best oarsman, who looks rather odd thus dressed in today's London. Maybe Doggett is having the last laugh. Again, there's a pub named after the race, right on Blackfriars Bridge.

ON THE ROAD TO ECCENTRICITY
Crustacean conversion

Should you be out driving and be overtaken by a garden shed, of the plain wooden variety, or a chap sitting on a sofa steering with a pizza pan on a coffee table in front of him with a standard lamp behind flapping in the wind, or a giant lobster-cum-Morris Minor, complete with snapping claws, then there are three possibilities. You are asleep and dreaming; you are far too drunk or drugged to drive; or you have encountered some of Britain's motoring eccentrics, a truly bizarre collection. There is also a motorised orange, a 70mph dodgem, and even a high-speed fireside armchair.

The Morris crustacean, named Claude by its owner at the time of writing (he was trying to sell it), probably outrages as many folk as it amuses, such is the reverence these cars are held in by some people, but the crustacean conversion is well done. It has a head made out of an old crash helmet, complete with antennae, above the windscreen. The claws are the best bit, for they actually snap open and shut as the car drives, being powered by windscreen wiper motors in the doors. Brilliant as it is, don't Morris fans object to one of their treasured cars being mutilated, I asked owner Phil Vincent of Burton Joyce, near Nottingham. 'Not when I explain it was done for a television series,' explains Phil, who has used the 150,000-mile car as a local runabout for so long that people in the village don't even turn round when a giant pink snapping lobster drives past. 'I work on making panels for Morris enthusiasts to restore the cars, and a mate of mine said he wanted a Morris Minor for a TV show by noon the next day, so I got him one. They spent about £8,000 on doing it up and used it in a children's TV series *Professor Lobster* during the 1980s. They had thought of using a VW Beetle, like in the Herbie films, but wanted something more British. When the series was over I bought it back and have been taking it to shows all round the country ever since. It's a bit heavy, with the tail full of filler and old inner tubes, but Claude goes all right with a tail wind,' he quipped. And goes better on Shell, no doubt.

Shed inhibitions

The garden shed, built on a quad bike frame and capable of 56mph, is fully roadworthy and street legal, as are the sofa-cum-living room, a motorised rubbish skip and a huge Outspan orange, which all met for a race at Donnington Park racing circuit in Leicestershire in 1998, organised by the *Sun* newspaper.

The shed, complete with trailing pot plants in a window box and rattling watering cans hung up, can potter along at 56mph, but the skip, despite its 1300cc engine, turned out to be, well, rubbish on corners. The giant orange, built for a fruit company, could manage 61mph, but was pipped at the post by Ed China's 79mph couch. Ed, a 27-year-old inventor-designer when I spoke to him, said it all started when he had to raise £4,500 to go on an Operation Raleigh adventure training trip to Belize. 'I thought I could raise sponsorship and so on, so I made it out of the front end of a Mini, and the front wheel of a Reliant Robin plus some bits of wood from the garage.' (A Robin is one of those quirky British three-wheel cars, themselves a bit eccentric in foreigners' estimation.) 'Being a three-wheeler it tends to go on only two

wheels on bends if you're doing the full 85mph but then it just planes down the wood underneath a bit more!' Ed's odd approach to motoring started two years before the Sitting Room, as he calls it, with a furry Beetle (the VW car, not the creature). Then came the sofa concept. 'We were sitting round in the pub talking about slobs who order pizzas from home, and we said it would be great it you could just drive down to the Pizza Hut in your living room, so we did it.'

As a fund-raising exercise, the Sitting Room was a complete flop. Pizza and cola companies, etc, approached for sponsorship, couldn't see what he was on about. But after the trip to Belize, more publicity began to earn appearance money at various arena events, and now Ed China is setting himself up as an agent for other wacky cars:

> 'The oranges – there were about four – were made for advertising back in the Sixties, but they made them too well. There's one in the National Motor Museum at Beaulieu (which also has a 1924 Daimler beer bottle) but the other ones have started to come out of storage.
>
> 'The guy with the shed – which is on a quad bike so it's quite stable – is George Shields of Derbyshire, and like the living room, it's completely street legal. He's working on a high-speed grand piano, and I've got commissions for a bathroom and a four-poster bed.'

Just try not to lose control of your own car if you see one of them coming round a corner...

Beaulieu

ODD ASSOCIATIONS
Tall stories and pillar boxes

There are societies for everything if you know where to look. Where do you start? The Left-Handers' Club (☎ 020 7437 3910) runs Left-Handers' Day and there are Anything Left-Handed shops in Brewer Street, London, and New Street, Worcester (☎ 020 8770 3722 and 01905 25798), where sinister (in the Latin sense) lefties can buy scissors, corkscrews, potato peelers, etc.

What other odd groups can one send a letter off to? To begin with, there is the Pillar Box Group. (This is a more serious affair than you might think. I once met author Jon Wynne-Tyson, a king of a tiny uninhabited Caribbean island who lived near Fontwell, Sussex, and had a remarkable collection of 30 or so boxes standing around his garden.) Have you seen a rare Edward VIII box? Try Chorleywood in Hertfordshire. A Queen Victoria hexagonal? Kensington, London, has plenty. A Victorian vertical slot octagonal with bad weather flap? The only one is at Barnes Cross, Holwell, Dorset. Then there are the elaborate pseudo-Tudor postboxes donated to the villages of Rous Lench and Radford, Worcestershire, by the eccentric local squire and parson, Dr Chaffy, at the end of the 19th century. Either you find this sort of stuff fascinating or you don't, but it is undeniably fascinating that some people, like trainspotters or bird twitchers, will drive hundreds of miles to bag a rare pillar box.

There is even a Talbot Society which holds reunions for anyone called Talbot. The Talbots travel to Port Talbot, Wales, in their Talbot cars, stopping off at the innumerable Talbot hotels (a talbot was a Norman hunting dog, if you must know). A Tall Persons' Club of Great Britain & Ireland (↘ 07000 TALL-1-2, or 07000 825512 with a numbers only phone), for people probably unkindly nicknamed 'Shorty' at school, meets in a Docklands tower block, where they have a high old time telling their kind of tall stories. Finally, the Bald-Headed Club of Great Britain recently had the bare-faced cheek to write to a leading Labour politician who is alleged to wear a wig, offering him a prominent position in the club.

ECCENTRICITY ON DISPLAY: BRITAIN'S TOP 21 ODD MUSEUMS

1 Advertising and Packaging Museum, Gloucester

Founder Robert Opie, with admirable foresight – although his friends may have thought him a little odd – started at the age of 16 in 1963 collecting, dating and price-labelling ordinary packaging of then contemporary household goods. A tad boring in 1963, but by 2000, absolutely fascinating. Since then his collection has mushroomed and gone back in time to the fascinating and unlikely origins of the things on our kitchen shelves. His greatest wish? 'Probably an early Heinz baked bean can, dating back to the end of the 19th century. Mine only go back to the 1930s,' he says wistfully.

Advertising and Packaging Museum, Albert Warehouse, The Docks, Gloucester; ↘ 01452 302309; web: www.themuseum.co.uk
Road M5 J11a, follow signs for Gloucester Docks.
Rail Gloucester station from London Paddington, Birmingham or Bristol, 15-min walk.
Tourist information ↘ 01452 421188.

2 Cinema Organ Museum, St Albans, Hertfordshire

See and hear a couple of those amazing Wurlitzer organs from the great days of giant 'dream palaces', mostly now demolished, and four gaudily decorated mechanical organs which, like those in fairgrounds, work automatically but equally rousingly off punched cards with the music on them.

Cinema Organ Museum, 320 Camp Rd, St Albans; ✎ 01727 851557.
Road Off M1, A1 or M25.
Rail St Albans City, from London St Pancras.
Tourist information ✎ 01727 864511.

Corkscrew Museum, Alfriston, Sussex

Actually just a display that's part of the English Wine Museum at the English Wine Centre, near Drusilla's Zoo. There is also an extensive corkscrew collection, not always on display, at the Victoria & Albert Museum, Kensington (✎ 020 7938 8500).
English Wine Museum at the English Wine Centre, Alfriston; ✎ 01323 870164; web:
www.englishwine.co.uk
Road Off A27 coast road between Brighton (M23 from London/M25) and Hastings. *Rail*
Berwick, from London Victoria, 1 mile walk south.
Tourist information ✎ 01323 442667.

Dental Museum, London

Mainly for the professional, though the public is welcome if visits are arranged by appointment ('Let's see, I can fit you in a week on Friday ...').
Dental Museum, 64 Wimpole Street, London W1; ✎ 020 7935 0875.
Tube: Bond St (Central/Jubilee lines).

Electric Shock Machine Museum, Salcombe, Devon

There is actually just the one machine, Overbeck's Rejuvenator, which made a huge fortune of £3 million for Otto Overbeck in the 1920s. The eccentric inventor of Bovril and alcohol-free beer left his peculiar collection of curios and his home at Overbecks to a possibly grateful nation.
Overbecks Museum (National Trust), Sharpitor, Salcombe; ✎ 01548 842893; web:
www.salcombe-online.co.uk
Road From end of M5, A38, then A382 to Newton Abbot, A381 to Salcombe.
Tourist information ✎ 01548 843927.

Gas Museum, Leicester

Not so much the gas itself, which would be rather difficult to pin down or display, but the history of the gas industry from the grimy Victorian coal gasworks to a 1920s kitchen full of appliances, to modern natural gas piped from the North Sea. Which of these is feasible: gas iron, gas hairdryer, gas fridge, gas curling tongs, gas projectors, gas radio? Answer: all of them and they're all on display. In the Victorian gatehouse of an old gasworks. Open Tuesday to Friday afternoons. Also, watch out for a future Gas Cooker Museum planned by a Cotswold building surveyor, James Bunce of Cirencester.
Gas Museum, 195 Aylestone Road, Leicester; ✎ 0116 250 3190; web:
www.emnet.co.uk/Museums/GasMuseum/
Road Off M1 (J21/22). From town centre ring road take Aylestone Rd (A426) and look out on right just after rail bridge.

Previous page It's considered lucky to meet the Burry man, who in August stalks the streets of South Queensferry, Lothian (RM)

Top Infernal goings-on at Burghead's dramatic Burning the Clavie (GB)

Right Historic figures make a torchlit parade through Lewes (BL)

Bottom right Competitors' dress must be 'smart, no jeans', for the World Bog Snorkelling Championship at Llanwrtyd Wells (CA)

Bottom left The Bognor Birdman event attracts all kinds of hopefuls who vie to fly off the Sussex resort's pier (BL)

Rail Leicester, from London St Pancras or cross-country. Walk south on ring road and then as above.
Tourist information ☎ 0116 2998888.

Inoculation Museum, Berkeley, Gloucestershire

This includes the hut where poor local children received jabs for free from the great Dr Edward Jenner, whose work on the now-eradicated scourge of smallpox means he saved more lives than anyone else on earth. He liked to call the hut the Temple of Vaccinnia, which could equally indicate a sense of humour or a complete lack of one. His study and medical equipment may be viewed in his former home. Open afternoons except Mondays.
Jenner Museum, Berkeley; ☎ 01453 810631; web:
www.fivevalleys.demon.co.uk/jenner.htm
Road Signed west of A38 midway between Bristol and Gloucester.
Tourist information ☎ 01452 421188.

Laurel and Hardy Museum, Ulverston, Cumbria

The local boy was the thin one in the globally famous comedy duo. The films, the music, the custard pies.
Stan Laurel Museum, Upper Brook St, Ulverston; ☎ 01229 582292; web:
www.furness.co.uk/on-line/laurelandhardy.htm
Road A590 west from M6 J36.
Rail Connecting services to Ulverston from London Euston–Glasgow line.
Tourist information ☎ 01229 587120.

Lavatory Museum, Armitage, Staffordshire

Armitage Shanks lifts the lid on its illustrious history. Exhibits dating back to the 9th century include an Armitage china bedpan recovered from a ship sunk in the Clyde. When you think about it, the subject is hardly a minority interest, so there's a lot to go on: not just the fascinating and heavily embellished Victorian contraptions, but also the answers to intriguing up-to-date questions such as how you make a bog-standard lavatory bowl in one piece without using two halves of a mould.
Lavatory Museum, Armitage, near Lichfield; ☎ 01543 490253.
Road Off A51 from Tamworth, off M42 J10.
Rail Rugely or Lichfield, from London Euston.
Tourist information ☎ 01543 308209.

Lawnmower Museum, Southport, Lancashire

Contains 150 vintage and celebrity machines (see page 39). Open 09.00–17.45 except Sundays. A smaller display at Trerice, a National Trust manor house near Newquay, Cornwall (☎ 01637 875404), has a mere 87 mowers.
Lawnmower Museum, above Brian and Sue Radam's lawnmower shop, Shakespeare St, Southport; ☎ 01704 535369; web: www.lawnmowerworld.co.uk
Road M6, follow signs.

Rail Southport, 15-min walk.
Tourist information ➘ 01704 533333.

11 Mechanical Music Museum and Doll Collection, Chichester, Sussex

One hundred china or wax-headed Victorian dolls amid the cacophony of 100 automatic music boxes, curios, and mechanical dance organs from the same period.

Mechanical Music Museum and Doll Collection, Church Road, Portfield, Chichester; ➘ 01243 785421.
Road A3 from London then A27 east.
Rail London Victoria and cross country.
Tourist information ➘ 01243 775888.

12 Mustard Museum, Norwich, Norfolk

Hotter than the Spice Girls ever were, Norfolk's mustard industry has a fascinating history illustrated here through the history of the Colman family, plus, of course, oodles of products to buy. And if that leaves you thirsty, try the Teapot Museum nearby (see below).

Mustard Museum, in the Mustard Shop, 3 Bridewell Alley, Norwich; ➘ 01603 627889; web: www.norwich.gov.uk/tourism/museums/museums
Road A11 from London, A47 from Midlands.
Rail Norwich from London Liverpool St or Birmingham and Peterborough.
Tourist information ➘ 01603 666071.

13 Needle Museum, Redditch, Worcestershire

An interesting remnant of a once-huge local industry that helped stitch the Empire together. This is in fact a water-powered needle scouring mill but you'll have to go along to see the point. One could naturally follow this with the **Button Museum**, Ross on Wye, but the owners were at the time of writing likely to retire ('sell our collection? Never!'), so check with tourist information.

Needle Museum Forge Mill, Needle Mill Lane, Redditch; ➘ 01527 62509
Road Off M40 London–Birmingham at J2, south on A441, signed at first roundabout.
Rail Redditch, on branch line from Birmingham.
Bus: The free shopper bus from Redditch bus station to Sainsbury's takes you near, then walk under dual carriageway to museum.
Tourist information ➘ 01527 60806.

14 Operating Theatre Museum, London Bridge

Return to the land of hope and gory when conscious, screaming patients in front of an audience (as in operating theatre) endured butchery that often killed them while sawdust soaked up the blood. The Old Operating Theatre and Herb Garret, near London Bridge, dates from 1822 and offers a fascinating insight into days before antiseptics and anaesthetics. If this makes you feel faint, there's always the **London Fan Museum** at Greenwich.

Old Operating Theatre and Herb Garret, 9A St Thomas's St, near London Bridge, London SE1; ℡ 020 7955 4791; web: www.southwark.gov.uk/tourism/attractions/ old_operating_theatre/index.htm
Rail Mainline and Northern Line tube: London Bridge.
London Fan Museum, 10–12 Groom Hill, Greenwich SE10; ℡ 020 8305 1441.
Rail Near Greenwich station mainline from London Charing Cross, North Greenwich on Jubilee tube (then bus or 1½-mile walk), or Cutty Sark on Docklands Light Railway from north of the river or Lewisham.

Pencil Museum, Keswick, Cumbria
Some may not see the point, to be blunt, but it's quite a draw on a rainy day in the Lake District where graphite mines provided the 'lead' for the famous Cumberland pencils. How about the world's biggest pencil, or spy pencils with secret maps in them? Plus all the 4Bs or 3Hs you can carry.
Pencil Museum, Greta Bridge, Keswick, Cumbria; ℡ 01768 773626; web: www.pencils.co.uk
Road From M6 J40, A66 west.
Tourist information ℡ 01768 772645.

Pilchard Museum, Newlyn, Penzance, Cornwall
A working museum where fish are still being processed, as well as telling the history of the industry. This is not a museum dedicated to your common tinned pilchard, but the last bastion of the traditional salted and pressed Cornish pilchard, for more than a century a vital ingredient of *Salacche Salate Inglesi* in certain northern Italian villages who still snap up most of the factory's output.
Pilchard Museum, Newlyn, Penzance, Cornwall; ℡ 01736 332112.
Road A30 to Penzance from end of M5 at Exeter.
Rail Penzance, from London Paddington and other centres.
Tourist information ℡ 01736 362207.

Shoe Museum, Street, Somerset
The home of Clark's shoes, but this family business is not the sole subject. It has the last word on footwear back to the 16th century and, on the way in, some early shoemaking machines.
Shoe Museum, Street.
Road Off M5 J23, A39 towards Glastonbury.
Tourist information ℡ 01458 832954.

Teapot Museum, Norwich Castle, Norfolk
This features a selection of the world's largest collection of British teapots, 3,000 varieties from short and stout to ancient and priceless and including the world's largest. And if that doesn't put the lid on it, 1,000 or so more of the same can be seen at the **Bramah Tea and Coffee Museum** at Butler's Wharf near Tower Bridge, London, including the largest teapot ever thrown on a potter's wheel, an 800-cup job, ancient coffee machines, etc.

For travel, see *Mustard Museum*.

Bramah Tea and Coffee Museum, The Clove Building, Maguire St, London SE1; ↘ 020 7378 0222.

Road East from A100 south side of Tower Bridge.

Rail/bus London Bridge (mainline/Northern Line tube), then walk or take 47 bus southeast on Tooley St or Tower Hill (Circle/District Line tubes) and cross Tower Bridge (itself a magnificently daft way to build a bridge). Maguire St runs south from Shad Thames, which follows the river bank east from the south side of Tower Bridge but at a lower level.

19 National Teddybear Museum, Stratford-upon-Avon, Warwickshire

Other similar museums include the **Teddy Museum**, 76 High St, Broadway, Worcestershire; ↘ 01386 858323; and another in the promising-sounding 38 Dragon St, Petersfield, Hampshire; ↘ 01730 265108.

Teddybear Museum, Greenhill St, Stratford-upon-Avon; ↘ 01789 293160.

Road Off M40 J15 then A46 southwest.

Rail Stratford from London Marylebone or Birmingham.

Tourist information ↘ 01789 293127.

20 Tramps, Villains and Paupers Museum, Ripon, North Yorkshire

There are actually two linked museums, the Prison and Police Museum which includes stocks and chains in an 1816 extension to a house of correction, and the Ripon Workhouse Museum housed in an 1854 building, including the delousing room and workyard. Curator Anthony Chadwick says: 'This place has a remarkable effect on people. About 90 per cent of visitors to the prison approve of everything that they see and wish to go back to those times, then they see the workhouse and their reaction is exactly the opposite.'

Ripon Museums, Allhallowgate, Ripon; ↘ 01765 690799.

Road Off A1 north of Wetherby, then A61 southwest.

Rail/bus London King's Cross to Leeds, then to Harrogate, then frequent bus 36.

Tourist information ↘ 01765 604625.

21 Wireless Museum, Ryde, Isle of Wight

Marconi transmitted from here to the mainland first before trying to bridge bigger and bigger stretches of water and installing his equipment on the *Titanic* which saved so many lives. There is a good collection of early radios and televisions, if that kind of thing is on your wavelength.

National Wireless Museum, Puckpool Park, Ryde; ↘ 01983 567665.

Road On A3054 on east edge of Ryde (towards Seaview). Car ferry from Portsmouth (reached by A3 from London/M25) lands 3 miles west on same road at Fishbourne.

Rail Ryde Esplanade, from London Waterloo, including ferry from Portsmouth Harbour.

Tourist information ↘ 01983 562905.

PS ... A REAL LIVE WIRE

Train-spotters are two-a-penny in his line of work, but West Country railwayman Harvey Brant is a little different – he's a pylon spotter. Electricity pylons, that is, those dull grey things that march uninvited across the countryside.

Mr Brant, 34, spends hours roaming the countryside to photograph the towering metal structures and record their serial numbers. And no, they're not all ugly and all the same, he says.

'Electricity pylons can really enhance the beauty of a landscape,' he claims. 'They are sadly unappreciated and are quite stunning feats of engineering. They provide a comforting reminder of Man's harnessing of the forces of nature.'

Mr Brant took up pylon-hunting in 1999 after being bored by his workmates' talk about train-spotting. He has now set up a website – http://users.tinyonline.co.uk/bigh/bigh/pylonof.htm – to log his findings. There's a Pylon of the Month – a sort of pin-up page. When I checked, it was, if you're interested, TP23 at Hindlip in Worcestershire. His favourite, however, is 4YX183 near the M4–M5 junction at Almondsbury, south Gloucestershire.

'Its design and backdrop are superb,' he enthuses. I couldn't possibly comment.

TRAVEL INFORMATION

Clog and Apron Race, Kew Gardens, Surrey; ↘ 020 8940 1171
Road South of Kew Bridge on the north/south circular roads and north of the A316 which links the M3 from the M25 to Chiswick.
Rail Kew Gardens, District Line tube and North London main line.

Coracle racing, Cilgerran, near Cardigan
Road From west end of M4, A48 to Carmarthen, then A484. Cilgerran is on left before Cardigan.
Rail Nearest station Carmarthen, from London Paddington.
Tourist information ↘ 01239 613230 (There is also an impressive castle above the river.)

National Motor Museum, Beaulieu, Hampshire; ↘ 01590 612345
Road Signed from M27 J2.
Rail From London Waterloo to Brockenhurst, then taxi. Keen walkers or cyclists could use Beaulieu Rd (3 miles).
Tourist information ↘ 01590 689000.

Woolsack Day, Tetbury, Gloucestershire
Road From M4 J17, north on A429 then west on B4014.
Rail Nearest station Kemble, from London Paddington.
Tourist information ↘ 01666 503552.

BARMY BUREAUCRACY & CURIOUS CHARITIES

ATLANTIC OCEAN

Thurso

Orkney Islands

Isle of Lewis

Outer Hebride

Isle of Skye

Inner Hebrides

Inverness

Aberdeen

Island of Mull

Islay

Arran

Glasgow

Edinburgh

North Sea

Isle of Man

Carlisle

Newcastle upon Tyne

Middlesbrough

York

Irish Sea

Bradford

Leeds

Kingston-upon-Hull

Anglesey

Manchester

Liverpool

Sheffield

Grimsby

Holyhead

Stoke-on-Trent

Derby

Nottingham

Oakham Castle

Norwich

Cardigan Bay

Wolverhampton

Bromsgrove Court Leet

Birmingham

Coventry

Cambridge

Ipswich

Fishguard

Dunmow Flitch Marriage Trials

Mayor Weighing, High Wycombe

Keys ceremony, Tower of London

Oxford

Guildhall processions

Admiralty Court, Rochester

0 100km
0 60 miles

Swansea

Cardiff

Bristol

LONDON

Stratfield Saye

Dover

Bristol Channel

Hungerford & the Tuttimen

Tichborne Dole of Crawls

Biddenden Dole of Siamese Twins

Southampton

Brighton

Exeter

Portsmouth

Isle of Wight

English Channel

Penzance

N

Barmy Bureaucracy and Curious Charities

PAYING THE RENT IN ROSES, NAILS AND PARSNIPS

Paying the rent might be one of life's less amusing chores, yet for some this droll routine is curiously colourful and the rent is even paid for centuries after the property in question has disappeared.

Every June 24 a single red Knollys Rose is carried on a velvet cushion by churchwardens of All-Hallows-by-the-Tower in the City of London to the Lord Mayor at Mansion House. This quit-rent was a penalty imposed on Sir Robert Knollys in 1381 because he built a gallery bridge between two of his properties – now long gone – across narrow Seething Lane. This rose is not unique as a form of rent: at Long Melford church, Suffolk, each Trinity Sunday (usually in June), the mayor and town council of Hadleigh pay the rent of one red rose to Sir William de Clopton, who donated the Guildhall to Hadleigh. The thorny problem with this is that the payment started in 1451 and his descendants have long since emigrated to America, but the arrangement still continues. The rent is placed on Sir William's tomb, without fail.

That this is not merely a medieval hangover was demonstrated in 1995 by the start of a 99-year lease of land by Mrs Mary Cornelius-Reid of Sutton Scotney, near Winchester, Hampshire. The rent is a dozen red roses payable each Midsummer's Day. The land was to be used by the Wessex Children's Hospice Trust. Similarly, a red rose is paid each August to the Duke of Northumberland as rent for a piece of land near Newburn church used as public open space.

Initially difficult to understand is the annual rent for the Rose and Lion pub in Bromyard, Hereford and Worcester, first paid in January 1997: a kilo of home-grown parsnips. Landlady Fran Hurdman handed over the token amount after Wye Valley Brewery owner Peter Amor decided to charge her in vegetables instead of cash, as a way of ensuring that the pub garden was kept full of crops to put off greedy developers.

Much harder to understand and more than 700 years older are the Horseshoe and Faggot Cutting ceremonies held at the High Court, London, on a Wednesday afternoon late each October ('between the morrow of St Michael and the morrow of St Martin'). The City Solicitor cuts hazel rods with two knives, which he then presents to the Queen's Remembrancer, who pronounces 'Good service'. This is the rent for a piece of ground called The Moors at Eardington in Shropshire. Six very large horseshoes and 61 nails are then counted out and the Remembrancer pronounces 'Good number'. This was the rent agreed after Walter le Brun was granted land in 1235 for a forge in St Clement Danes parish, probably where Australia House now stands. This may be the oldest surviving English ceremony, apart from the Coronation. It is as if the Rose and Lion pub (above) had been demolished for several centuries, totally forgotten about, the site redeveloped several times over, yet the parsnips still handed over each year for an unknown reason.

Penalties for not paying ancient rents can be severe. The Wroth Silver is paid by the 25 parishes of Knightlow Hundred (a hundred being an old rural district) to the Duke of Buccleuch, Lord of the Hundred. The rent must be paid before sunrise each St Martin's Day (November 11) at Knightlow Cross near Dunchurch, Warwickshire. The representatives gather in the often freezing darkness to hear the duke's agent read the Charter of Assembly and in turn walk three times round the stone, say 'Wroth Silver' and drop coins into the hole where the cross used to be – the sums varying from one penny to about 12p. The entire company then repairs to a pub nearby to breakfast, some at the duke's expense, and drink his health in rum and milk.

Although the duke must make a loss on the whole operation – he receives less than 50p in total Wroth Silver – non-payment is rigorously enforced at a rate of £1 per old penny unpaid, or a fine of a white bull with red ears and a red nose. Such old English cattle are now hard to find, yet this fine was imposed at least once in the 19th century.

Some quit rents certainly seem a good bargain for both sides. The Duke of Wellington's enormous **Stratfield Saye** estate on the Hampshire–Berkshire border is paid for each June 18 with the presentation of a memento of the Iron Duke's victory at Waterloo in 1815 – a small silk tricolour flag is given to the monarch before noon and is hung on the duke's bust in the Guard Room at Windsor Castle.

Perhaps the most exclusive rent – or rather tax – in the kingdom is applied only to peers of the realm passing through Oakham, Leicestershire, who must give a shoe from his or her horse, or enough money to have one made, so they may be hung in **Oakham Castle** Hall to go with the 218 others to be seen today – including one from the Queen.

BRITAIN'S WEIRD COURTS THAT COURT DISBELIEF
Putting your marriage on trial

The Rule of Law is often upheld as one of those Great British virtues – like sporting fair play – spread by the Empire to the four corners of the globe (by such smug people as always ignore the planet's complete lack of corners). But when you examine the peculiar way some of Britain's oldest and oddest courts actually operate, you could be forgiven for thinking them not much of a role model, with the daftest goings-on you could imagine.

There is the Big Court Night, for example, at Laugharne, Carmarthenshire, where on the first Monday of each October the new Portreeve is elected with much pomp and ceremony, then adorned with a fabulous three-strand chain of golden cockleshells (engraved with the names of the previous Portreeves) and carried three times round the town hall shoulder high by the constables.

This is just part of the paraphernalia created in the 13th-century charter, including not only the Portreeve, but a Grand Jury, Recorder, Common Attorneys, Constables, Halbadiers and a Bailiff.

Older and yet odder is the Court of Arraye at Lichfield, Staffordshire, each Spring bank holiday, which dates back to before 1176 in the reign of Henry II and was once part of a nationwide array of men-at-arms, to assess all men between 14 and 60 years of age and inspect their arms and armour. Today the High Constable still presides but the Bowers Procession is a less warlike event, with the crowning of a local maid as Bower Queen, plus a market and a fair.

One of the oldest, oddest, yet ever-relevant courts in the country must be the **Dunmow Flitch** trials, held in June or July every leap year at Great Dunmow, Essex. It dates from 1104 when the lord of the manor, Robert Fitzwalter, established a priory there. To test it he and his wife went in disguise and asked for a blessing on their marriage, according to the local legend. The prior quizzed them about it closely and was so impressed he gave the couple a side of bacon. After that Sir Robert gave the priory some lands, on condition that they offered a flitch of bacon to whichever man could show that within a year and a day of his marriage he did not repent of his wedding, nor quarrel nor dispute with his wife in any way. The claimants – or the pilgrims as then termed – were for centuries required to swear the oath of their testimony while kneeling on sharp stones in their churchyard.

By the 14th century the Dunmow Flitch, meaning a good marriage, was well known enough for Chaucer to put a reference to it in the mouth of one of his most ribald characters, the five-times married Wife of Bath, without further explanation. At least two other works of literature in that century referred to it as if common knowledge.

Today, the proceedings take the form of a properly argued trial, presided over by the Flitch Judge and with a jury of six maids and six bachelors. There is often a well-known figure as counsel for the couple and another as counsel for the bacon. In 1996, for example, the legal teams were led amid much ribaldry – but with some seriousness too – by agony aunt Claire Rayner and Tory MP Jerry Hayes. In fact there are two sessions, in the afternoon and evening, with two couples in each. The trials are held at Talberds Ley in a marquee – tickets are sold for charity – at the same time as a special fair, and end with a procession to the marketplace, the couple being carried shoulder-high in the Flitch Chair, accompanied by Morris dancers, the bachelors, maids and the flitch in a frame like a gibbet, all amid much merriment. Finally they make their oath and take home the bacon.

Pyx, pageantry and Black Death

Less accessible to the public but just as relevant, despite its name, is the Trial of the Pyx held in February or March at the Goldsmiths' Hall, London. The exact purpose of the trial – which dates from 1280 or earlier – is to provide independent scrutiny of the quality and size of coins of the realm made by the Royal Mint in the previous year. Officers of the Mint are required to place samples in the Pyx (a box) and these are brought before a jury of goldsmiths sworn in by the Queen's Remembrancer (a shadowy figure who appeared in the Horseshoe and Faggot Cutting Ceremony earlier in this chapter). It is not open to the public, unlike another colourful court held in a nearby building every other Thursday, the **Court of Common Council**. Here the Lord Mayor of London ceremonially enters the **Guildhall**, preceded by his or her City Sword and Mace, borne by the mayor's household officers. The mayor then pronounces the City's motto: 'Domine, Dirige Nos' ('O Lord, guide us').

Despite all the pageantry, this is serious local government for the Square Mile of the City of London – it has been thus ruled for more than a millennium. The Court of Common Council includes 25 aldermen and 130 common councilmen. The election of two sheriffs (held every Midsummer's Day since 1132) in a ceremony at the Guildhall called Common Hall, is a further occasion for pageantry: the procession to the husting (a raised platform strewn with herbs as a precaution against Black Death) is led by the Sheriff's chaplains, City officers, sheriffs, and aldermen in violet gowns, then the Sword and Mace being borne before the mayor dressed in scarlet robes. A similarly colourful procession on September 28, or the previous Friday if it falls on a weekend, sees the admission of the new Sheriffs. The admission itself is not public.

Michaelmas Day sees another procession from Mansion House to the Guildhall for the election of Lord Mayor. In Bristol, just as colourful a procession takes place at the Council House in May each year, for their mayor-making ceremony.

Do these jobs really exist?

Other ancient local courts are largely ceremonial talking shops, although a few retain real powers. There is one ancient type of court dating back to baronial times called the **Court Leet** which was once aimed at preserving local liberties and ending grievances (although at times it worked vice versa).

The Court Leet, which had much rather strange ceremonial, and a whole gamut of frankly unbelievable, office-holders and titles, should have been abolished many times over as the court system went through its evolution into Assizes, Quarter Sessions, County and Crown Courts. Somehow a few weren't, and stubbornly survive, such as the Court Leet at Southampton on the first Tuesday after Michaelmas; at Ashburton, Devon, on the fourth Tuesday in November; at Wareham, Dorset, on the four evenings before the last Friday in November; and at **Bromsgrove**, Worcestershire, on the Saturday nearest to Midsummer's Day, where it involves a procession through the town at 10.30, the proclamation of the 1199 charter, the assize of

Bread, Ale and Leather and the Walking of the Fayre, a carnival which begins at 14.00. Probably the best collection of these comic-opera titles is at Lichfield, Staffordshire, at the St George's Day court, which sees two High Constables, four Clerks of the Market, two Dozeners for each street, two Pinners or Pound Keppers, four Commoners, an Ale Taster and a Gamekeeper. All these courts hear local grievances or nuisances, sometimes lightheartedly, and few do anything about them. But each town's rights to hold these courts, however meaningless to the outsider, has been jealously guarded down the centuries.

In the last week of June at Ashburton, Devon, the Portreeve and the official Ale Tasters visit every tavern in turn to taste the beer. If it is of good quality, the landlord is handed an evergreen bough to put over the pub door. The Ale Tasters' procession includes the official Bread Weighers, who visit all the town's bakeries, weighing two loaves in each.

At Wareham, the Court Leet goes on patrol in its strange garb with ancient bread scales and an 18th-century ale measure, but is accompanied by officers such as the Leather Sealer, the Scavengers – for enforcing refuse removal – and the Surveyors and Searchers of Mantels and Chimneys or Chimney Peepers. The fine for having an unswept chimney is a double whisky.

Not any old court

'New' and 'from time immemorial' are relative terms but when it comes to two specialist courts still held in England, complete with eccentric traditions, they mean much the same thing.

One, the New Forest Verderers' Court, is held in Lyndhurst, Hampshire, on the third Monday of odd numbered months. The word 'New' refers to the laws of William the Conqueror who, after 1066, sought to establish a new royal hunting domain. This is a real court, in effect a specialised magistrates' court dealing with forest by-laws, and is opened with the proclamation: 'Oyez! Oyez! Oyez! All manner of person who have any presentment or matter or thing to do with this Court of Swaincote let him come forward and he shall be heard. God Save the King!' The court starts at 10.00 and is public.

The **Admiralty Court**, held at Rochester Pier, Kent, on the other hand, is supposedly the opposite of new – it has been in operation since 'time immemorial'. This phrase, also referred to as 'time out of mind' in the law confirming the procedure in 1727, actually means in English law before 1189. A procession is held of the mayor, aldermen, and civic bigwigs, notably the Principal Water Bailiff carrying a large silver oar to the civic barge, where the court is held to regulate the fishery. Twelve jurymen and a chamberlain are sworn in to oversee the oyster and floating fishery for the coming year. The court is held on the first or second Saturday in July, according to the tides.

A few weeks earlier – again variable – the mayor of Rochester in his barge, and accompanied by a small flotilla, beats the bounds in the Admiral of Medway's Cruise from Hawkwood Stone at Burham to Garriston Point, Sheerness.

WORTH THE WEIGHT

If MPs really are getting too many free lunches, then an ancient method of checking such things in High Wycombe, Buckinghamshire, each May could provide the proof of the pudding.

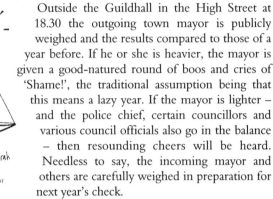

Outside the Guildhall in the High Street at 18.30 the outgoing town mayor is publicly weighed and the results compared to those of a year before. If he or she is heavier, the mayor is given a good-natured round of boos and cries of 'Shame!', the traditional assumption being that this means a lazy year. If the mayor is lighter – and the police chief, certain councillors and various council officials also go in the balance – then resounding cheers will be heard. Needless to say, the incoming mayor and others are carefully weighed in preparation for next year's check.

The ceremonial weighing is carried out with the full pomp the Chilterns town can muster, with berobed processions before and after, led by a Beadle carrying a mace. It is his job to proclaim the weight after crying: 'Oyez, oyez, oyez!' It could make state openings of Parliament worth the weight.

Not that locals can't bodge things. It is, or was, a highly valued skill in the beautiful beech forests round here and bodgers are the people who turn fancy legs and arms for the furniture that the Chilterns have long been famous for. Hence the High Wycombe pub name, the Jolly Bodger.

YOUR TAXES OR A KISS

Not many people smile and dance, or sport flowers, blue ribbons and balloons when the taxman comes, nor offer him foaming pints of ale. But they do in **Hungerford**, Berkshire, at Hocktide – that's the Monday and Tuesday of the second week after Easter, if you had forgotten. Actually most towns and villages have forgotten that Hocktide was the date for collecting tithes or church and parish taxes, and maybe the fact that Hungerford's Tuttimen ('tutti' is a West Country term for flowers) collect only the 13th-century penny per household makes them less feared than the Inland Revenue. Or is it because they usually throw all the taxes – including larger coins donated – for local children to scramble after?

In fact Hocktide is the day Hungerford goes to town. Proceedings start at 08.00 on the Tuesday with a blast from the Lucas horn summoning the Commoners to the Hocktide Court in the gloriously over-the-top town hall. The original horn was donated by John of Gaunt in 1343 and is kept in a bank vault for safety, so a modern replica is used. John of Gaunt gave the town certain rights over fisheries on the Rivers Kennet and Dun and common land – still held at Port Down, as a trip down the picturesque valley towards Newbury will show. The Hocktide Court is called in 14th-century style to regulate these ancient rights and appoint officers.

The Constable sends the tuttimen out on their rounds of the town at 09.00, carrying their flower-bedecked tutti poles and accompanied by the orangeman who wears a hat decorated with pheasant feathers and gives an orange in exchange for the penny, or kiss, collected. The tuttimen's work goes on all day and they have been known to return at dusk in wheelbarrows, such is the exhaustion caused by drinking the health of many a Commoner. Meanwhile the Hocktide lunch is held, with the principal toast being to 'The Immortal Memory of John O'Gaunt'.

The burghers of Hungerford also have a way of dealing with those characters who do anything to avoid buying a round of drinks but always partake of one bought by others. (Such individuals employ tricks such as dropping to tie a shoelace while a group approaches the bar and then catching up while the round is being bought.) This isn't a problem in Hungerford, where, after a civic lunch, newcomers are approached by a blacksmith in apron and another man with a box of farrier's nails. The initiate's foot is pulled up – even if this means being heel over head – and a nail is driven into the heel in a custom called 'Shoeing the colt'. The 'colt' can stop the process by crying 'Punch!', which is taken as an order for a round of drinks, and is thus admitted to the company of Hungerford men.

KEY TO ECCENTRICITIES

Locking a door or a gate would seem to be a fairly simple matter. Not, however, if the gates are of the **Tower of London** and the strange ceremony is more than 700 years old. At 21.53 each day for all those centuries the Chief Warder, in Tudor uniform, carrying a lantern and the keys, sets off from the Byward Tower to meet the Escort of the Key, all bedecked in Beefeater garb. They tour the various gates, ceremonially locking them.

On returning to the Bloody Tower Archway, however, the party is challenged by a sentry with the words: 'Halt! Who comes there?' as if he wouldn't know after 700 years. The reply is bellowed out: 'The Keys.'

'Whose Keys?'

'Queen Elizabeth's Keys.'

'Advance Queen Elizabeth's Keys.'

'All's well.'

The party passes through the arch and the chief warder raises his hat, saying: 'God preserve Queen Elizabeth.' All reply: 'Amen.' A bugler plays the Last Post and the keys are carried to the Resident Governor of the Tower for the night.

The same Yeomen of the Guard make a ceremonial search of the Houses of Parliament before the Queen arrives for the state opening of parliament, recalling the Gunpowder Plot which nearly succeeded in blowing king and parliament to pieces in 1605. The state opening involves another ritual challenge when Black Rod, the Queen's messenger sent to summon the House of Commons to the House of Lords to hear the Queen's speech outlining coming legislation, has the Commons' door slammed in his face. He has to bash his black staff three times on the oaken door to overcome this show of hard-won independence.

BIZARRE BIDDING

The trouble with auctions is knowing when to stop bidding, and this obviously taxed the minds of ancient village worthies, who came up with the bright idea of candle auctions. These are still surprisingly common, and usually involve setting the rent for a piece of land someone left centuries ago to pay for bread, or prayer-books, for the poor. Usually they are conducted behind closed doors.

The classic candle auction, such as that which takes place every three years at Aldermaston, Berkshire, to fix the rent for a piece of land called Church Acre, involves a nail stuck 1 inch down from the top of a tallow candle. The vicar lights it, bidding begins, and stops when the nail drops on to a tin tray beneath. The Aldermaston candle auction takes place on December 13 2001, 2004, etc, at 20.00 in the village hall.

Exactly the same technique is used at the parish meeting at Old Bolingbroke, Lincolnshire, each March to determine the rent for grazing rights; and for the Poor's Pasture at Hubberholme, North Yorkshire on the first Monday of each year.

In Chedzoy, Somerset they save money on pins by using a half-inch of candle every 21 years to time the bidding for an acre of land (next due in 2009), but at Tatworth in the same county, annually on the Tuesday following the first Saturday following April 6, when the 25-member Stowell Court gathers to eat watercress and cheese, they use a whole inch. This must be tedious because no one is allowed to rise from their seat or speak except to bid, until the candle goes out. The rules don't say anything about sneezing, though …

Lastly there is a running auction at Bourne, Lincolnshire, every Easter Monday, which sets the rent for White Bread Meadow to buy bread for the poor. Small boys are set running back and forth and the bidding begins. The last bid before the winner returns gains the rights, says one villager. Another insists that the last bid made before a complete back and forth of the boys without another bid stands, which could be exhausting for the boys involved. Then it's a well-earned supper of white bread, cheese, spring onions and beer for all concerned.

WEIRD AND WONDERFUL WAYS TO GET THE DOLE

Plenty of people can remember the complex system of private charity that operated before the welfare state came into being. But few realise that around the countryside of Britain even today the bizarre, the moving and the curious older systems of welfare charity still operate.

These range from little-known tales, such as that of the agonised Hampshire wife who went through torture to make her skinflint husband help the poor, to the relatively well-known customs, such as the monks of Prinknash Abbey in the Vale of Gloucester, who have been serving free meals to poor wayfarers since 1096. They hit the headlines in 1993 when feckless wastrels who arrived in luxury cars abused their hospitality. After that, the splendid three-course roast dinners were replaced by a more humble soup, bread and tea. But the monks are not alone in offering chivalrous hospitality dating back to the Middle Ages. At the Hospital of St Cross, Winchester, for example, the first few callers of the day at the porter's lodge have received the 'wayfarer's dole' of bread and beer daily since 1136.

Nearby, real pathos can be found with the curious story of the **Tichborne Dole**, distributed each March 25 at the Hampshire village. Given to the needy since the 13th century, the dole consists of a gallon of flour and dates from the time a dying Lady Tichborne asked her skinflint husband to leave food for the poor in her memory. The heartless Sir Roger said he would give grain grown on as much land as the bedridden Lady Mabella could go round before a burning firebrand went out. She managed to crawl round a 23-acre field, still called The Crawls, and every Lady Day villagers assemble at Tichborne House to be given a gallon of flour per adult, and half a gallon for children ... a life saver in famines past.

There's nothing like a good curse to ensure that the terms of a will are observed, and there was one in this case. If ever the Tichbornes failed to give the dole, the curse said, the house would fall down and there would be a generation of seven daughters, the family name dying out. In 1796 the dole caused such a commotion, with riff-raff from other villages trying to muscle in – a precursor of the more recent row over Prinknash Abbey's dole - that alarmed gentry had the local magistrates ban it in following years. Part of the house did subside in 1803 – you can see that it still leans – and Sir Henry Tichborne produced seven daughters but no male heir, which in turn led to Britain's longest yet court case at 291 days in 1874 (only displaced by the

'MacLibel' trial of 314 days in 1996) when an Australian impersonator claimed to be the rightful heir. The dole was resumed to stop the whole house and family name collapsing.

The court case involved and divided the whole country. The Tichborne Dole subsequently became the name of a pub, a play and a film.

Another poignant tale of suffering is remembered in the **Biddenden Dole**, given each Easter Monday. It recalls the 12th-century Siamese twins Mary and Elisa Chulkhurst who, despite being joined at the hips and shoulders, lived happily in the Kent village until one of them died at the age of 34. Friends of the survivor begged her to save herself by having the 'ligaments' joining her to her dead sister cut, but the tale is told how she refused, saying as they had come into the world together so they must leave together. Six hours later, they did. The sisters left land to provide for bread and cheese to be handed out to the poor of the parish. Widows and pensioners still receive this, together with tea, butter and a special biscuit bearing an image of the twins and their names.

Those who moan about social security benefits being too easily given out to today's idle, ill-educated young people might approve of a graveside dole in Wotton, Surrey, intended to benefit local youths – on one condition. In 1717 William Glanville left 40 shillings each (then a considerable sum) to five poor boys on condition that they each lay their hands on his tomb, recite the Lord's Prayer, the Apostles' Creed and the Ten Commandments from memory, read aloud from Corinthians and write two verses in a clear hand. Older villagers in Wotton can remember the dole was held each February 2, but it is now seldom given out.

Graveside doles were once common ways to ensure that the dead were not forgotten. A 13th-century dole table over which loaves were distributed before the Reformation can be seen in Powerstock churchyard, near Dorchester, Dorset. Another dole which should have ceased 500 years ago at Selborne, Hampshire, sees the village's old people receive a loaf each on St Thomas's Day (December 21) although the priory which ordered this closed in 1486. Magdalen College, Oxford, took over because of its interest in priory lands, for the next 500 years, but recently sold the lordship of the manor. The new owner continues the tradition, however.

St Thomas's Day also sees the inhabitants of the Cathedral Close, Lichfield, Staffordshire, each receive a loaf from the Dean's Vicar.

George Carlow's gravestone in the back garden of the Bull Hotel, Woodbridge, Suffolk, is actually inscribed with directions of how penny loaves – Carlow's Bread – are to be given to the poor from his gravetop from 1738 'for ever'. Landlord Neville Allen said: 'We mark it some years with children coming from one of the local schools to get rolls which we have baked. Of course they're not that poor nowadays, but it's very educational.' 'For ever' was the hopeful term also used in Peter Symonds' will of 1587, instructing that 60 Christ's Hospital boys receive a packet of raisins and a new penny on Good Friday.

Similarly, 21 coins are supposed to be laid on a tomb in St Bartholomew-the-Great in Smithfield, London, also on Good Fridays, for 21 poor widows to pick up as they step across the unnamed grave. As a church spokesman says: 'Not so many people live round here any more, so we've run out of poor widows in the parish. We still have the open-air service, then spend the money not picked up on hot cross buns for children.' But if remembering the dead was the aim of that bequest, it has failed, for records of how it came into being were found to be already long forgotten in 1686.

Such bequests are by no means all in the distant past. In 1997 farm worker Jack Palmer, 83, died and left money to buy the pensioners of Great Massingham, Norfolk a slap-up Christmas dinner for ten years – even though Jack had left the village 50 years earlier.

DICE, VICE AND HOUSES OF ILL REPUTE

The problem with bequeathing charitable amounts with all sorts of conditions 'for ever and ever' is that things change in unforeseeable ways. This particularly applies to three unusual charities of 17th-century origins that use dice or casting lots.

Dicing For Maids' Money takes place in late January in Guildford's Guildhall in Surrey, the interest on £400 being diced for by two maidservants in the service of the same Guildford household for two years, providing it was not an inn, hotel or house of ill repute, according to a will of 1674. This condition assumes that, as then, many people are in domestic service, that they stayed in their jobs, and that the interest on £400 was a great deal of money which poor servants would value. Today's Surrey nannies don't stay long and may well have mobile phones and the use of the pool and BMW, although one hopes they still stay clear of houses of ill repute …

A second charity set up in Guildford to benefit seven-year apprentices who could swear before the justices that they had property of less than £20 is similarly outdated. Such long craft apprenticeships have been largely forgotten, and if there are any such apprentices in Guildford they could spend much more than £20 on just one night out. So, as foreseen in the 1702 will, the money goes to the loser of the dicing ceremony (which is, sadly, not a public event), who therefore gets to be the real winner.

A similar maids' charity operates in Reading, Berkshire, although it specifies that money generated by a trust should go to a 'poor maiden servant' who has served in Reading 'in good name and fame five years at the least' for her 'preferment in marriage', the winner decided by casting lots. This was admirable stuff, to be done in the town hall on Good Friday for ever, according to the mathematician John Blagrave's 1611 will. So it takes place on the Thursday after Easter at Church House and one supposes there is similar latitude with regard to the maids' circumstances.

In St Ives, Cambridgeshire, one dice-decided charity runs almost chapter and verse according to Dr Robert Wilde's 1675 will. Six children who should be poor and able to read the Bible dice for copies of the Good Book, bought from the rent of a piece of land known as Bible Orchard. That six children still want to read the Scriptures is admirable, of course, and as for being poor, even today's overfed, mobile-phone-wielding video-owning types can be spiritually poor.

TRAVEL INFORMATION

Admiralty Court, Rochester, Kent
Road A2 from London/M25 J2.
Rail From London Victoria or London Bridge.
Tourist information ✆ 01634 843666.

Biddenden Dole, Kent
Pretty village in rolling countryside. Note twins on elaborate village sign on the green, and buy a Biddenden Twins mug at the village shop.
Road On A274 south from Maidstone, accessed from J7 of M20 which links London/M25 with Dover.
Rail Nearest station Headcorn, on main line from London Victoria to Dover.
Tourist information ✆ 01580 763572.

Bromsgrove Court Leet and Carnival, Worcestershire
Road Off M5 at J4A, or from London via M40 then M42. Some motorway junctions are limited in direction, so follow signs.
Rail On Birmingham–Hereford or Cardiff–Nottingham route, then 15-min walk to town.
Bus 144 Worcester–Birmingham, reached by National Express coaches from London and elsewhere.
Tourist information ✆ 01527 831809.

Court of Common Council and other processions, Guildhall, City of London
Rail Bank (Central, Northern and Waterloo & City lines, and Docklands Light Railway).

Dunmow Flitch trials, Essex
Road M11 from London/M25 to J8, then A120 east
Rail Bishops Stortford from London Liverpool St, then bus.
Tourist information ✆ 01376 550066.

High Wycombe, Buckinghamshire
Road On M40 between M25 and Oxford.
Rail From London Marylebone.
Tourist information ✆ 01494 421892.

Hungerford Hocktide and Tuttimen, Berkshire
Road From M4 J14, take A338 south for 3 miles.
Rail From London Paddington.
Tourist information ✆ 01635 30267.

Keys Ceremony, Tower of London, EC3
Tube Tower Hill (Circle and District Lines).
NB: Admission to the Keys Ceremony is only by written application and invitation. Apply to Ceremony of the Keys, HM Tower of London, EC3N 4AB.
Tower information ✆ 020 7680 9004

Oakham Castle, Rutland; ↘ 01572 723654
Road In town centre, east of church. From A1 near Stamford, take A606 west for 11 miles.
Rail Oakham, on Peterborough–Leicester line.
Tourist information ↘ 01572 724329.

Stratfield Saye, Hampshire; ↘ 01256 882882
Includes grave of Copenhagen, the Iron Duke's horse.
Road Off A33, south from Reading M4 J11, or north from Basingstoke M3 J6.
Tourist information ↘ 0118 956 6226.

Tichborne Dole, Hampshire
Tichborne is a sleepy village with a good pub just a mile south down a pretty lane from New Alresford, which is not new but a charming 18th-century small town stuffed with interest and worth a visit.
Road New Alresford is on A31 which connects Winchester M3 J10 with Guildford (A3 from London).
Rail/bus London Waterloo–Alton, then either Watercress Steam Railway (see page 220) through hills 10 miles to Alresford, or bus 64; or same bus from Winchester which has train services from more centres.
Tourist information ↘ 01962 840500.

Part Two

Eccentric People

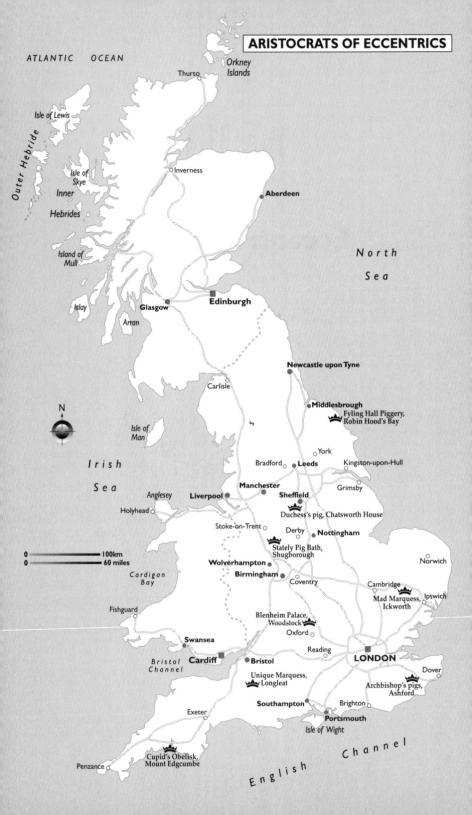

ARISTOCRATS OF ECCENTRICS

ATLANTIC OCEAN

Orkney Islands

Thurso

Isle of Lewis

Outer Hebrides

Isle of Skye

Inner

Inverness

Hebrides

Aberdeen

Island of Mull

N o r t h

S e a

Islay

Glasgow   **Edinburgh**

Arran

Newcastle upon Tyne

Carlisle

Middlesbrough
Fyling Hall Piggery,
Robin Hood's Bay

Isle of Man

York

Bradford   **Leeds**   Kingston-upon-Hull

Irish

Sea

Anglesey   **Liverpool**   **Manchester**   **Sheffield**   Grimsby

Holyhead

Duchess's pig, Chatsworth House

Stoke-on-Trent   Derby   **Nottingham**

Stately Pig Bath,
Shugborough

Wolverhampton   Norwich

Cardigan Bay

Birmingham   Coventry

Cambridge   Ipswich

N

Mad Marquess,
Ickworth

Fishguard

Blenheim Palace,
Woodstock

Swansea   Oxford

Reading   **LONDON**

Cardiff   **Bristol**   Dover

Bristol Channel

Unique Marquess,
Longleat

Archbishop's pigs,
Ashford

Southampton   Brighton

Exeter   **Portsmouth**

Isle of Wight

Cupid's Obelisk,
Mount Edgcumbe   *E n g l i s h*   *C h a n n e l*

Penzance

0 ─── 100km

0 ─── 60 miles

The Aristocrats of Eccentrics

THE TUNNELLING DUKE AND OTHER STRANGE ARISTOS

One might assume that the reputation for eccentricity of British aristocrats is because their wealth, and general mischief-making idleness, meant their whims had a more lasting impact than those more modest extravagances of more lowly Britons. This would be a simplification of a much more fascinating phenomenon than mere excess. Although fabulous riches obviously played their part in the legacy of flamboyant characters such as the third Marquess of Bute, who in the 19th century left Cardiff with the quite extraordinarily embellished **Cardiff Castle** and the almost Bavarian fantasy retreat of **Castell Coch** some five miles to the north (see Chapter 11), there is no denying that many a British aristocrat has been deeply strange as well as rich and powerful (or, sometimes, just deeply strange).

Take the fifth Duke of Portland, the eccentric Lord William John Cavendish-Scott-Bentinck (1800–75), who was shy to Howard Hughes extremes. When travelling, he would have his curtained carriage unhitched from the horses and then hoisted aboard a railway truck with him inside it. He wore a 2ft-high silk hat and carried a deep umbrella when out walking to shield himself from strangers' eyes. The penalty if any of his 500 workmen doffed a hat to him was instant dismissal. He used only four rooms in Welbeck Abbey, Nottinghamshire, his ancestral seat – now the Army's Welbeck College for educating would-be officers. Each room had two letterboxes on the doors – one for incoming and one for outgoing messages – so he need not see anyone. A roast chicken was passed through every day, one half for lunch and one for supper. All other rooms were painted pink and left bare except for an unscreened lavatory pan in the corner of each room.

In old age the duke went to ground by constructing a vast network of underground rooms. Miles of passages, stables and kitchens were all hewn out by hand, together with a 1½-mile long gaslit tunnel wide enough for two carriages to pass, a vast underground ballroom, the largest in Europe, where no one danced, and even a riding school – at 400ft by 600ft the second largest in the world, supported by 50 pillars and lit by 40,000 gas jets – where no-one ever rode.

Those recruited to be estate workers were surprised to find mushroom-like ventilators in their cottage gardens, and were told these were for underground washrooms so his lordship would not have to see washing rudely displayed.

Rumour has it that the duke's curtained carriage went all the way to

Worksop station by underground tunnel, so it could be hoisted aboard the train, but this is not quite true. The main 1½-mile Skylight Tunnel from the Abbey to the outskirts of the estate has an exit at the estate's northern boundary, known as the Tunnel End. From here the Duke, in a covered coach, travelled a further 3½ miles overland, through the Duke of Newcastle's Worksop Manor estate, to reach Worksop station.

Incidentally, he caused a crisis for Benjamin Disraeli in 1857 when he demanded the repayment of huge loans he had made to the prime minister, presumably to finance further mad mole-like behaviour. The suggested reasons for the underground extravagance by the former MP vary from being thwarted in love to wanting to create work for local unemployed labourers, but a true eccentric needs no reasonable explanation.

Another aristo who did not appreciate the presence of his servants was the third Lord Wallscourt, who had few peers in terms of eccentricity. He used to wander round his draughty stately home stark naked, ringing a cowbell to warn maidservants, who ran screaming from the sight. He died – whether of a chill or not is not recorded – in 1849.

More fun was Lord Delaval Beresford, although it was sadly ironic that he died in a train crash in 1906, since his uncle, the third Marquess of Waterford, once asked a railway company to crash two railway engines just for fun. But then Beresford once put aniseed, a scent loved by bloodhounds, on the hooves of a parson's horse before hunting the terrified clergyman and placed a donkey in the bed of a traveller at a wayside inn as another jolly jape. Lord Beresford's brother Admiral Lord Charles Beresford had a love of the chase too – he had a hunt in full cry tattooed down his back, with the fox going to earth at the appropriate aperture.

A penchant for railways and hunts was also shared by the ninth Earl of Lanesborough, who died in late 1998. This seemed to run in the family, judging by his recollections of childhood holidays in the 1920s.

> 'We used to travel though the night down to the French Riviera. My grandfather, Sir Anthony Abdy, would not spend the night in the sleeping car with us, however, because he would have had a word with the driver in Paris and would the next morning step down from the loco footplate at Nice, black with soot, but most pleased.'

Lord Lanesborough himself trained as an LNER engine driver during the war and, before he lost his fortune and had to sell his family house, Swithland Hall in Leicestershire, had 600ft of toy track running through the house with detailed scenery, including a miniature Quorn Hunt in full cry.

Many years before that, also in Paris, the Victorian Earl of Bridgewater used to hold formal banquets at his Paris mansion for his best friends who were required to wear full evening dress. Nothing odd in that, except that the guests were all his favourite dogs.

HELLFIRE AND HEROISM

The eccentricity of the British upper classes, if we are allowed to use such a politically incorrect but honest term, seems to be nothing new. A couple of centuries ago, John Mytton, sheriff of Shropshire despite having been expelled from Westminster and Harrow schools, went hunting naked, owned 1,000 hats and drank eight bottles of port a day. He once astounded his dinner guests by riding into the dining room astride a bear, which became so excited it bit part of his leg off. He died after he set his shirt alight to 'show how Jack Mytton cures the hiccups'. His last words are said to have been: 'Well, the hiccups is gone, by God.'

The 18th century saw the debauched excesses and whimsical creations of the Hellfire Club (see Chapter 5, *Some very strange organs*), with their satanic caves, very strange church and odd mausoleum. But what of the 20th century? Did the upper classes retain their eccentricities?

Sometimes it was a question of mere direct pragmatism, which could be amusing in small ways. The former prime minister Sir Anthony Eden's father Sir William was in the habit of tapping the barometer in his hall each morning. Once, when it was pouring with rain, but the barometer forecast sunshine, he hurled the instrument outside, yelling: 'Go on, you damned fool, go and see for yourself.'

In the 1930s, conductor Sir Thomas Beecham met a woman he vaguely recognised in the exclusive emporium of Fortnum & Mason's. After exchanging greetings, he asked: 'What's your husband doing nowadays?' The answer was: 'Oh, he's still king.' But he could be more forthright as a conductor. To a cellist he once thundered: 'Madam, you have between your legs that which could give pleasure to thousands. All you do is sit there and scratch it.'

The seventh Lord Newborough, who died in 1998, was a war hero of the first order and a true eccentric to boot. His war record included rescuing men in five trips to Dunkirk with a yacht, taking part in the incredibly brave and successful St Nazaire raid in 1942, where he was wounded and captured when stopping under the German guns to rescue men in the water; and various escapades at the notorious Colditz prison, from where he, of course, escaped. His post-war record, which concerns us here, included various cannon-firing incidents at his family estate in Denbighshire, north Wales. He liked to fire his cannon (plural) from Beland Fort for special occasions, such as birthdays, and was convicted of firing a 9lb cannonball through the spinnaker of a yacht passing through the Menai Strait, which he denied. He hit the headlines for removing the roof of the home of a gamekeeper to whom he had taken a dislike.

His parting shot was to have his ashes blasted from a gun fired by his son in front of 700 startled guests. His remains hurtled through the air in a cannister he had designed himself into one of his favourite places, the Big Wood, to resounding cheers from his many friends. The family motto is 'Gentle in manner, vigorous in action.'

BONKERS, AND BONKING, MPS

Modern politicians are not so colourless, either. Sir Nicholas Fairbairn, the flamboyant Tory MP for Perth and Kinross who died in 1995, designed his own clothes, the results sometimes execrable, leaving him wearing what looked like a skirt and patent leather high-heeled boots. A member of his family recalled: 'He once wore a see-through négligé top, with a huge black cross beneath it and white flared trousers: that was especially vile.' When he had a German guest at his ruined Fifeshire castle, Fordell, he even insisted on the guest goosestepping through the house wearing a spiked German helmet: about as subtle as Basil Fawlty in the *Fawlty Towers* television comedy.

He rarely said the right thing and often the horribly wrong one – such as lecturing his daughter about gonorrhea on her wedding day. He once summed it all up in *Who's Who* when he described his recreations as 'making love, ends meet, people laugh'. In a later edition he changed this to 'drawing ships, making quips, confounding Whips, scuttling drips'.

David Mellor, the philandering former member for Putney turned media moneyspinner, was famous as Minister for Fun for making love to an actress in an Earls Court flat while wearing Chelsea football kit. Whatever turns you on, I suppose, but Chelsea! Eventually Mellor, who clearly had something to offer besides good looks, ran off with the Viscountess Cobham, whose husband was distant heir to the second Lord Lyttleton, a Hellfire Club member (see page 99) and a Jack-the-lad, who ate himself to death 200 years ago in a three-day binge at Hagley Hall.

To maintain a semblance of balance, a third example was not a Tory MP at all but a baron, and half-brother to a Tory minister. The late third Baron Moynihan of Leeds, Anthony Patrick Andrew Cairnes Berkeley Moynihan, died from a stroke in 1991 while running a chain of brothels in the Philippines, leaving a string of small boys in the Orient whose mothers claimed him as their father and at least three Lady Moynihans in Manila. He had fled there in 1970 to evade a string of arrest warrants concerning 57 charges over gambling debts and other frauds, building up a £3 million sex industry fortune and acquiring himself the soubriquet, the Ermine Pimpernel.

Meanwhile he took out an advertisement in *The Times* to call the British police 'one of the most corrupt forces in the world'. His half-brother Colin Moynihan, a former Olympic rowing medallist, who while a Tory sports minister was himself controversially photographed with the exotic Pamella Bordes, witnessed an extraordinary court battle in 1996 when one of the third baron's alleged offspring tried to claim the title. In the event, the lawsuit failed and Colin became the fourth Baron Moynihan.

MODERN MARQUESSES OF B

Not all today's aristocrats live up to their eccentric heritage; some confuse mere spoilt brat bad behaviour with truly creative craziness.

At the start of this chapter I mentioned a Marquess of Bute. So let's take modern people with the title of Marquess of B, to limit the rather wide field. The mildly misbehaving (for drugs and motoring offences) Marquess of Blandford, heir to Blenheim Palace, turns out to be rather bland: most people would think him from his record in the 1980s and 1990s somewhat spoilt and silly.

Blenheim Palace

The seventh Marquess of Bristol, also a partaker of substances, whose main achievement seemed to have been to quit one of Europe's most astounding stately homes, **Ickworth** in Suffolk, and flog off the treasures therein, was eccentric only in a negative way – he managed to lose a real fortune more unwisely. He died in January 1999, aged 44, having achieved only notoriety. If he was at all eccentric, it was in carrying a hint of Marquis de Sade cruelty from his schooldays at Harrow to his arrogant, sneering adulthood. He would set his dogs on innocent visitors to Ickworth; he drove at speed through screaming visitors in his fast playboy cars; he sent an American woman visitor out on the lake at Ickworth in a rubber dinghy and shot at it with an air-rifle until it sank; he read out begging letters from parents of very sick children to amuse his dinner guests.

Are all marquesses of B's as vile, or as dull? Far from it: the Marquess of Bath upholds the fine tradition of aristocratic eccentricities. He openly maintained a set of 'wifelets' – put by some commentators at a number hard to credit, around 62 – and had a predilection for mad murals on sexual themes, rhino horns and suchlike, at his family seat, **Longleat**, made famous by his father for the Lions of Longleat. Predictably, Fleet Street christened the current marquess 'Loins of Longleat', which I imagine delighted him. The title is being aired yet again as I write and another alleged newborn Bathlet was found in the Wiltshire countryside.

His lordship is down to earth and eccentric all at once: his favourite dish is said to be squirrel in mushroom sauce, yet the Eton-educated Father Christmas figure sent his children to the local comprehensive school to give them a sense of the real world.

Is the eccentricity merely a convenient persona for Bath, who when he inherited the title proved himself a canny businessman, allowing Center Parcs to build a holiday village at Longleat (without even correcting their spelling)? Not entirely. The 'hippy peer' is just honest about his unconventional love life, and those murals dripping off miles of corridors ('pornographic pizza' as a family member put it), represent hundreds of hours of dedicated daubing. He is a truly eccentric Marquess of B, but not a crackpot.

As to the 21st century, I don't think we'll have to wait too long for evidence of continuing crackpotism among Britain's aristocrats and politicians. But whatever it is, it will be totally unpredictable.

STATELY PIGS OF OLD ENGLAND AND STY SOCIETY

That pigs and aristocrats have much in common is no mere fancy of novelist P G Wodehouse. Lord Emsworth's devotion to Empress of Blandings merely represented the esteem held between many a noble family and their porkers of equally good breeding.

This symbiosis of swine and toff goes back a long way. On a hill overlooking Plymouth Sound, a massive **obelisk** is popularly said to record Cupid the pig, social darling of Devonshire in the 18th century, who followed the Countess of Mount Edgcumbe everywhere. Historians say the pig monument was probably an urn which has been lost and that the obelisk is instead a redundant navigation mark. What is undeniable is that the aristocrat and her pig were inseparable – even on her visits to London.

Things aren't that different today. The Duchess of Devonshire, for example, has a soft spot for a 36-stone Gloucestershire Old Spot called Primrose, whose perfect and massive proportions complement the vast 365-windowed **Chatsworth House** in Derbyshire. As the Duchess confided: 'One can grow very affectionate towards pigs – there is something comforting about them.'

Chatsworth House

The comforting quality about pigs, so lauded by Lord Emsworth, is acknowledged by the former Archbishop of Canterbury, Lord Runcie. 'I wish I could turn my attention to such things as tranquil as my Berkshires.' The Berkshire is one of several breeds of British pig threatened with extinction, and good breeding has been a concern of British aristocrats since at least 1884 when the Earl of Ellesmere started the National Pig Breeders' Association to look after such pearls among swine as the Large Black, the Middle White, the Tamworth and the British Lop. Today the Rare Breeds Survival Trust keeps the flag flying for the breeds which have fallen out of favour with commercial pig farmers because we no longer like such fatty meat. There are fewer than 100 Berkshire boars left, so Lord Runcie's contribution is vital.

He first met the breed in the 1940s at a country rectory, which was backing the war effort by having a Pig for Victory. Later, in the 1970s, he created a Berkshire herd, albeit in Hertfordshire, when he was Bishop of St Albans. Later still the herd moved to the **South of England Rare Breeds Centre** in Kent. But Lord Runcie's delight in the animal is almost paternal: 'They are splendid and their skin shines. The tiny piglets are like advertisements for polish.' He modestly describes himself as a 'bogus pig-keeper'.

Royalty, too, values the decent sort of pig: the Princess Royal keeps Gloucestershire Old Spots at Gatcombe Park, and the Earls of Lichfield have long kept pigs in appropriate splendour at **Shugborough**, their Staffordshire seat. They – the pigs – occupy a splendid lead pig bath designed by Samuel Wyatt in the 18th century, and the farm itself is now open to the public. Lord Lichfield recognises the pigs' special charm: 'I find them relaxing. Contemplating pigs can be a peaceful occupation. In this regard I identify with Lord Emsworth.'

Even the Shugborough pigs cannot aspire to the porcine poshness of **Fyling Hall** in North Yorkshire (near those more famous golf balls which were supposed to give us four minutes' warning of being turned into pork scratchings ourselves during the Cold War). In the 19th century Squire Barry decided to build his pigs a sty, and built them a veritable Grecian temple complete with pillars, pediment and portico ... a shrine to swine, perhaps.

Whether he considered his pigs had divine qualities or whether it was simply to improve his view is not recorded, but Fyling Hall surely offered the world's most exclusive sty. Broadcaster John Timpson described this sty as 'piggery jokery' in his book *Timpson's England*, but the splendid view the beasts enjoyed over Robin Hood's Bay can be appreciated instead by weekenders in search of somewhere different to stay, thanks to the Landmark Trust's conversion of the piggery (see *Chapter 12*).

Of course, affection for porkers is not confined to the upper classes. In 1998 two Tamworth pigs hit the headlines when they fled the butcher's knife in a Wiltshire slaughterhouse, barged their way under a wire fence, swam a river and disappeared in thick vegetation, evading a huge search, only emerging to snack on gardeners' vegetables at night. Their story earned the admiration of the nation, partly due to headline writers who dubbed the duo Butch and Sundance. Tabloid newspapers fell over themselves to bid for the Tamworth

Two, and when they were recaptured, they were installed in a centrally heated thatched piggery, with private pool, mudbath, closed-circuit TV and the best possible food. It all made for good reading over your breakfast sausages and bacon, I suppose.

In Blandings Castle country, at Elmstone near Cheltenham, the **Gloucester Old Spot** pub reveres the name which keeps bringing home the bacon. And, not so far from Wodehouse's fictional Blandings Castle, at the village of **Pillerton Hersey** in Warwickshire, Glascote Dictator XVIII, a 58-stone Essex boar, hit the headlines a few years back for not only having his own bank account but also visiting the branch in question. Not to make a deposit, you understand – perish the thought. It was in protest at the closure of the branch where he held his prize money (£31 plus interest) that the great Dictator's owner, barrister Iain Whitney, decided to take him along to withdraw his funds. Piggy banks are not, after all, adequate for the posher porker. Dictator eventually headed for the pigsty in the sky, but his stuffed head will embellish Mr Whitney's cottage for years to come as a reminder of an honourable companion. Mr Whitney has spent the past ten years in a one-man campaign to have the Essex saddleback breed of pigs reinstated after an ill-starred attempt to merge them and Wessex saddlebacks into one breed. 'I've spent ten years campaigning to prove I have one of only two herds of the genuine Essex pigs, which were deemed to be extinct from 1967. Now I've won, the Essex is saved and I've won the Royal Show Supreme Champion too.' It would be a rasher man than myself who would question the importance of this.

The current apple sauce of Mr Whitney's eye is Bunkers Hill Dictator V, who will probably never become several hundred bacon sandwiches and joints of ham, succulent though his offspring may be. 'I enjoy his company. He'll probably die of old age.'

Mr Whitney even followed in Lord Emsworth's footsteps in 1996 with a classic Wodehouse-style ding-dong with the village bobby. This involved an allegedly truculent police sergeant who owned land next to Mr Whitney's piggery and seemed to dislike the animals. The force farce ended with police waiting for Mr Whitney outside a pub and Mr Whitney lying prostrate and speechless when stopped from driving his car as if having some kind of fit.

The jury clearly believed his story of police harassment and Mr Whitney's bacon was saved. It's all rather curious when you consider that his job is prosecuting in police cases in the courts. 'I only do it to pay for my hobby with the pigs,' avers the barrister. All he needs now is a minor peerage.

Perhaps, as W H Hudson noted, it's the hail-fellow-well-met air of the pig which endears him to the British and particularly the aristocracy, surrounded as they are by cap-doffing creeps or forelock-tugging envy. And as Churchill said (and one of his wife's nicknames for him was, after all, Pig): 'Dogs look up to us, cats look down on us, but pigs treat us as equals.' Quite.

TRAVEL INFORMATION

Blenheim Palace, Woodstock, Oxfordshire; ↘ 01993 811325
Road M40 to J9, then A34 towards Oxford, then A44 to Woodstock.
Rail/bus From London Paddington to Oxford, walk or taxi to Gloucester Green bus station, then bus 20 to Woodstock or taxi direct.
Tourist information ↘ 01865 726871

Chatsworth House, Derbyshire; ↘ 01246 565300
Top rate stately home with fabulous waterfall gardens.
Road Signed from M1 J29.
Rail/bus Nearest station Chesterfield, then bus 170 to Baslow, nearby village. Coach firms offer day trips from various centres.
Midland Mainline offers a discount midweek day out including rail, special return coach and admission ticket, from London St Pancras, Luton and various stations *en route*.
Tourist information ↘ 01246 345777.

Cupid's Obelisk, Mount Edgcumbe House and Country Park, near Plymouth, Devon; ↘ 01752 822236.
Road From M5 end at Exeter, take A38 to Plymouth, through city to Devonport for ferry to Torpoint, then follow signs.
Rail/bus Plymouth station, from London Paddington and many other centres, then walk to Royal Parade and catch bus 33 to Admiral's Hard in Stonehouse district. Then Cremyll foot ferry (a great, inexpensive ride) direct to country park.
Tourist information ↘ 01752 266030

Fyling Hall Piggery, above picturesque Robin Hood's Bay, near historic Whitby, North Yorkshire
Road Off A1(M) at Thirsk, take A61, A19, A172, A171.
Rail/bus Nearest station Whitby, end of branch from York or Darlington on London King's Cross–Edinburgh line. Bus 93 to Robin Hood's Bay then steep walk.
Tourist information ↘ 01947 602674.

Longleat, Wiltshire; ↘ 01985 844400
The Marquess of Bath's home welcomes visitors both to the house and the safari park.
Road From M4 J17, take A350 south, join A36 near Warminster and follow signs.
Rail/bus Nearest stations Warminster (on the Salisbury–Bath line, or less frequently, Waterloo–Cardiff). Then Lionlink bus, not Sun.
Tourist information ↘ 01985 218548 (check times in advance).

Ickworth, Suffolk; ☎ 01284 735270 (National Trust)
Road A14 turn off at first Bury St Edmunds exit then follow signs.
Rail/bus Trains to Bury St Edmunds then bus to Horringer, then less than a mile walk.
Tourist information ☎ 01284 764667.

Ickworth

South of England Rare Breeds Centre, near Ashford, Kent;
☎ 01233 861493
Road On B2067 Tenterden/Folkestone road. From London and M25, take M20 to J10, A2070 to, appropriately, Hamstreet, turn right on B2067 and go west for 3 miles.
Rail/bus Nearest mainline station Ashford (from London Victoria, Paris or Brussels). Bus 295 leaves Ashford International direct to centre at 10.52 weekdays with two return options. Hamstreet also has a railway station on Ashford–Hastings branch, but then 3-mile walk or cycle.
Tourist information ☎ 01233 629165.

Shugborough Hall, Staffordshire; ☎ 01889 881388
Major stately home in landscaped setting filled with magnificent monumental follies, plus Park Farm.
Road From M6 J13, follow signs.
Rail/bus Stafford or Lichfield City stations, then Arriva North Midlands bus 825.
Tourist information ☎ 01785 619619.

Above The spire of St Mary's Church, Chesterfield, was twisted by the Devil, locals say, in fury that a virgin married there (PA)

Above right Grave robbers were foiled by mortsafes such as these at Logierait north of Perth (BL)

Right The extraordinary Maharajah's Well at Stoke Row, Oxfordshire, is topped by a hidden gilded elephant (BL)

Dead Eccentric

BIZARRE LAST WISHES

Most people settle for burial or cremation. The odd eccentric asks to be frozen or mummified. Brian Cromblehome, 28, announced in 1994 he'd like the services of a good taxidermist. The father-of-two shocked his neighbours in Blackpool with his wish to be stuffed and put on display after death, but he would not be unique if his wishes were carried out.

Hannah Beswick, presumably terrified of waking up in her coffin, left a fortune to her physician in 1758 on condition that he regularly checked her for signs of life. To save himself trouble, the Lancashire doctor had her embalmed and mounted inside a glass-fronted grandfather clock on his landing so he could check her along with the barometer on his way out each morning. It was only 110 years later that her trustees decided she was safely dead and could be buried at last.

People still make strange requests about their deaths. A Bristol housewife astonished tabloid readers in 1994 by asking to be buried with her faithful gas cooker, appropriately a New World model. This gave plenty of scope for headline writers: Roast in Peace, or possibly, Rust in Peace.

People also make odd last requests for their ashes. When scientist Jeff Thorp died aged 72 in 1992, his family were determined to honour his last wishes to go out with a bang. In fact, in the form of specially made rockets, his ashes lit up the night sky for miles around. And as befits a brilliant biochemist who invented a major heart drug, he took the preparations seriously and researched rocket propulsion and the specific gravity of human ashes before calculating the best trajectory. He even staged a test run with coal fire ashes.

On the day, it took 28 rockets to blast all his remains into the sky from Kerridge Hill, near Macclesfield, Cheshire. Planes from nearby Manchester airport were diverted from the airspace as silver, red and green stars exploded in the heavens. A fellow scientist was quoted as saying: 'I came to this unusual event to honour Jeff. He was a fine colleague and an outstanding scientist – and he had a wicked sense of humour.' He got his last laugh.

Mr Thorp is not alone in having taken this direct route to the heavens – the

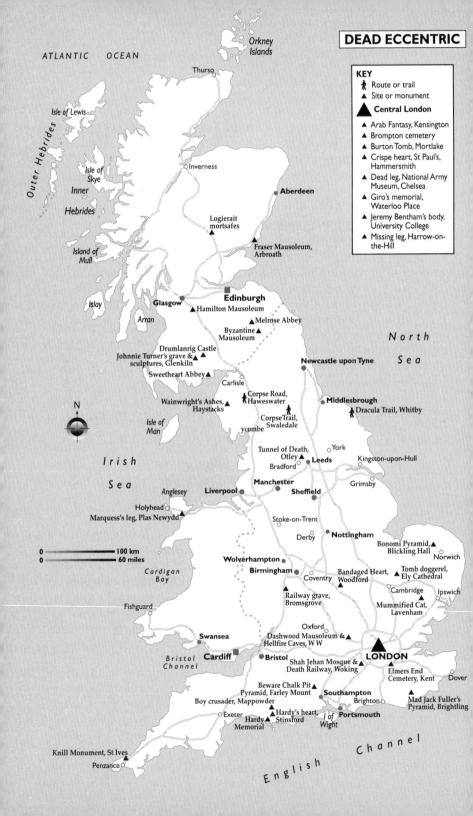

DEAD ECCENTRIC

ATLANTIC OCEAN

Orkney Islands

Thurso

Isle of Lewis

Outer Hebrides

Isle of Skye

Inner Hebrides

Inverness

Aberdeen

Island of Mull

Logierait mortsafes

Islay

Fraser Mausoleum, Arbroath

Arran

Glasgow

Edinburgh

Hamilton Mausoleum

Melrose Abbey

Byzantine Mausoleum

Drumlanrig Castle

Johnnie Turner's grave & sculptures, Glenkiln

Newcastle upon Tyne

North Sea

Sweetheart Abbey

Carlisle

Corpse Road, Haweswater

Middlesbrough

Dracula Trail, Whitby

Wainwright's Ashes, Haystacks

Isle of Man

Corpse Trail, Swaledale ycombe

Irish Sea

Tunnel of Death, Otley

York

Bradford

Leeds

Kingston-upon-Hull

Anglesey

Liverpool

Manchester

Sheffield

Grimsby

Holyhead

Marquess's leg, Plas Newydd

Stoke-on-Trent

Derby

Nottingham

Bonomi Pyramid, Blickling Hall

Norwich

100 km

60 miles

Wolverhampton

Birmingham

Coventry

Bandaged Heart, Woodford

Tomb doggerel, Ely Cathedral

Cardigan Bay

Railway grave, Bromsgrove

Cambridge

Ipswich

Fishguard

Mummified Cat, Lavenham

Oxford

Swansea

Dashwood Mausoleum & Hellfire Caves, W W

LONDON

Bristol Channel

Cardiff

Bristol

Shah Jehan Mosque & Death Railway, Woking

Elmers End Cemetery, Kent

Dover

Beware Chalk Pit Pyramid, Farley Mount

Southampton

Brighton

Mad Jack Fuller's Pyramid, Brightling

Boy crusader, Mappowder

Portsmouth

Exeter

Hardy's heart, Stinsford

Hardy Memorial

I of Wight

Knill Monument, St Ives

Penzance

English Channel

KEY

Route or trail

Site or monument

Central London

▲ Arab Fantasy, Kensington
▲ Brompton cemetery
▲ Burton Tomb, Mortlake
▲ Crispe heart, St Paul's, Hammersmith
▲ Dead leg, National Army Museum, Chelsea
▲ Giro's memorial, Waterloo Place
▲ Jeremy Bentham's body, University College
▲ Missing leg, Harrow-on-the-Hill

remains of a Welsh poet were blasted into the sky from a funeral wake a few years later.

But could anything beat, for happy aptness, the great Lake District fell walker A W Wainwright's last request? He asked for his ashes to be scattered on **Haystacks**, one of his favourite fells, and so they were in 1991. It is a place of pilgrimage for latter-day Wainwrighters, the be-backpacked followers of the goat-like guru, and it is indeed wonderful on a half-decent day. If you walk up from Buttermere, where you will have looked at the window to his memory in the church, go round the far side of this incomparably lovely lake and up through Scarth Gap round Haystacks to the peaceful Innominate Tarn; you can come back down Warnscale Beck to the lake, completing the circuit of Haystacks, perhaps seven miles in all.

The great man wrote with his dry humour of this place: 'Should you get a bit of grit in your boots as you are crossing Haystacks, please treat it with respect. It could be me.' It would be going too far, as I usually do, to say if you get a bit of grit in your eye, shed a tear for him. But don't be too sad on his behalf. He said of Buttermere church, where his memorial is: 'Buttermere is a foretaste of heaven.'

People ask to be deposited in the goal of their favourite football team (to make a posthumous save, possibly), whizzed round in pneumatic message carriers or blasted from the chimneys of their favourite steam locomotives. Wanting to be buried with a much-loved car is understandable but unlikely to find favour in the average churchyard. Grieving relatives of Jaguar owner Ian Ashton of County Durham made a compromise by screwing his personalised number plate to his coffin before his burial in 1996. His was a fine tradition which has been long-lived.

Britain is littered with bizarre relics of the dead eccentric, delightfully dotty deceased and buried bufoons. Some even had the last laugh *en route* to the grave.

The 17th-century English eccentric Jemmy Hurst, who during his life had ridden round town on a bull and printed his own 5*d* banknotes, directed in his will that his coffin should be carried by 12 elderly local virgins. No doubt he would have chuckled to know that his executors, at their wits' end, could find only two.

Perhaps the oddest case concerns a woman who never reached her grave at all. When the first wife of the king of 18th-century eccentrics, Martin van Butchell, died in 1775, he had her embalmed with turpentine and camphor, fitted with glass eyes, coloured to appear lifelike and mounted in a display case in the front room of his Mayfair home. She was wearing full wedding dress and van Butchell charged the public to see her. Van Butchell, who made a fortune supplying dentures and trusses to the gentry, although qualified in neither field, refused to visit his rich clients despite, in one case, being sent a horse and carriage and the small fortune of 500 guineas. On the other hand, he regularly visited Newgate jail to treat prisoners free of charge. His bizarre preservation of his first wife's corpse may have been brought on by her will, which stated that her fortune was to go to a distant relative 'the moment I am dead and buried'. She had been offered, incidentally, the choice of wearing black or white for the rest of her life on her wedding day – she chose black – and when van Butchell married his second wife (in fact, his maid Elizabeth, perhaps so he no longer had to pay her a wage) she chose white. Still the first wife was not buried, and in 1815 his son Edmund offered the body to the Royal College of Surgeons. There she remained unburied until blown to bits by a Nazi bomb in the Blitz of 1941. From dust to dust.

LAND OF ODD PYRAMIDS

The Pyramids have fascinated our nation since Briton Howard Carter discovered the tomb of Tutankhamun in 1922. But the British interest in things Egyptian goes back much further than that. There are a surprising number of old pyramids dotted around this country, often connected with death in some bizarre way.

Brightling Pyramid

At **Brightling** in East Sussex, for example, local eccentric 'Mad Jack' Fuller has been entombed in a fair-sized pyramid he built in the churchyard in 1811. Village lore has it that his 22-stone corpse sits in an iron chair with a bottle of port and a roast chicken before him, waiting for the Resurrection. The floor of the pyramid is said to be covered in broken glass to deter the Devil from trying to snatch him away in the meantime.

A similar, surprisingly large pyramid is the grave of Dr Francis Douce in the Hampshire village of Nether Wallop, where again it dominates the churchyard. Just in case Dr Douce's egotistical monument is overlooked, a plaque in the bell tower tells how in 1761 he left money for a village school and also for 'the relief of poor people past their labour'. Another handsome 18th-century pyramid, somewhat smaller, is in the churchyard of St Mary's Church, Painswick, Gloucestershire, famed for its strange clipping rituals (see page 111).

One pyramid you can enter is at **Farley Mount Country Park** near Winchester. The deceased is buried in the mound beneath – it is the favourite horse of Paulet St John who, while hunting in 1733, survived an amazing leap over a hedge on the horse's back and down into a 25ft-deep chalk pit. In the following year the horse won the Hunters' Plate at Worthy Downs races, again ridden by St John, under the somewhat cautionary name Beware Chalk Pit.

A cautionary tale attaches to a probably unique pyramidical village lock-up still to be seen in the centre of **Wheatley**, near Oxford. It was, local legend has it, used to detain 'loose women'. Swanage, Dorset, has yet another pyramid, a tomb for the 19th-century entrepreneur-builder John Mowlem; and there is a fine bunch of pyramids at Castle Howard, Yorkshire. One is stunningly mounted above an arch in the massive fortified wall through which passes an approach road to the great house, with an obelisk perfectly aligned to be visible through the arch.

Definitely unique is the ceremony attached to a splendid pyramid which takes place at St Ives, Cornwall. At the **Knill Monument** of 18th-century mayor John Knill, on every fifth anniversary of his death – the next is on July 25 2001 – ten virgins dressed in white must dance for 15 minutes and then sing a psalm. Two elderly widows in black must supervise, says his will, and the mayor and town council attend for good measure.

Perhaps the most elegant pyramid in Britain is that at **Blicking Hall**, Norfolk, built by Bonomi as a tribute to the Earl of Buckingham who died in 1793. The great house is run by the National Trust.

LEG-END IN HIS OWN LIFETIME

One of the odder possessions of the National Trust, along with all the stately homes and beauty spots, is a part of its heritage which should not be forgotten – the first Marquess of Anglesey's leg.

During the battle of Waterloo, as the cannon roared, the marquess (then merely Lord Uxbridge but later elevated for his heroism) cried out: 'My God, Sir, I've lost a leg!' The Duke of Wellington remarked: 'Have you, by God!' and carried on observing the French lines through his telescope. It is not recorded whether the Iron Duke dismounted to lend a hand, as it were – the two were hardly friends and later were political enemies – but amputation was performed in the field and the leg buried under a willow tree with full military honours.

The marquess later had the world's first articulated artificial limb made and the patented 'Anglesey leg' may be seen at the National Trust's neo-gothic **Plas Newydd** on the Menai Straits, north Wales. The house was given to the Trust by the seventh marquess in 1976 and contains a military museum, including a sprig of willow from the tree at Waterloo where the real leg was buried. That spot was marked with a monument and gave the marquess the peculiar prospect of being able to visit part of his own tomb.

Not only was the wooden leg only one of three made for the marquess – there was a riding leg, a walking leg and a best leg – but the National Trust's leg is just one of three monuments to the historic limb. At the **National Army Museum** in Chelsea a somewhat grisly display recreates the scene as the leg was detached on a farmhouse table,

with the surgeon's 15-inch bloodstained saw and his once-white glove. Recently the Waterloo site was redeveloped and the real leg disinterred, and reburied in a nearby cemetery alongside whole people, the spot being marked by a plaque.

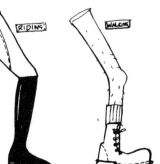

What about the rest of the marquess, minus his leg? Is he forgotten? Not at all: there's a one-legged but 91ft monument on the island of Anglesey. The monument, at the exhaustively named spot of Llanfairpwllgwngyllgogerychwyrndrobwllllantysiliogogogoch (see *Place names,* page 150), is a column ascended by an internal spiral staircase, with a statue on top. The hero's loss was others' gain: the marquess's pioneering limb enabled thousands of disabled people worldwide to stand on two feet, if not their own.

LONDON'S ONLY NAZI MEMORIAL

For how many more years will someone put a flower, as they have every February for decades, on the only Nazi memorial in London? In February 1934, **Giro**, the faithful hound of the German ambassador Leopold von Hoesch, was buried complete with tombstone near the then German embassy at 7 Carlton House Terrace.

The memorial, with touching epithet *Ein Treuer Begleiter* ('a true companion'), is tucked under a tree at the top of the steps from the Institute of Contemporary Art on the Mall to Waterloo Place, perhaps somewhat cheekily given that the area is laden with vast monuments to heroes of the British Empire. Indeed, the statues of Field Marshal Lord Clyde and the mounted Edward VII show serious bomb damage inflicted by Giro's master's master fewer than ten years later. Giro's tombstone, however, was undamaged – as was the splendid Nazi interior nearby designed by Hitler's architect Albert Speer – and has been encased in glass to preserve it further.

PIGEONS AT WAR

There is a splendidly conceived and charming, if somewhat stained, war memorial for pigeons in Worthing, Sussex. It consists of inscribed boulders and a pond on a mound in Beach House Park and is perfectly serious. One stone reads: 'In memory of warrior birds who gave their lives on active service 1939–45 and for the use and pleasure of living birds.'

Hundreds of homing pigeons were dropped into Nazi-occupied Europe to the Resistance and many made it home. Others were with troops on secret missions. Naturally, the Germans tried to shoot down any pigeons they thought might be carrying messages. An astounding 31 of the 53 Dickin medals, the 'animal VCs', went to pigeons, so these brave creatures were not, when it came to it, doves.

AMAZING GRACE

Incomprehensibly, it was decided in Hastings, East Sussex, in 1997 not to erect a statue to 19th-century cricket legend Dr W G Grace in a new shopping centre built over the ground where he scored a double century against Australia; instead, they just portrayed some vague cricketing figures.

Devotees of the good doctor should direct their pilgrimage further north and discover a few fascinating relics of cricketing greatness. At **Elmers End Cemetery**, Beckenham, Kent, may be found his grave inscribed with bat and ball. Fans who marvel at the first man to score one hundred centuries (just over a century ago, in 1895) can slake their thirst in the nearby W G Grace pub.

Another grave marked with a stone bat and ball is that of cricketing chronicler John Wisden at **Brompton Cemetery**, Earls Court, London. It was he who said on seeing the mountainous waves of the Atlantic Ocean for the first time: 'What this pitch needs is ten minutes of the heavy roller.' This sentiment may have been shared by groundsman-turned-ground-owner Thomas Lord, who in 1787 created the hallowed turf of Lord's Cricket Ground. He lies beneath the equally hallowed turf of peaceful West Meon churchyard, Hampshire, his innings having ended in 1832. The thirsty cricket pilgrim could continue to the – yes, hallowed – cricket ground at Hambledon where it all began, and where a pint may be enjoyed in the legendary Bat and Ball pub.

The south of England also holds the remains of John Willes, credited with introducing round-arm bowling to cricket. He died in 1852 and his grave is at Sutton Valence, Kent.

PICKLED BRAINS AND RESTLESS HEADS

A controversial exhibition at London's Serpentine Gallery in 1995 included, beside a totally naked nude actress sleeping in a box, the pickled brain of mathematician Charles Babbage.

Babbage's brilliant ideas on calculating machines in the early 19th century laid the groundwork for today's computers more than a century before such machines were actually made to work. But the bizarre preservation of his brain – it normally resides at the Royal College of Surgeons of England – isn't at all unique.

Not far away the embalmed body of philosopher **Jeremy Bentham** (1748–1832) sits in state within a glass case in University College, Gower Street, London. In the 19th century his head was replaced with a replica, as disrespectful students had the macabre habit of playing football with the real thing, even if this followed his famed principle of utilitarianism – matters should be arranged to be useful for 'the happiness of the greatest number'.

People can become very pompous when writing their wills and Bentham was no exception. He directed how his body was to be displayed in great detail, including:

'my executor will cause the skeleton to be clad in one of the suits of black occasionally worn by me. The body so clothed shall together with the chair and staff in my later years bourne by me he will take charge of and for containing the whole apparatus he will cause to be prepared an appropriate box or case and will cause to be engraved in conspicuous characters on a plate to be fixed thereon and also on labels on the glass cases in which the preparation of the soft parts of my body will be preserved ... etc, etc'

This suggests not only that Bentham's lectures might in real life have been less than riveting, but also that he had that delusion of the self-appointed great and the good that the world's fascination with them cannot end with their death. Now whom does that remind me of today?

Like Bentham's, the Lord Protector Oliver Cromwell's head has not had a restful time in the three centuries since it was ripped from his remains in the 1660 Restoration and impaled on a pole at Westminster Hall. It supposedly blew down in a storm and was buried in various places before ending up in the grounds of Sidney Sussex College, Cambridge. Its location is unmarked in case Royalists, still angry after all those years at his part in chopping off the head of King Charles I, dig it up again.

SURREY'S MYSTERY MOSQUE AND A DEATH RAILWAY

Generations of commuters, schoolchildren returning from boarding school and holidaymakers using the main railway line from London's Waterloo will have all, momentarily, wondered exactly the same thing. Why, just before Woking, in the leafy gin and Jag belt beloved of stockbrokers, is there a sizeable mosque, complete with handsome dome and crescent moon?

After all, it is an area where few Muslim immigrants have ever lived and religion is more likely thought of in terms of old ladies cycling to evensong. The eccentric character behind this puzzle can be found a couple of miles further down the main line in the massive **Brookwood Cemetery**, itself a rather bizarre answer to Victorian London's burial space crisis. Both stories are most peculiar.

Things in the capital were so bad in the early 19th century that the poor were buried in shallow graves on top of one another. The poor scavenged

FUNERAL TRAINS

Funeral trains have started running again at Ripley, Derbyshire, this time aimed at dead steam-train enthusiasts. A new cemetery has been created a two-mile ride down the line from Butterley station and the coffins are unloaded at a special platform, with the wake held in the buffet car. The dead puff buffs are buried so close to the tracks that their bones must be shaken by the giants of yesteryear rolling past.

coffin wood from the inadequately buried, whom they were often doomed soon to join in a capital rife with disease and lacking basic sewerage systems.

Human bones were shipped north to be used as fertiliser. Churchyards even today bulge higher than the paths through them, such was the burial upon burial, often after an indecently short interval. One solution to this, along with the great Victorian cemeteries such as Hampstead, Kensal Green and West Brompton, was the macabrely fascinating Brookwood Necropolis Railway which started running in 1854.

It was exclusive in that you only travelled once, and then only in one direction. The service was run for the dead, so the 'coffin tickets' issued right up to the 1950s were not available as returns. Funeral trains ran from the discreet London Necropolis station near Waterloo, where steam-powered hoists would raise coffins to the level of the hearse vans. In the spirit of the age, there was segregation between Anglicans and the rest, as there was in the mourners' waiting rooms and carriages.

At Brookwood, a part of Woking, a vast city of the dead was laid out with every possible nationality and creed catered for (and indeed, judging by the number of graves marked 'resting' or 'fell asleep', waking Woking might still be a possibility). If today you take the pleasant and fascinating walk along the route of the long siding which these mournful trains took from Brookwood station, to two truly terminal stations (one Anglican, one for the rest), many interesting things will come to light. For instance, the reason why the further station is now occupied by Orthodox monks, incongruously set with their chickens on a former platform for the dead in deepest Surrey, is that they are venerating the relics of the English king Edward the Martyr, an important saint for them, in the nearby special chapel.

On the right of the tracks, the solution to the mosque puzzle comes with an impressive monument to Gottlieb William Leitner, featuring a noble bust framed by an arch inscribed 'The Learned are Honoured in their Work' (as untrue for him as for many another forgotten eccentric). Undoubtedly a gifted linguist, Dr Leitner, who had been born in Budapest in 1840, was the kind of self-obsessed, self-driven, self-publicising oddball who would make little impact today, unless he could find a sponsor for an expedition by yak to the South Pole or host a television show.

But this was the apogee of the British Empire, and an indifferent white man could become a great man in some remote country, such were the opportunities. Leitner, flawed as he was, was *not* indifferent. Having learned five languages by the age of five, and 15 by the time he set off for the Crimean War in 1855 (gaining an honorary British Army colonelship at that astounding age as an invaluable interpreter), he continued to add approximately one language per year of his life.

After creating an oriental section at King's College, London and becoming its professor by 1861, Leitner saw a job advertised running Government College, Lahore, then in British India. Although only 21, he was appointed, a decision the authorities came to regret. Despite churning out English-speaking *babus* (clerks) for the massive bureaucracy that the British were creating – it endures even today – Leitner wanted to blend Indian and European cultures. He published a stream of works on Indian languages (an Urdu *Macbeth*, for example) and set up the Punjab University and about ten other schools and colleges. But as John Keay writes in his excellent book *Eccentric Travellers* (John Murray/BBC Books, 1982): 'Sadly, Leitner's was a genius untempered by judgment; he never knew where to stop.' He started a bank and other organisations for 'native people' in a way which annoyed the authorities who believed they had run India perfectly well for years without him.

His expeditions for linguistic researches into remote parts of the North-West Frontier, the Hindu Kush and Ladakh produced some scattered information, which few took any notice of, about languages and peoples he encountered, sitting, as he put it, by a camp fire with a pen in one hand and a revolver in the other. He lost too many men and became entangled in endless political intrigues and small wars between various potentates and maharajas. He even managed to lose an important travelling companion, Henry Cowie, brother of the advocate-general of Bengal, who fell from one of those flimsy rope bridges over a torrent, now so beloved of Indiana Jones films. Months later he even recovered the body after its burial, and an attempted body-kidnapping, and carted the remains himself hundreds of miles, according to his own account.

On his trips back to Europe, Leitner not only brought Oriental artefacts but several native people who were paraded like specimens before learned societies' soirées. On leave in 1884 he purchased the Royal Dramatic College, Woking, a failed charitable project earlier backed by Charles Dickens, and eventually made it into the Indian University Institute affiliated to his own Punjab University. In his retirement at Woking he continued to rail against 'British imperialism' in northwest India as the British agents tried to pacify the local tribes, ignoring the bigger picture – this was part of the 'Great Game' in stopping Russian imperialism spreading south.

Like many of his creations, the Indian University at Woking did not outlive him. But the beautiful **Shah Jehan Mosque**, built in its grounds in Oriental Road, still surprises and delights passengers of the adjacent railway line.

HOW THE LIVING CAN FOLLOW THE DEAD

The increasingly popular Coast-to-Coast walk across the most beautiful bits of the north of England – from the Lakes across the Pennines to the North Yorkshire Moors and the North Sea – has the merit, and I write from footsore experience, of making a hiker feel really alive. But, oddly enough, the route has often been rather popular with the dead.

'Corpse roads' feature strongly in the pre-motor road days of these then-remote areas, when some settlements could only be reached by foot or packhorse. The dead from remoter farms and hamlets still had to be buried in consecrated ground, and as parishes in these thinly populated areas could be huge, the church might be a dozen miles away. There were set routes for the dead to reach these graveyards, the corpses being slung over packhorses, or being carried by mourners or bearers.

One of the more tiring but rewarding days of the Coast-to-Coast walk brings the hiker down to **Haweswater**, a reservoir that today fills Mardale, once home to a pretty village and a more modest natural lake. Across the lake from the hiker's long track, beside the road on the other side, a trail can be seen zig-zagging up the hill. This is the corpse road which once led from Mardale Green up and over the hill to consecrated ground at Shap. The dead would have been strapped to a horse and carried across in all weathers, followed up the fellside by windswept mourners. This happened until 1729, when Mardale Green at last gained its own church and consecrated ground.

In 1936 the church was taken down and used in building the dam that was to flood the valley. That left the awkward question of the dead, and whether being under 100ft of water as well as 6ft of earth would cause problems. It certainly would have done for those wishing to visit graves without diving gear – although in times of droughts the eerie remains of the village, the lane and drystone walls emerge as the water levels fall. So the dead were exhumed and reburied at Shap, where they would have gone anyway up the corpse road, had no church been built. It is all fuel for thought for hikers who also feel pretty near dead when, exhausted, they reach Shap's welcoming pubs.

Two days further along the Coast-to-Coast walk, which by now has crossed the Pennine watershed heading east, the walk follows the length of lovely **Swaledale**. This entire valley was the prescribed route for those carrying – often on a mourner's back – their dead to Grinton, a journey which could take two or three days. Side routes led from other hamlets in the bleak and sparsely populated upland. The corpse stone at Ivelet, where there is now a handsome bridge, was the spot for laying down the body for the bearers to rest before fording the river, and at Blades a dead-house, now ruined, provided the overnight stop for those who started way up the valley. Eventually, today's hiker passes St Andrew's, Grinton, the dead end for that particular corpse trail. (Some 15 miles south of Swaledale, another Yorkshire road for the dead links remote Hubberholme church, northwest of Buckden, which had no consecrated graveyard, to Arncliffe, via the Corpse Way which reaches 2,000ft in bleak moorland.)

The macabre theme goes on. As the North Yorkshire Moors are reached, the route converges with that famous route of the dead, the Lyke Wake Walk, immortalised by the Cleveland Lyke Wake Dirge, a dialect folksong about death and the Devil, naming several features along the route. There is a tradition among trekking fanatics to do the whole thing in one go, right through the bleak windswept night.

Despite all this, and despite the fact that a party in recent years made the 40-mile trek carrying a coffin, the authors of the dirge admit that the song and the route were created in the 20th century as a bit of instant folklore, albeit representative of the customs in the hills all around. After all, there was no reason to take bodies *away* from the perfectly adequate graveyards at either end of the trail. Dead peculiar, one might think, heading on towards the North Sea.

Yet further along the Coast-to-Coast walk for the dead, near Grosmont, on a track not open to cars, walkers pass an old toll-house sign still saying: 'Hearses, 6d'. After all that, when you hit Whitby, its Dracula Trail might seem a little dead.

GONE FOR A BURTON: THE ARAB TENT IN DEEPEST MORTLAKE

The most eccentric tomb in London must be that of **Richard Burton**. Not the Richard Burton who kept marrying Elizabeth Taylor – surely rather eccentric behaviour in itself – but the great explorer who opened up the vast and unknown lands of Arabia to the eyes of an enchanted Western world. Thus, a full-scale Arab sheik's tent – complete with stone folds of cloth frozen in mid-flap of a desert breeze as if touched by a Narnian witch's wand – stands somewhat incongruously in a sleepy corner of suburban Mortlake.

Aptly, finding Burton's mausoleum is something of an exploration in itself. It is not in the vast municipal Mortlake Cemetery, nor in the graveyard of the confusingly named St Mary the Virgin church fronting Mortlake High Street near the Thames. But behind there, through a labyrinth of paths such as Tinderbox Alley, lined by Victorian cottages, lies St Mary Magdalen, a Catholic church, where the extraordinary monument can be found by following a well-worn track through the undergrowth.

Close up, one can see an iron star romantically hidden in the foliage above the tent, a valedictory poem typical of the era and, behind, the most fascinating aspect: a window in the tent's roof with a handy steel ladder, enabling one to peer at the coffins of Burton and his wife. They are surrounded by some of their favourite objects from his explorations, and well-withered wreaths, a century of dust and decrepitude having failed to spoil the oddly cosy, domestic scene.

Another half-forgotten gem in London from this era of exotic Arabists is the home of the great Victorian artist Frederic, Lord Leighton. The creator of the familiar *Flaming June* picture lived at the extraordinary **Leighton House**, in a quiet road off Kensington High Street, where one can experience (for no admission fee) heady incense in the exotic, bejewelled Arab hall where Leighton's unique collection of Moorish tilework is employed, complete with tinkling fountain and the lofty dome described in its day as the eighth wonder of the world.

Lord Lloyd-Webber and Lady Lucinda Lambton are great fans of what the latter calls 'the secret heart of Kensington'. Leighton, whose career received a huge boost when Queen Victoria bought one of his pictures, was made a peer – the only artist so honoured – shortly before his death in 1896.

The real Richard Burton

Burton, born in Torquay in 1821, was a typical Victorian flawed genius. He was eccentrically brilliant and a high achiever, obsessively driven to the ends of the earth, but unconventional and totally unable to see that his fascination with unusual sexual practices and erotic perversions was bound to alienate him from the straight-laced Establishment.

This does not detract from the fact that he was a consummate master of languages and daring disguise who was the first European to penetrate forbidden Muslim cities without being executed, who made a great spy and was also the first white man to see Lake Tanganyika. He had been expelled from Trinity College in 1842 over some disciplinary matter, having become fluent in Greek, Latin, French and the various forms of Italian then in use. He soon turned disgrace to advantage.

While serving in India as a subaltern in the 18th regiment of Bombay Native Infantry during the war with the Sind, he added Arabic, Hindi, Marathi, Sindhi, Punjabi, Telegu, Pashtu and Milani to his linguistic cornucopia. He was eventually to acquire 25 languages and many dialects. Burton became intelligence officer for the commander of British forces in the Sind, Sir Charles Napier (and would have appreciated the greatest pun ever telegraphed to London, Napier's one word Latin victory message: *Peccavi*, or, 'I have sinned', which he meant to be understood as 'I have Sind').

Burton was sent by Napier to investigate the homosexual brothels of Karachi, and although this led to them being destroyed, it also led to Burton's disgrace through his association with perhaps over-zealously detailed reports on the sexual peccadillos he discovered there. Burton returned home ill and in disgrace. Again he turned this disgrace to advantage by writing great scholarly works on India, and then voyaging to Mecca in disguise, daringly sketching and measuring the mosque and holy shrine, then travelling to the equally forbidden East African city of Harar, both voyages being described in books that brought him fame. Burton then developed an obsessive interest in the source of the White Nile; his 1855 expedition with John Speke ended after the party was attacked and Burton had a spear thrown through his jaw.

Undaunted, he volunteered to go to the Crimea to fight against Russia. He would have been there at the same time as Gottlieb Leitner, another flawed genius who rubbed the Establishment up the wrong way. After the Crimean War, Burton and Speke resumed the search for the source of the Nile. They became very ill and split up: Speke's discovery of Lake Victoria led to a bitter row which ended in Speke's mysterious death from a gunshot wound in 1864. The inquest said it was a hunting accident; Burton thought it was suicide, and believed others secretly blamed him for shooting Speke, who had gained much of the fame Burton had sought over the source of the Nile.

Burton married the aristocratic English rose Isabell Arundell (a now extinct great family, not connected with the equally Catholic Earls of Arundel) and spent the rest of his life working as British consul at various corners of the globe. He and Isabell had become secretly engaged in 1856 before he left for Africa, and when he asked in Hyde Park if she would mind giving up civilisation for him, she said: 'I have prayed for you every morning and night, I have followed your career minutely, I have read every word you have ever written and I would rather have a crust and a tent with you than be Queen of all the world.'

Foreign Office mandarins, despairing of Burton ever keeping his mouth shut, sent him to the West African hell-hole of Fernando Po where most Europeans conveniently died of horrible diseases within a year or two. Burton not only survived but turned out five books detailing tribal fetishism, ritual murder, cannibalism and bizarre sexual perversions – this in a prim age where lesbianism, for example, did not officially exist – which did not nothing to dent his reputation as maverick eccentric. He made several discoveries, including a squirrel, still called *Scirius Isabella* after his wife. One consulship, in Damascus, ended in dismissal and disgrace because the Christian proselytising of Isabell annoyed the authorities and because Burton had made so many enemies within the diplomatic service.

But his last years as consul in Trieste saw his flowering as a truly great translator, including his masterful version of the unexpurgated *Arabian Nights*. He also secretly published the *Kama Sutra of Vatsyayana* and the *Perfumed Garden of the Cheik Nefzaoui*. There were plenty of detailed footnotes about pornography, homosexuality and the odd sexual practices which most of Victorian Britain found appalling, if secretly fascinating.

Knighted at last in 1886 for his services to the Empire, Sir Richard Burton died in Trieste in 1890. His Catholic wife promptly burned all his notes, diaries and manuscripts, fearing they would offend presumably for their sexual content, and wrote a biography which recreated her husband as a faithful Catholic, which he never was. His great collection of diaries and notebooks about various corners of the globe were thus mostly lost to posterity, his secrets confined to that very strange Arab tent where one can but peer down on the Burtons apparently slumbering in sleepy Mortlake and wonder.

TOMBS ALONG ODD LINES

Railwaymen whose lives are ruled by unemotional iron and steel have often been most loyal and strangely sentimental, as their bizarre tombs dotted around the country, adorned with fantastic if not appalling doggerel, testify.

One of the most elaborate rhymes is on the memorial to William Pickering and Richard Hedger in the south porch of **Ely Cathedral**, Cambridgeshire. They were killed on Christmas Eve 1845 aged 30 and 24 respectively on the Norfolk Railway near Thetford. An inquest blamed their death on excessive speed, although some of the jury thought the engine construction deficient – these were very early days and the technology primitive, although Norfolk jurors can't have known much about it.

Their memorial, however, happily compares the new-fangled railway journeys to the trip to heaven in a wonderful poem known as the *Spiritual Railway*. Either the Norfolk accent was then a lot stronger or the writer was an atrocious rhymer, but the conclusion was clearly on the right lines:

'The Line to heaven by Christ was made
With heavenly truth the Rails are laid ...
God's Love the Fire, his Truth the Steam,
Which drives the Engine and the Train ...
In First and Second, and Third Class,
Repentence, Faith and Holiness ...
Come then poor Sinners, now's the time
At any station on the Line.
If you'll repent and turn from sin
The Train will stop and take you in.'

Train-surfing, an insanely dangerous American game of riding train roofs or sides, and the mass roof-riding phenomenon that the Indians euphemistically call ticketless travel, are nothing new, judging by an 1838 tombstone at **St Mary's, Harrow-on-the-Hill**, northwest London. But one hopes that the gruesomely detailed doggerel is not copied elsewhere. The inscription says that Thomas Port, who used to ride wagons on the nearby London and Birmingham Railway, lost his legs in 1838 after falling from the train. 'With the greatest fortitude he bore a second amputation by the surgeons and died from loss of blood.'

The macabre doggerel states:

'Bright rose the morn and vig'rous Port,
Gay on the train he used his wonted sport
Ere noon arrived his mangled form they bore
With pain distorted and overwhelmed with gore
When evening came to close the fateful day
A mutilated corpse the sufferer lay.'

A shudder went though me as I stood there pondering gay sport on trains. Did they chuck all the bits into his grave?

Another fine piece of railway disaster doggerel, at **St John's Church** in Bromsgrove, Worcestershire, also dates from the very early days. It is a memorial to Thomas Scaife, 28, and Joseph Rutherford, 30, engineers on the Birmingham and Gloucester Railway, who were killed by a boiler explosion in November 1840. As the tombstone of Scaife records:

'My engine now is cold and still
No water does my boiler fill
My coke affords its flame no more
My days of usefulness are o'er.
My wheels deny their noted speed
No more my guiding hands they heed
My whistle too has lost its tone
Its shrill and thrilling sounds are gone ...
No more I feel each urging breath
My steam is now condens'd in death ...'

This is brilliant stuff, but the wonderfully detailed carvings on the graves show one of the American-built Norris banking engines normally used near here to bank (push) heavy trains up the notorious Lickey Incline. In fact, poor Scaife and Rutherford were using an experimental locomotive which was blown to pieces and therefore could not be copied. Its name was '*Surprise*'.

Another railway disaster is commemorated in the churchyard at **Otley**, near the Leeds to Harrogate line. This time there is no verse, but a splendid miniature tunnel portal, stone-built and crenellated with towers. It would grace the best garden train layout and one can happily imagine puffing models bringing truckloads of scones to ladies at vicarage tea parties. However, the truth is somewhat more sombre. The miniature is a replica of the portal of nearby Bramhope Tunnel, and a memorial to the 23 men who died in its appallingly troublesome construction, 280ft beneath the ridge between Leeds and Wharfedale. Some 1,500 million gallons of water had to be pumped out to prevent flooding during construction.

ABOVE OUR HEADS

Some mortgage holders feel the bank owns them body and soul, but Henry Trigg's coffin in Stevenage old town in Hertfordshire takes the notion to an extreme. It is installed in the rafters of the National Westminster Bank.

In 1724 he instructed that his coffin be 'buried' in the roof of what was then a barn, his will perhaps being motivated by the contemporary fear of grave robbers. Later, the barn became part of a bank and the coffin is still there.

Various eccentrics have asked to be 'buried' at the tops of towers (see page 199) but another corpse which ended up closer to heaven than usual was a mummified cat, installed in the roof of the half-timbered Guildhall of Corpus Christi in the charming small town of **Lavenham**, Suffolk. It was probably put there for superstitious reasons when the Guildhall was built in the 16th century and may still be seen in the splendid building in this exceptionally pretty town, with its timbered houses and pargetted fronts.

SOME VERY STRANGE ORGANS
Hearts that were strangely moved

Just as rushing living hearts around to save lives in transplants seized the imagination of late 20th-century society, so the location of even dead people's hearts has been thought in the past to have immense significance.

The explorer Livingstone's heart is buried where he was searching for the source of the Nile in his beloved Africa, while **Thomas Hardy's heart** can be found beneath a tombstone at Stinsford near Dorchester, Dorset – appropriately, as Dorchester was the Casterbridge of Hardy's great novel.

Hardy actually wanted to buried whole at Stinsford next to his wife, but against his wishes the rest of him was cremated and the ashes taken to Poets' Corner in Westminster Abbey. Local legend has it that the 'heart' was another bit of meat, as the cat got in and stole the real organ. But a spokesman for the Thomas Hardy Society said sniffily: 'We've never lent any credence to this local gossip. It's just a myth which probably had its origin in the fact that Hardy wasn't very popular locally.'

By the way, the nearby ugly factory chimney of a **Hardy Monument** uphill from Portesham near Weymouth is often assumed to commemorate Thomas Hardy the author. But actually it remembers the other Thomas Hardy – the 'kiss me' or *kismet* ('fate' in Arabic) Hardy of Trafalgar fame, not the writer of a century later. The view, nevertheless, is fantastic.

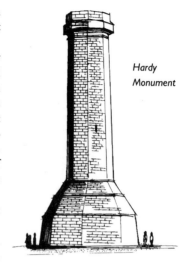

Hardy
Monument

A yet stranger story can be traced at **St Paul's, Hammersmith**, West London. At the back of the nave stands an urn in which Sir Nicholas Crispe requested his heart be put on his death in 1665. The urn is below a bronze bust of 'that glorious martyr Kinge Charles the first of blessed memory' and symbolises Crispe's role as a 'loyall sharer in the sufferings of his late and present majesty'.

Curiously, the urn is empty. In 1898 the Royalist knight's body was moved to Hammersmith from St Mildred's, Bread Street, London, and someone with a strong stomach took the two-centuries-old, and probably crisp, heart from the urn and reunited it with Crispe's body in the churchyard. There it lies today, beneath the thundering A4 flyover.

Another heart missing from its urn is at that altogether amazing collection of eccentricities at **West Wycombe**, Buckinghamshire, where Sir Francis Dashwood and his Hellfire Club (motto: 'Do What You Will') met for feasts (some say orgies), deep in labyrinthine caves he had carved hundreds of feet inside West Wycombe Hill. The club had an initiation rite which involved a naked woman lying on a table, and on one occasion a dozen 'vestal virgins' were ordered from a London brothel. They were plied with champagne and danced with leading members of parliament, while a band played behind a screen.

A typical Hellfire Club practical joke was that played by MP John Wilkes on Lord Sandwich, First Lord of the Admiralty. During a Black Mass, Wilkes released a baboon dressed as the Devil. The creature leapt on to the shoulders of Lord Sandwich who fled screaming into woodland, convinced he was being chased by Satan.

Today, the caves can be toured and their colourful past is illustrated deep in the hill. Above, the church of St Lawrence, with its extraordinary golden ball 646ft above sea level, forms a dramatic landmark at the end of A40 from High Wycombe, a road built on chalk dug from the caves. Sir Francis and up to nine of his pals could sit drinking on seats within the ball, accessed by a curved trapdoor let down as if from a spaceship or diving bell. Until 1950 the public could enter too, but now you can reach only the top of the tower a few feet below, drinking in merely the exceptional view, which is heady enough after climbing the 113 steps.

Dashwood Mausoleum

Between the church and A40 leading to London sits the extraordinary **Dashwood Mausoleum**, a vast flint hexagon open to the skies. One of Dashwood's greatest fans was the poet Paul Whitehead, Steward of the Hellfire Club, who left his heart plus £50 for an urn, with a request for it to be placed in the mausoleum. This was done with much pomp, six soldiers carrying the heavy urn up the hill and firing a salute. But there seem to have been almost as many curious visitors to West Wycombe 200 years ago as now, and they had a habit of taking out poor Whitehead's heart and disrespectfully throwing it round. In about 1820, someone failed to replace the heart in its urn. Heartless.

The baronet at the time of writing, another Sir Francis Dashwood, also has his foibles. There was once staged a re-enactment of the battle of Trafalgar on West Wycombe's lake and in 1996 he was noted regularly catching the Green Line bus to London, despite being 'England's premier baronet'. The separate, but not nearly so eccentric, West Wycombe Park and the quite remarkably preserved village either side of the main road are in the care of the National Trust.

Broken hearts and a visible organ

Another heart that tells a story can be found at West Parley church, Dorset, just north of Bournemouth, the rest of the lady's body being buried at Lydlinch, about 20 miles away. Her name is modestly not recorded, but it is thought that in the 14th century a lady of the manor of West Parley was compelled on her marriage to leave her home village to live at Lydlinch. She said before she died that as her heart had always been at West Parley, she wished it be buried there. The heart was buried in an urn under a circular stone, but the urn was excavated in 1895 and can now be seen behind an iron grille on the east wall of the church. Her body lies in a tomb outside the entrance of Lydlinch church with an inscription recording the tithes she left 'for ever' for the rector of that church.

Of course in the days before refrigeration, there was no way of moving the dead around unless they were thoroughly embalmed, and even then it was, frankly, dead difficult over long distances. In **Mappowder**, another Dorset village, can be seen a small stone effigy of a crusader with chain mail, sword and shield, his legs crossed, indicating that he died in action. This led to a local legend of a 'boy crusader', but in fact it is the heart of a knight, who died fighting in the Holy Land, which is buried here, his embalmed heart having been sent back to his grieving family – the body bag of its day.

This tradition even involved the heart of one of the late Princess Diana's ancestors. In the crypt at St Mary the Virgin at Great Brington, near the Spencer family home at Althorp, lies the embalmed heart of the third Baron Spencer, who died at the battle of Newbury in 1643. The ashes of Diana's father are also interred in the crypt, which was entered over the centuries by lifting a heavy stone slab embedded with an iron ring. No doubt Diana would have been buried there – and not on a lake island on the estate – had not her global fame meant that the tiny village would have been overwhelmed.

At **St Mary's Church, Woodford**, Northamptonshire, a bandaged heart may be seen, and, again, its story is convoluted and linked with the great events of English history. It is a reminder of John Styles, a 16th-century priest who refused to accept the Reformation and fled to the Low Countries, taking with him a valuable chalice which belonged to the church. A later minister hunted down the chalice, and brought it back with Styles' heart; later still, both were lost. Then in the 19th century, after a ghost, apparently, pointed the way, the chalice was rediscovered concealed in a wall at the vicarage. It did not contain the heart, but it did contain a letter saying where the heart was hidden in a church pillar. There it may still be seen, through a glass panel.

Faith given a hand

It may seem rather bizarre and macabre nowadays, but going even further back, relics of the saints such as alleged bits of their bodies – along with stained glass windows – were common visual aids in the illiterate Middle Ages. Most of these were destroyed by the Puritans, but at St Peter's Church, Marlow, Buckinghamshire, may be seen a mummified hand, said to have belonged to St James the apostle.

One hand that apparently reached from beyond the grave to help today's faithful is that of 17th-century martyr St John Kemble. The Roman Catholic was hanged, drawn and quartered in Hereford in 1679 at the grand old age of 80 after the Titus Oates plot – a conspiracy to kill King Charles II – was exposed. After the execution, the severed hand of Kemble was picked up by a woman sympathiser and for the past two centuries the relic has been at St Francis Xavier's Church, Hereford.

In July 1995 a local Catholic priest, Father Christopher Jenkins, lay in a coma after a stroke and doctors said that only 'the hand of God' could save him. This gave churchmen the idea of taking the relic – Kemble's hand — from the church to the hospital bedside. Father Anthony Tumelty took the relic from its oak casket and placed it on Father Jenkins' forehead. The 63-year-old priest made an astonishing recovery.

Brave heart into battle

A heart that went into battle without its body in the crusades can be found at **Melrose Abbey**, in Scotland's Borders. It belongs to Robert the Bruce, best known for thrashing the English at Bannockburn in 1314. A month before his death he wrote to his son asking to be buried at the abbey, but on his deathbed asked his loyal friend Sir James Douglas to take his heart to the Holy Land to fight the Infidel. Sir James, the 'Black Douglas', was mortally wounded in battle despite carrying the heart as protection. As he died, he hurled the casket at the enemy with the cry: 'Forward brave heart!' Everywhere in **Drumlanrig Castle**, built on the site of Sir James's stronghold, can be seen the emblem of the winged heart.

As for Robert the Bruce's heart, a lead casket was excavated at Melrose in 1921, and a further archaeological dig in 1996 saw it reburied without being opened, but with a new marker stone locating it easily for the visitor. 'Good' Sir James Douglas's heart can similarly be found at St Bride's Chapel, Douglas, Lanarkshire, in a lead casket, as can that of Archibald, fifth Earl of Angus.

A great Scottish love story

Perhaps the most poignant heart burial is the one behind the romantic red stone ruin of **Sweetheart Abbey**, near Dumfries. This is one of many relics of a renowned 13th-century beauty, Lady Devorgilla, and her enduring love for her husband John Balliol, founder of Balliol College, Oxford. They lived at Buittle Castle near Dalbeattie and were utterly devoted to each other. Thus Balliol's early death in 1269 caused a grief and mourning not unlike Queen Victoria's, six centuries later, for Albert. Devorgilla had his heart embalmed and placed in an ivory casket bound with enamelled silver bands. She kept this 'silent, sweet companion' with her until she died in 1289, aged 81. The casket was buried with her in the monastery which she had founded and which the Cistercian monks came to know as Sweetheart Abbey. Her tomb-top effigy showed her still clasping the heart to her bosom.

Devorgilla's beauty and bounty were sung of by minstrels and renowned by poets in Scotland for centuries afterwards. She also left the handsome Devorgilla Bridge in Dumfries, set up friaries in Wigtown and Dundee and confirmed and endowed Balliol College – enduring testimonies to one of Scotland's greatest love affairs.

EVASION OF THE BODY-SNATCHERS

Edinburgh having been the setting for Burke and Hare's grisly grave-robbing exploits – the pair were hanged in 1829 – the Scots could be forgiven for being a wee bit cautious about their mortal remains. But at times the precautions seemed excessive.

In Perthshire, at **Logierait** on the north bank of the Tay, the churchyard contains three mortsafes – coffin-shaped iron cages whose grilles extend above and below the ground to prevent digging. By a low wall, there are two adult mortsafes and a child's alongside. (Similar iron hoops can be seen across the border at Warden, Northumberland, where a vicar ordered hoops for himself, his wife and his children, and, predictably, in Edinburgh graveyards.) It is likely that coffins were left here until the body was in no condition for the medical students (who paid the grave robbers so well) and then buried.

At Udny Green in Aberdeenshire, the churchyard of the beautiful village contains a circular stone building erected by local subscription as a mortsafe in 1832 to combat the body-snatching hysteria. A turntable in the centre facilitates the handling of coffins – like those roundhouses in which steam engines used to gather round.

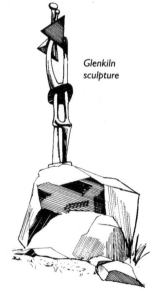

Glenkiln
sculpture

Perhaps the most extreme is the remote grave of eccentric shepherd **Johnnie Turner** high above Glenkiln Reservoir, seven miles west of Dumfries. Turner, terrified of body-snatchers, hewed his own grave out of solid rock at an altitude of 1,300ft, and it is now marked with a monument. This is rather eccentric country, with some of the greatest sculptures by Rodin, Moore, Epstein and Renoir gazing around the bleak landscape. This has to be God's own wonderful art gallery. The superb Moore King and Queen were beheaded by morons in 1995, and the sculpture was away being mended when I visited but they left Turner's remains alone, so perhaps he was right. There are no concessions to tourists, who have no rights of access to the sculptures off the lonely road, and no signs to help you find the spot.

When the great and the powerful in Scotland wanted to be buried, they built some of the most magnificent mausoleums in Europe. In Hamilton, Lanarkshire, the **Hamilton Mausoleum** soars 120ft high with its glass-topped cupola. It was designed by the tenth Duke of Hamilton in 1840 for his own funeral in 1852. The entrance is flanked by two huge stone lions. The interior is marble floored and has bizarre acoustic qualities. The tenth Duke, it was said, was obsessed with a classical sarcophagus he had brought to Hamilton and frequently lay down in it to ensure he would fit when the time came. However, he forgot the thickness of the necessary casket, so his feet had to be cut off and put in beside him.

The duke's Hamilton Palace has long since been demolished but the mausoleum remains, as does the Chatelherault Hunting Lodge and Country Park, from where one can book a place on the thrice-weekly tours of the mausoleum.

A far more attractive and artistically eccentric mausoleum is that of Patrick Alan Fraser of Hospital Field at **Arbroath** in Angus. Beautifully detailed carving adorns the extraordinary building to the rooftops. It was begun in 1875 and took local stonemason James Peters 25 years to execute. The exquisiteness of his sandstone carvings deserves greater recognition. It is in Western Cemetery, and is opened once a year (in September) for visitors to inspect the interior.

Another attractive Scottish mausoleum worth stopping to inspect is on the A68. It has an attractive **Byzantine** dome, glazed stars in the roof, and, as at Hamilton, two lions guarding the door, one sleeping and one awake. This is the resting place of one General Sir Thomas Monteath Douglas, who died in 1868.

TRAVEL INFORMATION

Beware Chalk Pit Pyramid, Farley Mount Country Park, Hampshire
Road On back roads west of Winchester, which is off M3 J12. Take B3049 and then turn south (left) through Sparsholt.
Tourist information ✆ 01962 840500.

Bonomi Pyramid, Blickling Hall, Norfolk; ✆ 01263 738030 (National Trust)
Road Just north of Aylsham, off A140 Norwich–Cromer road. Norwich is reached from London/M25 by A11.
Rail For the enthusiast, possible by reaching Wroxham on the Norwich–Sheringham branch and changing to the Bure Valley Railway (miniature) to reach Aylsham.
Tourist information ✆ 01603 666071.

Boy crusader, Mappowder, Dorset
Road From M3 J8 take A303 west about 40 miles to Wincanton turn (north from A303) then take A357 south 18 miles, A3030 (right) and B3143 (left) to continue south; take lane left (east) before Duntish through Brockhampton Green.
Tourist information ✆ 01305 267992.

Brompton Cemetery, Earls Court, London SW10
Rail West Brompton (District Line and main line from Clapham Junction).

Brookwood Cemetery
See Shah Jehan Mosque, page 108.

Burton Tomb, Mortlake, Surrey
Road Off High St, Mortlake, accessed from south end of London's Chiswick Bridge, or approach from White Hart Lane along North Worple Way.

Rail Mortlake station (from Waterloo), then walk back 200 yards towards Barnes on north (right) side of railway.
Bus 9A from Hammersmith terminates a few yards away.
Byzantine Mausoleum, Borders
Road On A68 going towards Edinburgh between Jedburgh and St Boswells, on the left just after Lilliardsedge.
Tourist information ↘ 01835 863435.

Corpse Road, Haweswater, Cumbria
Road Reached from Shap through lanes to northwest via Rosgill and Bampton. *Rail/bus* The London–Glasgow train whistles through Shap to Penrith. Return to Shap on bus 107, then walk or taxi 5 miles.
Foot Use *Wainwright's Coast to Coast Walk* (Westmorland Gazette, £7.95) to reach it from Patterdale or Shap. Get the pocket-sized book, not the coffee-table colour picture one.
Tourist information ↘ 01768 867466.

Corpse Trail, Swaledale, and the corpse stone at Ivelet, Yorkshire
Road From A1 at Scotch Corner near Darlington, take A6108 southeast through Richmond, then right on to B6270. The Corpse Trail mostly follows the north side of the Swale, and the corpse stone is near the north side of the pretty bridge at Ivelet. The wonderful path down this valley from Keld, with its numerous waterfalls and outstanding beauty, is recommended. If you see any Wainwright Coast-to-Coast walkers, pretend to look the other way. They are dodging the high-level route that mountain goat of a walker prescribed, just as I did, and taking the more pleasant option along the valley.
Tourist information ↘ 01748 850252.

Crispe heart, St Paul's, Hammersmith, London W6
Road Below A4 flyover.
Tube Hammersmith (District and Piccadilly lines).

Dashwood Mausoleum, Hellfire Caves, etc, West Wycombe, Buckinghamshire
Not to be confused with West Wycombe Park (↘ National Trust 01628 488675).
Road Off M40 J4, then A4010.
Rail/bus High Wycombe, then bus 300, 75, 321, 323.
Tourist information ↘ 01494 421892.

Dracula Trail, Whitby, and **Grosmont**, North Yorkshire
Road Off A1(M) near Thirsk, then A61, A19, A172, A171.
Rail/bus On picturesque Esk Valley branch line from London King's Cross–Edinburgh line.
Tourist information ↘ 01947 602674.

Drumlanrig Castle, Dumfries; ↘ 01848 330248
Road Off A76 about 18 miles north of Dumfries. From M6 Carlisle take A74, A75.
Rail Dumfries, then bus 246.
Tourist information ↘ 01387 253862.

Elmers End Cemetery, Kent
Rail Elmers End from London Bridge.
Road Straight down A214 Anerley Hill from landmark Crystal Palace. A214 joins A23 Brighton Rd in Streatham.

Ely Cathedral, Cambridgeshire
Architectural gem with rare lantern roof in charming small town set on hill (once Isle of Ely in surrounding marshes) northeast of Cambridge.
Rail Trains to Ely from King's Cross, London, and Cambridge—Kings Lynn on the Norfolk coast stop here, as do some cross-country trains from Liverpool, Birmingham and Peterborough to Norwich. 10-min walk to cathedral.
Bus National Express from London to Cambridge, then change to 109 bus to Ely.
Road From London or M25 take M11 to J14 near Cambridge then A14 east, A10 north (or use all A10 from London for far slower, more interesting journey). From Midlands and north, use M1, M6 or A1 to connect with A14.
Tourist information ✆ 01353 662062.

Fraser Mausoleum, Arbroath, Angus
Road Take A92 towards Dundee from town centre, right on to Westway after a mile or so, then left into Keptie Rd.
Rail On London King's Cross and Edinburgh–Aberdeen line.
Tourist information ✆ 01241 872609.

Giro's Memorial, Waterloo Place, London SW1
Tube Piccadilly Circus or Charing Cross (Piccadilly, Northern and Bakerloo lines or main line at Charing Cross).

Hamilton Mausoleum, Lanarkshire (book a tour ✆ 01698 426213)
Road Near Carlisle–Glasgow M74 J6.
Rail Hamilton Central, from Glasgow or London Euston then 10-min walk.
Tourist information ✆ 01698 285590.

Hardy's heart, Stinsford, Dorset
Road M3 to south end, M27 west, A31 and A35. Stinsford is on the left just before Dorchester.
Rail Dorchester South station from London Waterloo and other centres.
Tourist information ✆ 01305 267992.

Haystacks, Cumbria
Road From M6 J40 take A66 east to past Keswick, fork left on B5292 over Whinlatter pass to Lorton, through village and then B5289 left (south, up valley) to Buttermere. Don't consider this on an August weekend or a fine bank holiday. Wainwright's vision of heaven here doesn't then apply, thanks to the brainless politicians who ripped up the railways to this part of the lakes. Take a map and suitable clothing for sudden changes in weather.
Tourist information ✆ 01768 772645.

Jeremy Bentham's body, south cloister, University College, Gower St, London W1
Tube Warren Street (Victoria and Northern lines).

Johnnie Turner's grave and sculptures, Glenkiln, near Dumfries
Road Take the A75 west from Dumfries and after about 7 miles turn right for
Shawhead. In the village a quick right and left will lead you to a left fork marked
Glenkiln. Fork left when you reach the reservoir and you can park next to a Rodin at
the far end. Walk onwards to see a Hepworth with cows grazing around.

Knill Monument, St Ives, Cornwall
Road End of M5 to Exeter, A30 through north Cornwall, then, before Penzance, A3074
to St Ives.
Rail Short branch line off London Paddington and other centres–Penzance main line.
Tourist information ↘ 01736 796297.

Lavenham Guildhall, Suffolk (National Trust)
Road From London/M25, use A12 to about 10 miles before Ipswich, turn left on B1070
to Hadleigh then A1141 towards Bury St Edmunds. From North and Midlands use A14
from M1/M6 junction.
Rail/bus London Liverpool St, to Sudbury (change at Marks Tey), then bus 753.
Tourist information ↘ 01787 248207.

Leighton House, Kensington, London W11; ↘ 020 7602 3316
Road Off Kensington High Street, up Melbury Road, then Holland Park Road.
Bus/rail High St Kensington (Circle and District lines) and walk west, or many buses
such as 9, 10 to Commonwealth Institute.

Logierait mortsafes, Perthshire
Road One mile off A9, north of Perth, on A827 towards Aberfeldy. Ignore the cemetery
sign to the right and the churchyard is on the left.
Rail Nearest station Pitlochry, on Perth–Inverness line.
Tourist information ↘ 01796 472215.

Mad Jack Fuller's Pyramid, Brightling, East Sussex
See page 211.

Melrose Abbey, Borders; ↘ 01896 822562
Road Melrose is between A7 Edinburgh–Carlisle road, A68 Edinburgh–Darlington on A6091.
Rail/bus Edinburgh, from London King's Cross and other centres, then bus.
Tourist information ↘ 0131 473 3800.

Midland Railway Centre, Derbyshire
Road Signed off A38 at Ripley, reached from M1 J28 (turn south).
Rail/bus Alfreton Parkway station, then bus 91, 92, 93 (4 miles).

National Army Museum, Chelsea, London SW3; tel: ↘ 020 7730 0717
Tube: Sloane Square (District and Circle lines) then short walk.

Otley Parish Church, Yorkshire
In hills northwest of Leeds.
Road From A1, take A659 west from Wetherby.
Rail Local trains from Leeds to Ilkley stop at Menstone, then 735 bus or 30-min walk.
Bus National Express from London, then X84 local bus.
Tourist information ↘ 0113 247 7707

Sweetheart Abbey

Plas Newydd, Menai Straits; ↘ 01248 714795 (National Trust)
Road Slow but picturesque A5 from English Midlands (M6 J10A) then M54 to end, or quicker A55 along north Wales coast from Chester.
Rail Llanfair PG (from London Euston).
Tourist information ↘ 01248 352786.

Shah Jehan Mosque and Brookwood Cemetery, Woking, Surrey
Rail Woking, on main line from London Waterloo to southwest. Walk along south side of tracks towards London, and the mosque is on the left. Brookwood is one stop further towards Basingstoke.
Road From M25 J11 to Woking. Brookwood is 3 miles further down A324.
Tourist information ↘ 01483 444333.

St John's Church, Bromsgrove, Worcestershire
In the town centre.
Road Off M5 at J4A, or from London via M40 then M42. Some motorway junctions are limited in direction, so follow signs.
Rail On Birmingham–Hereford or Cardiff–Nottingham route (if your engine doesn't blow up on the hill), then 15-min walk to town.
Bus 144 Worcester–Birmingham, reached by National Express coaches from London and elsewhere.
Tourist information ↘ 01527 831809.

St Mary's, Harrow-on-the-Hill, Middlesex
Landmark spire in historic village with famous public school and great views of north-west London.
Road From London, take A4005 from A406 (north circular) junction with A40 at Hanger Lane. From M25, turn off at J16 on M40 towards London then A40 to Hanger Lane, then A4005.
Rail/bus Tube to South Harrow (Piccadilly Line), turn right out of station, walk half a mile to traffic lights and turn right up Roxeth Hill; turn left at top into picturesque old village centre, Church Hill being on left. Or take 258 bus from tube.
Tourist information ↘ 020 8424 1103.

Sweetheart Abbey, Dumfries; ↘ 01387 850397
Road A75 to Dumfries from Gretna at top of M6/bottom of M74, then A710 south.
Rail Nearest station Dumfries, on branch from Carlisle, then bus 372.
Tourist information ↘ 01387 253862.

Wheatley Lock-up, Oxfordshire
Road Off A40 London–Oxford road 3 miles before Oxford.
Rail/bus On London–Oxford coach routes. Nearest railway station: Oxford, then local bus.
Tourist information ↘ 01865 726871.

Woodford bandaged heart, Northamptonshire
Road From M1 J15A near Northampton follow A43 to Kettering, then A14 east and
Woodford is on the right (south).
Rail Kettering, from London St Pancras.
Tourist information ↘ 01536 410266.

Wrong Hardy Monument, Portesham, Dorset
Road From Dorchester bypass southwestern corner roundabout (reached from M3 via
M27 west, A3 and A35), take minor road through Martinstown over the top towards
Portesham and it's on the left at a high point.
Tourist information ↘ 01305 267992.

THE ECCENTRIC CHURCH

KEY
- 🛕 Buddhist site
- ✝ Christian site
- 🛕 Hindu site or group of temples
- ☾ Muslim
- 🔺 Pagoda
- ⚬ Prehistoric site
- △ **Central London**
- 🔺 Peace Pagoda, Battersea
- ✝ St John's, Hyde Park
- 🛕 Swaminarayan Hindu Temple, Neasden

Orkney Islands

Thurso

ATLANTIC OCEAN

Isle of Lewis

Outer Hebrides

Isle of Skye

Inner Hebrides

Aberdeen

Inverness

Island of Mull

Islay

Arran

Glasgow

■ **Edinburgh**

✝ Whuppity Scourie, Lanark

Samye Ling Buddhist Monastery, Eskdalemuir 🛕

North Sea

Newcastle upon Tyne

Carlisle

Middlesbrough

Milton Keynes

York

Bradford ○ **Leeds**

Kingston-upon-Hull

Irish Sea

Isle of Man

Mormon Temple, Preston ✝

Manchester

Liverpool

Sheffield

Grimsby

Anglesey

Holyhead ○

Plague Service, Eyam ✝

Stoke-on-Trent ○

✝ St Mary's Church, Chesterfield

Derby ○

Nottingham

| 0 | 100km |
| 0 | 60 miles |

Cardigan Bay

Wolverhampton

🛕 Leicester temples

Norwich ○

Birmingham

Coventry ○

Cambridge ○

Ipswich ○

Peace Pagoda 🔺

St Non's Well, St David's ✝ Fishguard ○

Clipping the Church, Painswick ✝

Oxford ○

✝ Tree Cathedral, Whipsnade

Swansea

Little India, Southall 🛕

Reading

△ **LONDON**

Cardiff ■

Bristol

Bristol Channel

⚬ Avebury

Shah Jehan Mosque, Woking ☾

Buddhapadipa Temple, Wimbledon 🛕

Dover

Southampton

Brighton

St Ia's Well, St Ives ✝

Penzance ○

Exeter

Portsmouth

Isle of Wight

English Channel

N

The Eccentric Church and Some Very Strange Churchmen

BEYOND BELIEF
The most unlikely church cannons

Those who think the Church is redolent with tedious traditions might be surprised how bizarre, obscure and fascinating some continuing ecclesiastical customs are.

In Fenny Stratford, near Woburn, Bedfordshire, for example, cannonfire rings out on November 11 as the vicar of St Martin's, the verger and churchwardens take part in Firing the Fenny Poppers – three salvoes of miniature tankard-shaped weapons which the churchwarden primes with gunpowder. The tradition, every St Martin's Day, was started by Dr Browne Willis who founded St Martin's in 1730 in memory of his grandfather who worshipped at St Martin-in-the-Fields, London, and died on St Martin's Day in St Martin's Lane.

A more ancient and less noisy ritual is the gift each Christmas to the reigning monarch of a clipping of the thorn tree in the grounds of St John's Church, Glastonbury, Somerset. Legend has it that when Joseph of Arimathea, having arrived in Britain carrying the Holy Grail, first saw the Isle of Avalon (Glastonbury Tor), he thrust his staff into the ground, and it flowered as a hawthorn.

Clipping the Church, on the other hand, is a form of embracing the church by dancing round it, a once widespread ritual. At **St Mary's** in Painswick, near Gloucester, hundreds of children wearing flowers still link hands to 'clip' the church on the third Sunday each September, and after the Clipping Hymn has been sung each child is given a bun and a silver coin. St Mary's, by the way, has a remarkable 99 topiary yews in the churchyard and the other sort of clippings – of the yew trees – are given by the church to fight ovarian cancer because of the rare chemical they contain. For a real tree cathedral, you need to go to **Whipsnade**, Bedfordshire, which has a nave and transept of trees laid out on the floor plan of a traditional cathedral; an annual service is held there in late June.

Similar customs are recorded in Yorkshire, Berkshire and Sussex and clipping still takes place at Burbage, near Buxton, Derbyshire, on the Sunday nearest August 2.

An annual service where the packed congregation is comprised of dozens of horses sounds too bizarre to be true, but for a sight of a priest in his vestments on horseback intoning to the gathered dozens of horses – or, perhaps,

their riders – make the trip to **St John's, Hyde Park**, in Hyde Park Crescent, London W2 (tube: Lancaster Gate).

Horseman's Sunday, also usually the third Sunday in September, is the occasion when the assembled posse can be seen bursting into a stirring blast of the hymn *Jerusalem*, after a sermon on the mount, before the horses take a trot round the block and are then announced one by one and given a rosette.

Things are more frenetic north of the border, at St Nicholas Church in Lanark, each March 1 when Whuppity Scourie involves dozens of children, each wielding a tightly packed paper ball on the end of a piece of string, dashing three times round the church on a signal from a bell, hitting each other over the head and then scrambling wildly for pennies thrown from a platform by local bigwigs.

But the most poignant of Britain's odd church customs does not involve a church building at all. When the Great Plague of 1655 arrived at **Eyam**, Derbyshire, the people, led by the rector, decided not to flee, to stop the disease spreading further. They put themselves in voluntary quarantine, leaving money for supplies at the parish boundaries in bowls of vinegar and shouting messages to well-wishers who kept their distance.

Four out of every five villagers died, including the rector's wife and one entire family of seven. Each August a Plague Sunday Service is held at Cucklet Church, a rocky spot where open-air services – with the congregation standing well apart – were held during the heroic village's ordeal.

Clergy's strange urges

The clergy – like aristocrats, press barons, the military, and colonials – have always provided Britain with a rich seam of eccentricity, an inexhaustible reserve of batty barminess.

The Revd F W Densham, the vicar of Warleggan in Cornwall who died in 1953, for example, had so offended his parishioners that they refused to attend church. He installed a row of cardboard cut-outs and preached at them instead.

There must be something about Cornwall and off-the-wall clerics. Take the Revd Robert Hawker, vicar of Morwenstow, who one night in July 1825 decided to play a trick on the superstitious people of Bude, who were

always going on about sea serpents and mythical creatures. Under a full moon he rowed out to some rocks, plaited himself a wig from seaweed and wrapped his legs in more weed to resemble a tail. He sang and crooned to awestruck crowds, returning each night as the 'mermaid' story spread. Eventually Hawker tired of this, sang 'God Save The King' and plunged into the waves.

When entering church to take services, he was always accompanied by nine cats; he rode a mule bareback around the parish, followed by a pet black pig called Gyp. Morwenstow Vicarage, which he built, is embellished by odd chimneystacks which are miniatures of various church towers which took his fancy. He is also credited with inventing the Harvest Festival service. When his first wife Charlotte died – at 20 years older she was also his godmother – he was so bereft he decided to eat nothing but clotted cream, morning, noon and night.

A modern Cornish priest and poultry enthusiast, the Revd Ray Trudgian, has been known to take a Maran hen with him into the pulpit. He now lives in Lincolnshire but keeps preaching (about poultry, at any rate). He says: 'I have been lucky as I have travelled around the country with my job and have always been able to find people who love their poultry and make friends.'

Back in Cornwall, one Bishop of Truro, checking up on his ministers, found one curate chained to the altar rail. He was so nervous that the slightest noise – such as the congregation making a liturgical response – would send him fleeing from the church, so the churchwarden had padlocked him there until the end of the service.

Luckily it was not this minister who had the misfortune to be the preacher in a Lancashire church where the pulpit exploded. It seems the churchwarden had been making elderflower champagne in the small cupboard underneath the steps.

In another church, the vicar point blank refused to enter the church, but was happy to stroll around outside, greeting parishioners, smoking a hookah pipe and wearing a floral dressing gown, as long as someone else took the service.

Parson Pike of Kirkby Mallory, Leicestershire, on the other hand, did want to get into the pulpit but was so gargantuan he could not ascend the narrow stairway. He had to be lowered in by a special crane, revolving slowly like some corpulent archangel.

Another vicar who loved his food was gourmet the Revd Edward Bragge of Charmouth, Dorset. His affection for his dining table was such that he asked to be buried with it. His friends obliged in 1747 by cutting the table up and making it into his coffin. His memorial may be seen in the church chancel.

A vicar in Manchester in about 1850 habitually used what would come to be known as mass production by marrying a dozen or more couples simultaneously. He once married the wrong pair, but they fancied the new partners more than the intended and ran off to Blackpool, despite the fury of four sets of relatives.

The early 19th-century cleric and wit Sydney Smith so feared for his health that he used to go about in a suit of armour, each part of which could be filled with hot water. It was Smith who retorted once: 'Quaker baby? Impossible! There is no such thing, there never was. They are always born broad-brimmed and in full quake.'

Another minister, recalled by Canon Wilfred Pemberton of Derby, would set his congregation singing all 176 verses of Psalm 119. He would then pop out to feed the chickens and finish his housework, invariably returning just as the panting singers exhaustedly reached the last verse, appropriately, 'I have strayed like a lost sheep. Seek your servant, for I have not forgotten your commands.'

The vicar of Heybridge in Essex at the beginning of the last century, one Francis Waring, put a small clock in front of him at the beginning of every service, which he read at gabbling speed, allowing the congregation no time to make any of the responses, before running out of the porch, and jumping on a horse to take two similar services nearby. Waring was also known for his eccentric garb. Once, when a bishop remonstrated with him: 'But you're wearing purple!' he replied: 'How very good of you to notice. Do let me recommend my tailor to you.'

The eccentricity of the former rector of Calthorpe in Leicestershire, William Stanesmore, lay in making the collection. Not just the coin collection from the faithful, but – as was discovered in the rectory after he died – 58 dogs, 60 horses, 50 saddles, 130 wheelbarrows, 200 pickaxes, 74 ladders and 400 pairs of shoes. Imelda Marcos would have been proud of him.

Such eccentricities can be found among present-day clergymen. The Revd Father B J Eager of St Catherine of Siena Church, Lowton, Warrington, admitted in a letter to *The Times* in December 1995 not only that he made his dog collars from slices of plastic detergent bottles but that at least once he wore his the wrong way round, so that the word 'Fairy' stood out on his collar. 'Either nobody noticed or they were too polite to mention it,' he added. And in 1997 Father Tim Williams, Anglican vicar of Knighton on the Shropshire border with Wales, was quoted as saying about himself: 'Vicars are often seen in frocks, but not often in frilly dresses, false eyelashes and a bra.' True, his appearance was odd indeed, even for a priest who has ridden down the aisle on a motorbike or on a camel borrowed from a circus. The last two were to make a point to the congregation, but the cross-dressing was less controversial. The village production of *Aladdin* had lost its Widow Twankey at the last minute and the game vicar stepped into her high heels.

The laity, too, can be somewhat peculiar about religion. The Victorian diarist Augustus Hare used to delete any words from the prayer book, before reading to his family, that he felt were too favourable to God. 'God', he said, 'is undoubtedly a gentleman, and no gentleman cares to be praised to his face.'

Equally direct was *Sunday Express* diarist Lord Castlerosse who once drove his golf ball into a bunker and dropped to his knees to pray for divine intervention. He was overheard saying: 'But don't send Jesus – this is no job for a boy.'

Above The eerie Callanish Standing Stones, on the Isle of Lewis, are atmospheric in the extreme (DR)

Below Henry Moore's King and Queen at Glenkiln near Dumfries overlook a lonely shepherd's grave (STB)

Previous page Norse raiders reappear with helmets and flaming torches for Up Helly Aa, in Lerwick (GB)

Above Mike Waters trims his topiary loco (BL)

Left Don't lose control of your own vehicle if you meet Claude, the lobster car (PV)

Below A steam engine at full tilt is what Max Bowker wanted on his garage (BL)

For the vicar of Farringdon's folly and a bid to keep out Methodists, see *Towering Eccentrics*, Chapter 11.

WELL, WELL, WELL – ECCENTRIC SAINTS

Villagers at Bradninch, near Exeter, appear to have been revering a holy spelling mistake for 196 years. They were told in 1831 that their church was dedicated to St Disen, assumed to be a medieval Irish missionary who might have brought Christianity to heathen Cornwall. St Disen was thereafter mentioned with all due respect, but it should have been St Denis all along, it was revealed recently.

But as residents and tourists in the West Country and Wales will know, the area is already riddled with plenty of oddly named saints and their legends are such that you couldn't make them up. There are those associated with ancient wells, for example.

St Nectan was beheaded in the 6th century and miraculously carried his head a mile to cast it into **St Nectan's Well**, Hartland Point, Devon. Where the blood dropped, the first foxgloves sprang up, a story recalled by the anniversary mass sometimes held there on St Nectan's Day (June 17) which includes a procession of children bearing foxgloves. They should, perhaps, wear gloves, for the poison digitalis is found in that beautiful plant.

St Neot, Cornwall, also has a holy well where the legendary 15-inch high saint kept three fish given to him by an angel, who said that if he ate just one a day, there would always be three the next day. One day when he fell ill, *two* were cooked for him. Praying for forgiveness, he returned one from the frying pan to the well, where it came back to life.

A third well, at **St Keyne**, near Liskeard, Cornwall, bears the legend that the first of a couple to drink from it after their wedding will dominate the marriage. The 19th-century ballad *The Well of St Keyne* by Robert Southey tells of a bride who outwitted her bossy groom by smuggling a bottle of the well water to church under her dress. It was just as well, because after she drank it, she wore the trousers in that marriage.

The delightfully named **St Endellion** was a Welsh princess who lived like a hermit near Wadebridge, Cornwall, in the 6th century, living on only the produce of her cow. When the beast wandered on to Lord Tregony's land, he killed it, and he was in turn killed by enraged friends of hers. Endellion not only brought Tregony back to life, but asked that when she died her body be put on a cart and drawn by another cow to wherever the beast chose as a last resting place. This was where her church, and today's village named after her, stand.

St Ives, Cornwall, is in fact named after an Irish virgin, St Ia, who landed there after fleeing pursuers in Ireland. She needed to be a saint because, legend says, she crossed the sea on a leaf. She is remembered when the extraordinary Hurling The Silver Ball takes place (see Chapter 1) and the ball has to be dipped in **St Ia's well**. It all makes St Disen seem positively dull.

Across the water in the rather magical peninsula of St David's, Pembrokeshire, another mystic well marks the birthplace of that Welsh patron saint. Near the tiny city of St David's, if you take St Non's Road off Goat

Street and head southeast towards St Non's Bay, you reach **St Non's Well**, still credited with great powers of healing.

St Non was St David's astoundingly beautiful mother. His father, a prince of Ceredigion, came across the maiden while out hunting and, the legend says,

one thing led to another (supporters of St Non said it must have been rape). The pregnancy meant that Non was cast out from her family. Indeed, after Non's father was told by a prophet that a baby was coming who would one day have power over all the land, he had vowed to kill Non and her unborn baby. She gave birth in an ancient cromlech (group of standing stones) and gripped the stones so hard that they split and a terrible dark storm sprang up all around to protect her during the labour. Yet she and the infant David were in the eye of this storm, bathed in a serene light. As he was born, a spring of pure water sprang up, and it is this St Non's Well that one can visit.

St Non's Well

One of the things known about the ascetic St David is that he drank just water all his long life. Near the well are the ruins of St Non's Chapel, a popular place of medieval pilgrimage, and also a more modern chapel to her, set in a place of peaceful beauty.

The story embodies two strands of Celtic culture. One is that disturbing the ancient stones disturbs the elements all around. Another is the interconnection of Celtic cultures even at this early date – before AD500 – as in the story of St Ia above. For St Non fled after the birth to Britanny, where for the next 1,300 years her story was annually re-enacted in a passion play.

BRITAIN'S TOP TEN MOST SURPRISING PLACES OF WORSHIP

Amid Britain's truly wondrous heritage of mainstream Christian churches, there are here and there some astounding, beautiful, surprising or just curious edifices of other religions. Here is a selection:

Avebury, Wiltshire
Why Stonehenge is so much better known than this more interesting site, the remains of Europe's largest stone circle, perhaps 4,000 years old, is a total mystery. Equally obscure are origin and purpose of a whole collection of extraordinary prehistoric monuments around the village of Avebury, which is on the Swindon to Devizes road. Nearby is the enigmatic Silbury Hill, an artificial earth cone 130ft high, again the largest in Europe. There are barrows and sarsens all around, set in a dramatic landscape.

Road A4361 from Swindon to Beckhampton passes through the stone circle. It doesn't connect with M4 so you need to leave at J16 and take B4005 east to Wroughton and turn right onto A4361 there.

Rail/bus Nearest station Swindon (London Paddington–south Wales line).

Tourist information ☎ 01672 539425.

Buddhapadipa Temple,

Calonne Road,

Wimbledon, London SW19

Only a good lob away from the tennis courts, this beautiful, glittering building sits serenely in a bubble of unlikely oriental tranquillity. The exquisite murals inside are fascinating in their blend of Buddhist teaching and the Western environment.

Road Signed off Wimbledon Parkside, which is south off A3 at Tibbet's Corner, Putney Heath.

Rail/bus Wimbledon station (District Line or main line from Waterloo) then bus 93 through Wimbledon village.

Buddhapadipa Temple

Leicester

With its cultural cornucopia, this Midlands city offers not just great South Asian food but the fascinating temples of its great religions, includings the Muslims, Jains, Hindus and Sikhs, many of which welcome visitors, to add to the usual churches and synagogues, so most days are the Sabbath of someone or other. The Sikhs' **Guru Nank Sikh Gurdwara** is, perhaps aptly, in a road called Holy Bones. The **Jain Samaj Europe** temple in Oxford St (due south of the Holiday Inn on the inner ring road), which features great carvings, is the only temple of this minority faith in Europe. Afternoons are a good time to visit, particularly Thursdays. There are two great Hindu temples, the **Shree Sanatan Mandir** in Weymouth St, which is the oldest temple in Leicester, and the **Shree Jalaran** in Narborough Rd. The best time to visit these is around 10.00, and they are likely to be closed in the early afternoon. The **Central Mosque** is on Conduit St, next to the railway station, and the main day of prayer is, of course, on Fridays.

Road From M1 J21.

Rail From London St Pancras.

Peace Pagodas, Willen Park, Milton Keynes, Buckinghamshire, and Battersea Park, beside the Thames in London

These startling apparitions in English landscapes make the point that those on the receiving end of the ultimate warfare, at Hiroshima, wish to promote global peace. The elegant constructions bring an exotic yet peaceful surprise to their waterside locations.

Battersea
Road Between Chelsea and Albert bridges on south bank of Thames.
Rail Battersea Park station (one stop from London Victoria) then cross park to river.

Milton Keynes
Road Off M1 J14.
Rail/bus Milton Keynes, on London Euston–Birmingham line, then bus.

Preston Temple
Another surprisingly giant place of worship has sprung up at Preston, Lancashire, where the Mormons have stuck their biggest temple outside Salt Lake City in what initially seems an oddly incongruous setting. This vast white box of a building – don't expect to be shown round the inside without an invitation – looms over nearby houses like a huge power station with a spire instead of a chimney. Still, the Mormons must like it.
Road Just west of J8 of the M61.
Rail Chorley station.

Samye Ling Buddhist Monastery, Eskdalemuir, Dumfries and Galloway
A place so windswept and cold that Tibetan monks must feel almost at home, although as the name means 'place beyond imagination' even they might find it a bit remote. It may be the place most often mentioned when weather forecasters pinpoint Britain's coldest place in the previous 24 hours, but the religion and art of oppressed Tibet are warmly alive here.
Road From A74(M) J17 at Lockerbie, take B723.

Shah Jehan Mosque, Oriental Rd, Woking
For many years this was Britain's only mosque, and its elegant dome rising through trees in leafy commuterland has long puzzled passengers on the Waterloo main line alongside. For its extraordinary full story, see Chapter 5.
Rail/bus Walk from Woking station, from London Waterloo.
Road Woking from M25 J11 or A3.

Southall, West London
Not so much one place of worship but a collection of temples where one can be the only chap not wearing a turban in a busy street (if one is a chap who doesn't wear turbans, that is). The authentic Indian food at authentic Indian prices plus the shops glittering with gaudy brassware, spices, carvings, over-the-top Ali Baba shoes and endless Indian clothes make this a cultural experience for visitors.
Road Just south of A4020 (from Shepherd's Bush to Uxbridge). From M4 J3 take A312 north, then A4020 east (right).
Rail Southall, from London Paddington.

Shah Jehan Mosque

10 **Swaminarayn Hindu Temple**, Neasden, London NW10
On a cathedral scale, this stone and marble edifice stands out like an exotic oriental gem amidst the dreariest North London suburbia. Has to be seen to be believed.

Road Between North Circular (A406) and Brentfield Rd.
Rail Neasden (Jubilee Line or Stonebridge Park mainline station (from Euston).

Note: These sites are, of course, not tourist destinations or theme park ornaments, but places of worship. Please make sure you have permission to enter any grounds or buildings; and observe rules about removing shoes, taking photographs, etc. I've seen enough Westerners – and other tourists in our own churches too – wandering in chewing gum, smoking, showing off bare flesh, bringing in screaming brats who fiddle with sacred ornaments, or photographing people praying, to be thoroughly ashamed.

TRAVEL INFORMATION

Clipping the Church, Painswick, Gloucestershire
Road From M5 J13 east, or M4 J18 north, to Stroud. Painswick is 3 miles north on A46 towards Cheltenham.
Rail/bus Stroud, on London Paddington–Gloucester line, then bus.
Tourist information ✆ 01452 813552.

St David's, Pembrokeshire
The smallest city in Britain – village size to some – with the oldest cathedral site in the country. A peninsula of pilgrimage and peace. Free map of one-hour circular walk, including St Non's Well, from tourist information.
Road M4 to far Western end, then A40 to Haverfordwest, then A487 to St David's.

THE MYSTERY OF TWISTERY

Chesterfield's St Mary's Church has a fantastically twisted spire and, as any local will tell you, it was twisted by the Devil when a virgin married there (and God will put it right as soon as another virgin weds there). It was not caused, as some may think, by Tony Benn becoming MP in the Derbyshire town (he was merely eccentric, not twisted, in the name-shortening department, starting off as Viscount Stansgate, then becoming Anthony Wedgwood-Benn, then Tony Benn). Here are some spire facts you probably didn't know:

- The 100ft spire isn't attached to the church, but is kept in place by 150 tons of timber and lead. On a windy day it sways.
- The 14th-century spire constantly twists and untwists slightly. Experts measured a one-and-a-half inch twist in a recent year.
- A hi-tech dendrochronologist of Nottingham University's tree-ring dating laboratory took a pencil-sized core sample from beams in the spire and fixed the construction date precisely at 1362.
- Chesterfield is one of no fewer then 79 spiral steeples in Europe, some built that way on purpose, but most have twisted of their own accord due to faults in construction or, as probably happened at Chesterfield, unseasoned timber being used.
- Spiral spire towns regularly hold twisted European conventions and tie themselves in knots discussing the cause of accidental spiralisation – for instance, one spire at Puiseaux in France was straight until vinegar was used to put a fire out in 1785.

Rail/coach/bus Swansea (from London Paddington and other centres), local train to Haverfordwest, then bus 411 to St Davids; or National Express coach to Haverfordwest. *Tourist information* ✆ 01437 720392.

Tree cathedral, Whipsnade, Bedfordshire (free; National Trust; tel: 01494 528051)
Road 2 miles south of Dunstable, which is signed off M1 J11. There is a car park signed off B4540.
Rail/bus London Euston–Hemel Hempstead or St Pancras–Luton, then Arriva bus 43 which goes between these points and past the tree cathedral.
Tourist information ✆ 01582 471012.

St Ives, Cornwall
Beautifully set fishing and holiday harbour with great artistic traditions and the modern Tate Gallery. Parking and access can be difficult during summer weekends (use branch line to avoid this).
Road M5 to western end, then A38 and A30 through Cornwall. 6 miles short of Penzance, turn right on A3074 to St Ives.
Rail St Ives has its own short branch off the London Paddington–Penzance line. Change at St Erth.
Tourist information ✆ 01736 796297.

Part Three

Eccentric Places

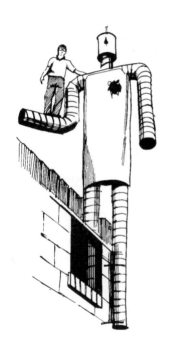

HOME OF THE ECCENTRIC

ATLANTIC OCEAN

Orkney Islands

Thurso

Isle of Lewis

Outer Hebrides

Isle of Skye

Inner Hebrides

Inverness

Aberdeen

Island of Mull

North Sea

Islay

Arran

Glasgow

Edinburgh

N

Newcastle upon Tyne

Carlisle

Middlesbrough

Isle of Man

York

Irish Sea

Bradford

Leeds

Kingston-upon-Hull

Anglesey

Liverpool

Manchester

Grimsby

Holyhead

Sheffield

Stoke-on-Trent

Midland Railway Centre, Ripley

0   100km
0   60 miles

Derby

Nottingham

Cardigan Bay

Wolverhampton

Birmingham

Coventry

Norwich

Cambridge

Ipswich

Fishguard

Mick Waters' Steam Hedge, Swanbourne

Shark house, Oxford

Swansea

Reading

LONDON

Peter Hook's water tower, Faversham

Cardiff

Bristol

Max Bowker's garage, Swallowfield

Dover

Bristol Channel

Southampton

Clayton Tunnel House & church

Brighton

Exeter

Portsmouth

English Channel

Penzance

Home of the Eccentric

UNLIKELY ADDITIONS

The Englishman's home is his castle, goes the cliché, but then it's all the more surprising how dull most of them are (the homes, that is). Most people live in suburban conformity, reinforced by planning restrictions that are exactingly petty in the prettier places – all part of the price of living on an overpopulated island with some of finest heritage going.

So it is in the suburbs, not in massive stately homes, that the occasional fantastic whims really stand out. There is a massive shark sculpture plunging from the sky into the roof of a staid Oxford terrace house, for example. The slates are scattered as if the dramatically unbelievable had just happened. The 25ft glass fibre shark is in fact supported against the gales by internal girders, and the house is otherwise quite habitable, although at the time of writing it seemed unkempt.

Despite much gnashing of teeth by the twitching net curtain brigade, the sculpture was eventually allowed to stay by junior planning minister Tony Baldry, who said, to his everlasting credit: 'I do not believe the purpose of planning control is to enforce a boring and mediocre conformity.'

Actually, planning control is the very reason many people feel driven to visual outbursts. South London businessman John Gladden was so incensed by Croydon Council that he erected a replica Spitfire fighter aircraft on his roof, plus a 14ft plastic marlin. Other features not normally found among the

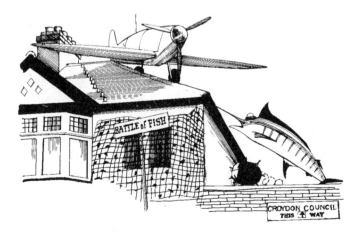

neat privet hedges of St Oswald's Road, Norbury, included a Churchill tank, a hand on a pole giving a giant V-sign towards the council offices, a 40ft replica of a Scud missile ... one could go on, and no doubt the neighbours do. One suspects Mr Gladden doesn't gladden all their hearts, but he does mine.

The original marlin – a replica of one he had caught in Hawaii – was what raised the planners' ire, and had they not made an issue of it, Mr Gladden would probably have been content without all the other clobber. In the end a court ordered it all to be removed except the marlin. I was under the impression that Mr Gladden was content to keep the marlin and peace had returned to Norbury ... until I checked the up-to-date situation in 1999.

> 'We're marching on the council with an army of sympathisers who all own tanks and military vehicles, about 50 in all. We've got our massive Churchill statue, and a huge condom mounted on a tank. When you press a button, it goes whoosh, twice as big.
>
> 'Then we're marching on Scotland Yard to give them a piece of our minds – actually a writ for a million pounds for harassment.'

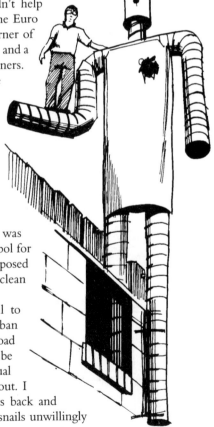

I ventured: 'I bet they wish they'd never started it.' Mr Gladden agreed, and I couldn't help wishing him the best of British. Come Euro rules or high water, there is some corner of Norbury that will forever be eccentric, and a pain in the backside to nit-picking planners.

A similar case enlivened the skyline in 1995 in the North Yorkshire village of Scorton. One Geoff Harper built a 30ft Tin Man as a protest at what he called years of frustration, misery and anger at battling council planners over attempts to alter his 200-year-old Malt Kiln House. He was quoted as explaining: 'In *The Wizard Of Oz* the Tin Man had no heart, so it was appropriate that I chose him as a symbol for the council.' To underline the supposed heartlessness, he punched a hole clean through the Tin Man's chest.

Such a creation would hardly fail to attract attention, but in suburban Worthing, Sussex, where road after road has a comfortable charm that could be characterised as dull, the truly unusual sometimes fails, somehow, to stand out. I went there to investigate a few years back and found that schoolboys, creeping like snails unwillingly to school, failed to lift their eyes to a female nude smiling at them, breasts thrust out like fullsome water melons. Perhaps it was overfamiliarity, for although the concrete sculpture *Reclining Woman* by Dhruva Mistry created a stir when she arrived in 1988, she had aged gracefully, acquiring the odd patch of lichen here and there but no stretch marks or cellulite.

Landscape consultant Wilf Simms bought her as an impulsive engagement present for art teacher Jan Wright when they visited the Glasgow Garden Festival. Jan told me then:

> 'It was a crazy gesture but we loved her straight away and intended to take her to a Scottish island. That was impossible then, and having spent about £20,000 on her, VAT and transport, we had to settle her in here in Worthing.
>
> 'Initially, there was strong reaction locally and nationally. The *Sun* wittily put her on page 3, opposite one of their pin-up pictures, but she was not nearly as beautiful as our girl.
>
> 'Sadly there was an attack by a vandal with spray paints, which was upsetting, but then she gradually became part of the garden. Now we want to find her a home where more people can view her and yet she can be protected from vandals. It's humiliating for her to be in a small garden – sculptures need space and should have views around them.'

The couple have now moved on, and the nude has been sold at auction to someone with rolling acres to match the rolling flesh.

LIVING IN A TIMEWARP

The eccentricity of others lies not in dramatically altering a 1930s semi with tin men, sharks or nudes, but in fanatically refusing to allow it to be anything other than exactly that – a 1930s semi. A colleague of mine visited Alex Woolliams' Bristol semi where everything dated from the year it was built – 1937, which he reckons was a great time to be British – which it was, providing it doesn't ever become 1939 in two years' time.

Beside his valve radio lay a 1937 copy of the *Radio Times*. The banisters, stairs, picture rails, were all brown: brilliant white was absurd on a 1930s house, he said, because it had not yet been invented. There was a 1937 Bakelite telephone, a 1937 Austin Ten and a 1937 bike in the 1937 garage. The books were from that date or earlier.

The eccentric English teacher, who often sported a suitable trilby hat and cravat, lived with his social worker wife Carol and their daughter Emma, who was allowed modern things as long as she kept them upstairs out of sight. Everything, from upholstery to Anaglypta wallpaper, from Ascot water heater to cast-iron gas cooker, was 1930s, British-made, and still worked. 'They didn't need to import anything then, and it was built to last. There was a solidity in things then. Things didn't change. You were brought up in a town, married there, died there,' Mr Woolliams proudly told my colleague, who I hope took it all down in pencil shorthand on a spiral-bound notebook.

When I last checked (1999) with my colleague, Julian Champkin, on the 1937 house, it seemed that the teacher had plans to sell up and – who knows? – possibly move directly to 2000 (rather like a Monopoly player being given the command 'move directly to Mayfair'), not a bad scheme when you consider that the intervening 60 years included the war, rationing, the Suez crisis, three-day week, mad cow disease and Des O'Connor.

Not everyone has hated the intervening decades. Glenn and Melanie Sanderson were born in the 1960s and live on a modern estate in Deepcar, South Yorkshire. They drew the national media's attention for taking the 1940s to their hearts – and, down to the tiniest detail, to the interior of their home. The phone is Bakelite, the *Picture Post* lies on a Utility sofa, the dress is wartime. The wind-up gramophone plays 78rpm Glenn Miller records, while the other Glenn dresses with Brylcreem and braces.

Melanie was quoted as explaining the fascination of the 1940s:

> 'Of course Britain suffered during the Forties but from all I've heard and read people were friendlier, more trusting and had greater respect for others. People also dressed smartly, not slovenly – women like women and men like men. We love the things from that era in fashions or furnishings much more than those of today.'

Who said nostalgia isn't as good as it used to be?

LIVING WITH THE RAILWAYS
A house above a tunnel

Britain's most eccentric, not to say exclusive, country cottage could well be **Clayton Tunnel House**, a rather unlikely bungalow perched between the towers of the even more unlikely castellated north entrance to Clayton Tunnel on the Brighton line.

On one side it has the appearance of a castle. Above soar the glorious South Downs topped by the Jack and Jill windmills; before it lies the verdant sweep of the rolling Sussex Weald. And right in front, there is a suicidal drop into a gaping hole below, through which hurtle dozens of trains a day carrying holidaymakers and commuters.

Clayton Tunnel House was until recently the home of railway workers, and has being completely restored and made into a family home. But its past contains a dark secret.

The house's origin and purpose are somewhat clouded, as indeed would have been its residents every few minutes in the age of steam and smoke. It hardly befits the extravagant Romanesque style of the tunnel portal created by John Ratrick, the genius responsible for Britain's most elegant and unsung railway viaduct across the Ouse valley, a few miles north on the same line. Being showered in smuts, having a near-cliff for a front lawn and a suicidal drop for a back garden would not be most people's idea of a nice country cottage.

It is ironic that the remarkable medieval doom paintings uncovered in Clayton church lie just a few steps to the east, depicting fearful scenes of death and the descent to the underworld. Fear of the underworld could account for

Clayton Tunnel House

the peculiar cottage's presence, and doom certainly lay in store for some early railway passengers.

When the railway, one of Britain's earliest main lines, was built in 1841, there was no way of avoiding the great ridge of the South Downs that so dramatically cuts off the Sussex Weald from the sea. Would the inexperienced passengers' fears – and at that time they were carried in open carriages behind engines belching fire, steam and smoke – prevent them from going underground in the line's longest tunnel?

The directors attempted to diminish these fears of the underworld by whitewashing the tunnel's brick lining and lighting the tunnel throughout with gas jets. The tunnel cottage's resident probably helped maintain these lights, in an attempt to convince naive people that heading into the tunnel wasn't to say farewell to daylight for ever.

But it was exactly that for the victims of the Clayton Tunnel Disaster of August 25, 1861, Britain's worst rail crash to that date. By then the Brighton line was booming as Britain's premier holiday route, but signalling technology was still based simply on dispatching trains at five-minute intervals. Rear-end collisions were thus greatly feared, particularly in tunnels.

Ironically, Clayton Tunnel was the only part of the line given more sophisticated protection, in the form of a single telegraph needle in each box at the ends of the tunnel, which dipped one way or the other to indicate 'train in tunnel' or 'line clear'.

The day disaster struck was a Sunday, which meant heavy excursion trains. It also meant that signalman Henry Killick at the south end was working a 24-hour shift so he could have his one day off later in the week. There was also a simple signal, the arm of which was supposed to be returned to 'danger' by the passing train wheels pressing a lever. This did not always work, and the Portsmouth excursion heading for London that morning failed to return it to 'danger'.

Signalman Killick telegraphed 'train in tunnel' to his colleague at the north end but failed to put the signal to 'danger' before the Brighton excursion passed some three minutes later. He did wave his red flag just as the heavy train steamed into the tunnel.

Now worried, he frantically telegraphed the north box and soon received the reassuring answer 'tunnel clear'. He assumed this meant that the second excursion train had left the tunnel; but in fact it hadn't – it was the first train the north box signalman meant. The second train's crew, having seen the red flag, had screwed down the feeble brakes of the era and the train's 17 packed carriages slowly came to a halt deep in the tunnel, then started to reverse slowly to see what was wrong.

At that moment, about four minutes after the Brighton excursion, came a third train – a regular timetabled train from Brighton to London. Killick, reassured by the telegraph's ambiguous message, waved his white flag (the equivalent of today's green). Had the earlier whitewash been kept clean and the gaslights still been lit, the driver might have seen his doom approaching. As it was, the tunnel was sooty black and filled with smoke. The resulting crash caused appalling carnage, with the third train's locomotive leaping up and crushing the earlier train's guard's van and rear carriage. Twenty-one people died and 176 were seriously injured.

More than 130 years later, Railtrack has completely restored the listed tunnel portal and cottage, and, unable to sell off the home as it sits on operational railway land, or rather over an operational hole, rents it out. Railtrack's Steve Tyler said: 'We believe the old railway policemen who controlled the trains by means of flags lived there. These characters wore frock coats, top hats and tails and were the reason why signalmen were known as "bobbies" well into this century. We have a record of a Mr Russell who lived there with his wife and nine children.' The parents must have had their work cut out stopping them falling into the underworld.

A signal success

Like others fortunate enough to live on the Sussex coast, Tim and Sylvia Stephens can gaze out to sea as they raise their glasses at dinner. More unusually, they can listen to telegraph bells tinkle, cast an eye over a railway section map, pull any one of a set of signal levers or wind the wheel of an old-fashioned level crossing.

Their dining room is high in a Victorian signalbox, far from any railway but not entirely incongruous in that their home, a few yards up the garden, is composed of two remarkable Victorian railway carriages, joined by a kitchen and a glassed-in conservatory whose roof groans with red grapes each autumn. Even the conservatory doors are recycled railwayana – shapely numbers that British Rail discarded when it revamped Hassocks station on the Brighton line. An unwillingness to see some railway gem trashed – nor to pass up a bargain – was central when Tim learned that Bosham signalbox, along with a whole set of others, was to be smashed into skips when BR modernised the Portsmouth–Chichester line in the early 1990s.

> 'I just found out from people living nearby who knew we lived in
> railway carriages and thought we might be interested. I took a look
> and then went to BR and got them to agree to give it to me,' says
> Tim, a photographer and college lecturer.
> 'Of course it wasn't that simple. There were heaps of paperwork.
> We had to build a steel cradle under the box, close the road at
> Bosham and lift it out onto a low loader with a massive crane.
> Unloading was simpler. The lowloader backed in through an
> understanding neighbour's garden, after we took the fence down,
> then we jacked it up and took the lorry out from underneath.'

But there were more problems to come. First there was the urgent task of buying back all the signal fittings which had been sent to BR's Collector's Corner near Euston, where such things are sold to enthusiasts and antique dealers. Then there was the small matter of planning permission – luckily forthcoming – and rebuilding the brick ground-floor section, which had earlier been taken to pieces at Bosham. Then followed months of refitting the box and its balcony, ideal as a sun-soaked verandah with sea views.

Curiously, Tim and Sylvia aren't the sort of railway nuts with whom Britain (with its 110 preserved steam railways) abounds. They couldn't tell you all the types of engines which used to whistle past Bosham box, still less their numbers or timetables, as thousands of fully grown men doubtless could. Tim mostly finds railways an infernal endurance test, with up to $2^1/2$ hours commuting each way to allow him to live this splendid life on the coast and yet work at various London colleges and studios.

In fact, living in grounded railway carriages (minus the wheels, that is) made into a bungalow isn't that unusual – but is becoming more so, as railway preservation fans rediscover more and more Victorian and Edwardian gems and put them back on wheels. It dates back to the time after World War I when seaside land was being divided up cheaply, with no planning controls, and communities were allowed to sprawl. The Portacabins of the day – that is cheap, instant accommodation – were the thousands of railway carriage bodies becoming surplus as the hundreds of small railway companies were grouped into the big four great railways. Just as thousands of dismounted goods vans can still be seen up and down the country as farmers' chicken coops or toolsheds, so the carriages tended to be absorbed into houses and were often soon unrecognisable within later alterations. The Stephens' two carriages have a regular pitched roof with an upstairs between them. Yet these two were far from the average commuter sardine cans. Both have an illustrious history dating back to Victorian elegance and including dramatic war service overseas, before they arrived on the beach in 1923. The one that greets your eye as you push open the front gate was built in 1874.

'It was almost royal train standard. Just a few were made,' says Tim. At some point it became an inspection saloon used by railway top brass, hence the unusually generous end windows through which directors would have viewed the line while being propelled by steam engine and served from the kitchen compartment, still complete with mahogany cupboards behind the saloon.

The illustrious story of the second carriage only came to light in 1994. It was built by the London and North Western Railway in 1878 as a picnic saloon. The gentry would have hired it by the day and enjoyed its then long leather longitudinal benches and dining table. In World War I it became part of Earl Haig's unique command train of 14 carriages complete with power generators, dining car, map room, central heating and staff sleeping quarters.

The Stephens were delighted when an expert turned up a picture of their then six-year-old son Etienne's bedroom as a not very different compartment where two of Haig's clerks slept during the war. This was a little more spartan than its previous use, but was much more comfortable than the trenches, from which men would attack on orders from this very train, so often with no return ticket.

The official photograph shows the partitions and the doors in the same positions as today, even down to the roller over which a leather belt ran to raise the windows. Now, after having seen all those miles of service in different eras and different places, the coach slumbers in a long retirement, the door opening onto a flower-lined garden path leading to the Stephens' splendidly eccentric signalbox dining room.

Thatching a train

A typical reroofed railway carriage is one at the Cornish village of St Giles on the Heath, which was all farm labourer Wilfrid Parnell could afford to rent in 1936 for a home for his wife Ivy and two young daughters. The London and South Western Railway carriage gained running water, electricity, two more daughters and a telephone over the next 60 years but retained its railway character. But in 1995 widow Ivy, then 82, faced an attempt by her farmer landlord to evict her or increase the rent, still at 1930s levels of £20 a year. The judge at Launceston County Court threw out the farmer's eviction case.

A truly glorious and possibly unique thatched carriage is the one at a village not far from Portsmouth. It is a beauty and its owner begged for its precise location not to be publicised as he intended to leave it to the National Trust, but it looks as though it might have been a London, Brighton and South Coast Railway brake-third, with the guard's special window for looking along the train for signals, stray passengers, zeppelin attacks or whatever. When I saw it, the paintwork was in first-class condition.

Hey, that's my home on Platform 3

Sometimes the carriages which were converted into homes are so old and rare (and so much better preserved than if they had spent a century thrashing up and down railways in all weathers) that enthusiasts actually reconvert them back into rail-going carriages. A case in point was a third-class coach which ran from 1865 until 1890 and was then converted into a bungalow at East Bridgford, near Nottingham. Three generations of the Curtis family were raised in the somewhat draughty but much-loved home. When the bungalow was demolished in 1983 the carriage was saved again, this time by railway enthusiasts who painstakingly restored it, mounted it on wheels again, and coupled it up at the **Midland Railway Centre**, Ripley, Derbyshire in 1996, an amazing 131 years after it first entered service.

Max impact

Car drivers in sleepy rural Berkshire can get a shock when they round a corner to see a 'Battle of Britain' class steam locomotive thundering out from under a bridge ahead of them. The train is a fabulous mural created on **Max Bowker's garage** door in Swallowfield by local artist Brian Matravers.

Quantity surveyor Max, who was never a trainspotter in the sense of writing down all the numbers, nevertheless had a good reason for choosing this subject when he decided to cover up some ugly double garage doors.

> 'I used to go to school by train from Emsworth, Hampshire, to Portsmouth, and the express engines on that line were almost always these Bulleids, known as Spam Cans because of their unusual boxy shape. I've always had an affection for them, so there was no alternative for the painting.
>
> 'I told Brian, a friend who lives in the next village, that if he got one detail of the engine wrong he wouldn't get a penny for his work! But he's done a brilliant job.'

Max gave Brian a set of photos to help, but didn't specify which one. 'As it happens he chose 257 Squadron, which still runs on the Swanage line, so it's not just memories. I can pop down and see the real thing.' But is his mural seen as a work of art or a dangerous eyesore?

> 'Most people like it, but as it's set down a drive at right angles to the road you don't have to look at it. Passengers in cars sometimes get drivers to back up for a look, but in five years we've not had any accidents caused by it. Actually, I'd quite like to add a bit more bridge over the top with two boys looking down and a plywood plume of smoke going up in the sky ...'

A step up the housing ladder

All kinds of people have moved into former railway stations, as the once-vast network has shrunk under competition from lorries and subsidised company cars and very good homes they can make too. Even goods sheds have become showrooms and offices, and a few signalboxes have sometimes found other uses, but water towers would not seem at all welcoming, as they usually consist of a whopping great iron tank on an unpretty brick or iron tower.

Peter Hook, luckily, didn't take that view, and as a consequence he enjoys a splendid view – from the top of a redundant water tower at **Faversham, Kent**, where he's made a unique home.

The railway reached Faversham from Chatham in January 1858, but plans to make the line branch there and run – as indeed it now does – to either Dover or Margate, had to be shelved for a couple of years because the promoters ran out of money. For those two years trains had to turn back to London from Faversham. This meant using all the town's water supply for topping up thirsty steam engines, much to the fury of townspeople. Hence the tower, which may have been supplied from a well, as Mr Hook recently discovered one under the

tower. It might seem odd that it is across a road from the railway, isolated from its fire-breathing customers, but that is because the railway moved, not the tower.

Peter isn't a rail nut, still less could he tell you the classes and numbers of the trains passing through, but he likes the distant bustle of the station. 'The only problem with the railway is that when it shuts for engineering work, or at Christmas, it seems too quiet and that's when I notice it,' he says, a sentiment I have heard from others living with a usually constant background noise.

The tower was bought from the British Rail Property Board. 'I first went up the old iron ladder on the outside in 1984', said Mr Hook, 'and saw the possibilities of the place. I thought the climb pretty hairy, but later I spoke to a railwayman who climbed it during a wartime blackout and air-raid on a winter's night with no torch, to deal with frozen valves, so my climb must have been relatively easy.'

Inside the brick tower was a vast cavity, the main features being half a dozen cast-iron pipes descending from the tank. Most were in the way of the conversion, but Peter has kept two as ornaments. To make the tower into a comfortable and different home with a splendid roof garden, internal stairs and floors were put in. An entrance hall, bedroom and bathroom are on the ground floor, and stairs lead up to an office or eating area, kitchen, then up to a double-height formal dining room; from there a spiral straircase leads to a gallery sitting room.

Finally a steep stair like a ship's ladder, through a 4ft by 8ft hole cut in the floor of the cast iron tank, reveals a sun-trap roof garden and terrace way above the other rooftops with sweeping views over picturesque Faversham and the Swale estuary.

For a rooftop party, or if someone's visiting, Peter runs a flag up the pole so the tower stands out even more than usual, and he has been known to fly various colours, and flags at half-mast for funerals. These are unlikely to include plummeting partygoers from the water tower (no doubt some wag has already said: 'Plenty to drink at the water tower, folks') because the original cast-iron side panels and railings strongly enclose the roof terrace. I only mention this macabre thought because anyone climbing up the ladder to the roof is met first by a stone plaque which says disconcertingly: 'He who dies for England is not dead while England lives.' Lord Berners would have seen the joke (see *Towering Eccentrics*, page 199).

Of course, the conversion of the tower wasn't quite as simple as it may sound. For instance, while the lower storey windows were pleasantly arched with elaborate iron grilles, the upper storey windows were not needed so were built as blind arches (that is, filled with brick). Not only did these have to be knocked out but matching grilles had to be manufactured. A schoolteacher turned local potter, Peter, in his forties, is now happy with his unusual home. 'It's nice being part of the town, down on the ground, and then I can go up there and be completely away from it.'

A railway romance

There's a certain romance about railway stations, as in the classic film *Brief Encounter*. And Lewis and Patricia Yates certainly haven't missed the connection. Patricia clearly wasn't as immune as many girls (from trains, that is).

As a teenager she used to go to Oxford station just to watch the trains, but the couple (both middle-aged divorcees) got to know each other at the steam railway at Quainton Road station, Buckinghamshire, many years later. They spent some of their courting sitting at a favourite spot beside the tracks of the Oxford–Birmingham line next to the abandoned Aynho station, watching the many trains go by and others joining from the Marylebone route on a viaduct in the background. 'We used to bring some sandwiches and a Thermos of tea and sit by the derelict Brunel-designed station building which dates from 1850. We thought it was a shame it was going to rack and ruin,' says Pat.

'Later on, when we heard the building was up for auction, we had to go for it.' Some people thought they were crazy, and indeed some may still doubt their sanity. For one thing, the place was derelict and crumbling fast. The windows were all smashed, and the floors were rotten because water from the roof was directed to huge Victorian lead tanks which had been stolen. The lintels above the windows were rotten and in another year or two they would have brought the stonework down. There was even a tree growing out of the roof.

When they viewed the property they had to pick their way over rubbish in the dim interior. All the movable Great Western Railway fittings and notices had long been sold or stolen. 'The girl from the estate agents couldn't get out fast enough. I've been given longer to buy a pair of trousers!' recalls Lewis. But didn't Pat at that moment see the whole project as a nightmare?

'Not at all. I knew Lewis, as a carpenter, could do it. I had faith in the outcome. There was nothing the pair of us couldn't cope with, as long as we had our health.' Lewis says: 'That day it was chucking it down with rain. We nicknamed one room Niagara Falls for obvious reasons. You could hardly get through the rubbish. It was in a right old state but being in the building trade I could see it could be saved.'

The couple moved into a caravan in the station yard in September 1994 but it was two years before the station was habitable. The roof timbers were solid and only a few slates needed replacing. Remarkably, although the interior doors had been ripped out, they were found nearby and rehung in frames painstakingly built in most cases by carpenter Lewis using the undamaged ones as models. The cast-iron roof brackets are Brunel's originals, as are the Bath stone walls and unusual dark raised pointing made with locomotive ashes.

Sadly, the longer brackets over the platforms were cut short with oxy-acetylene torches when the railways abandoned the station and let it out as a coal office, but one unique feature could be restored.

'There were just three original stations between Oxford and Banbury and this is the only one that survives. Although the design was something of a GWR standard, our collection of steam-age photos shows only these three stations had unusual cast-iron lion shields on the ends of the roof brackets. Which would be great if they hadn't been stolen or sold too.

'We have tracked one of these down in a local museum and have got permission to have replicas cast so the station will look perfect as the only example.'

Inside, the priority has been to make a comfortable home. The sitting room is in the former first-class waiting room, and the couple have done a first-class job of converting it, opening up the original fireplace. The only area where they would like to recreate the railway interior is in the booking hall. With the original fittings lost, this, like the roof bracket shields, would be an expensive project for the retired couple.

The second reason that people may have thought the couple a little odd in their choice of home is that their proposed home is a few feet from a busy main line. This is not one of Britain's hundreds of pretty former stations on an abandoned trackbed, or some rural mountain branch with two trains a day. InterCity 125s from Virgin Trains hurtle through a few feet from the couple's bedroom. Local trains speed through more quietly, while massive freights rumble and thunder past, carrying coal for Didcot power station, containers for Southampton, or freight for the Channel Tunnel.

When I visited the Yates, I soon saw that the 'up' track on the far side had what railwaymen call a dipped joint right opposite their home. While I was there a half-mile long monster of a train from Solihull carrying hundreds of export Range Rovers and Land Rovers came through, every axle bending the rail down slightly at the joint – quite safely – and thumping over on to the next rail. Isn't this an endurance test, particularly as much freight travels at night?

'We sleep soundly. We like the trains, and the noise is occasional, unlike the non-stop roar of a motorway,' says Lewis. 'It probably adds up to just half-an-hour of noise a day.' A visitor from Canada carried back the story and Canadian Broadcasting called to arrange a live radio show, asking to fix a time when a train would be thundering past.

> 'I just told him to interview us there and then, and sure enough our talk was livened up by the sound of several trains going past. I suppose the Canadian listeners may have thought we were a little eccentric. I don't mind. I'm just glad we saved this place.
> 'The noise isn't a problem at all. Really, for us the biggest bonus is some 300 trains a day thundering past. The rush of sound is music to our ears.'

They mean it. For most people living next to a railway line, the sight and sound soon becomes unnoticed, but not for these two. They actually look at each train, call out to the other if something interesting is coming and discuss recent oddities. Pat says:

> 'It's wonderful when I'm hanging up my washing or in my greenhouse next to the platform and see one of these old steam engines thunder by. We saw Britannia come through the other day, running light on the way to do some work somewhere. That was a treat.
> 'We see new Tube trains being hauled to London or back for repair. There's plenty of interest.
> 'This station has been described as a token of our love because trains are part of us and that's fair enough. I'd far rather have this little station than the Taj Mahal.'

One-man rail 'privetisation'

Mick Waters of Swanbourne, Buckinghamshire, also lives in a station beside a track. His is still owned by Railtrack, the company that took over from nationalised British Rail. But he saw the last train rattle through on the

Bletchley–Winslow section of the former Oxford–Cambridge route six or seven years ago and the mothballed, rusted track sees only rabbits and pheasants passing.

The station – sitting prettily on a curve above a stream – is hopefully named Swanbourne, but is really nowhere near that village and is only reached by a long lane up hill and down dale. Now it is left in what most people would surely judge idyllic rural peace. What Mick wants more than anything, however, is for the train service to be restored along his line. He was brought up in the railway-owned house, his late father Reg being a permanent way man. As with many thousands of railwaymen, Reg found the 'permanent' way (so called to differentiate it from temporary construction tracks) was not so permanent after all. The nearby hamlet of Verney Junction marks where Metropolitan Line trains from London with dining cars once reached far into rural Buckinghamshire to connect with this route. That line has long gone, as has another from there to Buckingham and Banbury.

The route through to Cambridge was severed – insanely, most planners would now agree – at Bedford, making any connection eastwards to the King's Cross–Edinburgh line impossible for want of half a dozen miles of track. That was done, typically, immediately after millions of pounds had been spent on new signalling and a flashy concrete flyover at Bletchley; equally typically the following and partly resulting boom in road traffic has meant many millions more being spent on bypass after bypass.

Mick's father Reg, who dressed the station in mourning flags for the last stopping passenger train, started cutting the privet hedge next to the platform in the shape of one of the tough freight locomotives that frequented the line, the 'Super D' 0-8-0 type, and Mick maintains this topiary ghost train to this day. 'I can remember them coming through as a child. We also had push-and-pull little 2-6-2 tank engines on local services with just one carriage. Many's the time as a lad I got a free ride down to Winslow on the footplate!'

Mick, a jolly man whose 50 years in the station house exactly encapsulates the birth and death of British Rail, is surprisingly optimistic about the line reopening. He's pinned up recent press clippings which show how planners, faced with the new rail freight boom clogging up the system with trains have realised that the route is part of a rail M25 which, for a few miles of cheap restoration, would link Cambridge to Oxford, then round to Reading, Guildford, Tonbridge and the Channel Tunnel, joining the lines in between. 'I think it's got a future for passengers too. They might not reopen this station but Winslow down the line a couple of miles is growing fast and needs a station. The part from Oxford to Bicester has been reopened for commuters in recent years and the bit from Bletchley to Bedford has never lost its trains.' Meanwhile Mick, who works, ironically, on the roads ('We could do with getting rid of some of this heavy traffic back on to the railway') looks after not only the old station but weedkills the one remaining track for half a mile or so before it disappears into knee-high foliage round the corner.

'I really don't know what my Dad would think of the state of some of the track, but I'm very hopeful the trains will come back. Everyone is in favour.

I'll still be here to see them through.' And with that, the cherry blossom from the station garden blowing around like snow in the sunshine, he takes his dog for a walk up the line his family has watched over for so many decades.

Slags and couplings

Like several well-to-do celebrities, Chris Donald, editor of the raucously rude comic *Viz*, has indulged himself by buying an old railway station. Except that Chris bought three, and is in the throes of restoring the whole branch line from Alnwick in Northumberland to the junction with the main London–Edinburgh line. Chris composes his schoolboy humour about Fat Slags and Bottom Inspectors in, aptly enough, an office made from an old gents' loo. Indeed, had he not restored the station so lovingly, he could have gained inspiration from the obscene graffiti that doubtless daubed the walls.

Chris, who cheerfully admits to having more money than sense when his comic took off in the late 1980s, bought his first station when it had been converted into a pretend real house, with every scrap of railwayness covered up. He soon dug up the garden to uncover the platform – 'great place for the kids to fall off' – and was delighted to uncover buffers too.

While his wife Dolores looked around auction houses for authentic London and North-Eastern Railway knick-knacks such as chamber pots or sugar bowls (there could be a *Viz* storyline in there somewhere), Chris bought two more stations – one for a restaurant, complete with recorded train noises precisely to the line's original timetable, and the other to house a homeless aunt.

Soon the odd inhabitants of these three stations may not have to play recorded train noises, as Chris is involved in a bold scheme to rebuild completely the branch to Alnwick, a tourist destination with Alnwick Castle, home to the ancient Dukes of Northumberland. It's not a modest scheme, involving a new bridge across the A1 dual carriageway which has irritatingly been built in the meantime (why not just close it, like the railway was?). But at least the *Viz* office would have authentic smut, inside and out.

TRAVEL INFORMATION

The eccentric railway homes described in this chapter are all private properties, except for the one restored to the Midland Railway Centre, and not open for general public visits. By all means have a discreet look from public rights-of-way, but please respect the owners' privacy.

Clayton Tunnel House, Sussex, is a private home and is best viewed from the road bridge to the north. It is difficult and indeed dangerous to see from trains. **Clayton church** and doom paintings is across the road.
Road From London/M25, take M23 and A23 then turn left.
Rail Nearest station Hassocks, from London Victoria.
Tourist information ☎ 01273 292599.

Max Bowker's garage, Swallowfield, south of Reading, Berkshire
Road Off M4 at J11, south on A33, and left to Swallowfield. Take care if you do have a look, as this is a narrow, dangerous road.

Mick Waters' steam hedge, Swanbourne, Buckinghamshire
Road Off M1 at J13, through Bletchley on A421 to Buckingham, south on A413 Aylesbury–Winslow, left (east) on B4032 to Swanbourne then look for lane to left (north).
Rail One day soon, we hope.

Midland Railway Centre, Derbyshire; ☎ 01773 570140
Road Signed off A38 at Ripley.
Rail/bus Alfreton Parkway station, then bus 91, 92, 93 (4 miles).

Oxford Shark House, New High Street, Headington. Almost opposite Oxford United football ground.
Road From London, M25 or Birmingham, use M40, turn off for Oxford. Headington is signed on a turning to the city centre from the northern ring road on the London side. From Birmingham, turn left on to this ring road.
Rail/bus Oxford, from London Paddington or Birmingham, then bus to Headington.
Tourist information ☎ 01865 726871.

Peter Hook's water tower, Faversham (an interesting historic town), Kent
Road Off M2 J6, look for station.
Rail Next to Faversham station, on London Victoria–East Kent line.

Eccentric Gardens

GARDEN WIT, WISDOM AND MASS WISTERIA

The British garden at its worst exhibits all the prim paranoia of the ghastly architecture it suits so well. Outside the endless rows of characterless suburban semis, with not a neurotically twitching lace curtain out of place, stand manicured square lawns, sprayed with this or that poison to prevent a wildflower or even a daisy spoiling their plastic perfection, and surrounded by municipal-style beds of totally predictable flowers, evenly spaced with all the flair and imagination of an amoeba on Valium. The odd gnome hardly makes up for this.

Yet surprisingly, for those not constrained by the regimented suburban approach, the garden offers a haven for oddball whimsy, fantastical flair or tawdry trivia which would never be allowed in the home. Around the country can be seen whimsical gardens with a dozen or more gnomes, complete with fake ponds, windmills, waterfalls, helter-skelters or whatever.

These small-time rebels against confomity are nothing compared to the exhibition – the Ideal Gnome Show, as it were – put on by the zealous Ann Atkin at West Putford, near Bideford, Devon. The four-acre **Gnome Reserve** features more than 1,000 of the red-capped characters, as well as various frogs, toadstools, kittens, ducks etc (all unreal) and a beech wood and wildflower plot (real). It attracts thousands of visitors every year, all of whom have to don the red cap, says Mrs Atkin, 'so as not to embarrass the gnomes'. Well, as long as they don't feel silly.

Xanadu, near Andover

Well beyond the gnome stage is the garden created by the late Stanley Norbury near Andover, Hampshire. In a fairly ordinary bungalow garden, squashed between the noisy A342 and a little-used military railway, he engineered the most escapist fantasy garden possible on an heroic scale. It is the Alhambra come to Andover, a surreal Xanadu off Salisbury Plain. Better

ECCENTRIC GARDENS

ATLANTIC OCEAN

Orkney Islands

Thurso

Isle of Lewis

Outer Hebrides

Isle of Skye

Inner Hebrides

Inverness

Aberdeen

Island of Mull

Meikleour Hedge, Perthshire

North Sea

Islay

Arran

Glasgow

Edinburgh

Newcastle-upon-Tyne

Carlisle

Middlesbrough

N

Isle of Man

Druids' Temple, Ilton Moor

York

Kingston-upon-Hull

Bradford

Leeds

Irish Sea

Anglesey

Liverpool

Manchester

Grimsby

Holyhead

Sheffield

Stoke-on-Trent

Derby

Nottingham

0   100 km
0   60 miles

Wolverhampton

Birmingham

Coventry

Norwich

Cambridge

Ipswich

Cardigan Bay

Fishguard

Oxford

Swansea

Reading

LONDON

Bristol Channel

Cardiff

Bristol

Dover

Gnome Reserve, West Putford

Exeter

Southampton

Garden of the Mind, Stansted Park

Brighton

Enchanted Forest, Groombridge Place

Portsmouth

Penzance

English Channel

THE HEDGE WITH AN EDGE

If you find trimming the hedge a bit of a bore, consider the world's tallest one, which looms cliff-like an average 100ft high and 580 yards long at **Meikleour** in Perthshire. Planted by Jean Mercer of Meikleour in about 1746, it is definitely still a beech hedge, not a grown-out line of trees, for the dense foliage reaches down to ground level. It takes four men with hydraulic cranes six weeks to trim, but this is only undertaken every ten years. Here we are near Birnam, and the trimmings would indeed be enough to camouflage an army, as in Shakespeare's *Macbeth*.

than a theme park because it is not plastic, nor for paying visitors, it is a quiet, very personal garden and, remarkably, it's all been constructed in solid concrete and Portland stone by one man working all hours on top of a full-time job. The planting was wisely restricted to species which thrive in the setting: chalky soil drained by giant beech trees lining the main road. The railway embankment, by the way, in springtime offers the most solid block of primroses I have ever seen.

Mr Norbury, who died in 1996 while this book was being prepared, had started the sunken garden in 1975 by converting a kidney-shaped swimming

pool he had excavated in the 1960s. He had lived on the site when a boy. Then the bungalow was a corrugated-iron former 'tin tabernacle' moved from elsewhere. After serving as a World War II pilot, he bought the much-loved property with his £150 gratuity and spent 12 years rebuilding the bungalow.

When it came to the stone and concrete garden, his realisation of a childhood dream became a little obsessive. He would get up at 05.00 to put in a few hours before work as a civil servant at the Ministry of Defence nearby, then work into the darkness in the long summer evenings.

> 'It was hard physical work – I must have shifted tons and tons of cement and stone. I had to use levers and wedges to shift the very heavy pieces because I was on my own. One time a big pierced arch, which I had pre-formed on the flat, collapsed as I was trying to erect it. It nearly killed me.
> 'A lot of the detail was carved with a knife while the cement was still wet. I made some of the pieces, such as the balustrading for the bridge, in boxes, then finished with a knife.'

Stanley married late, in 1981, at the age of 60. His wife Jean, luckily, loved the fantasy garden too. 'It's the way he likes it and I'm not going to change it,' she told me a month before he died. Someone ought to preserve this garden – they would have a hard time of a job shifting it, after all – because it is remarkable what can be achieved on a modest site with modest means. If the same thing had been built 200 years ago the great and the good of the heritage industry would be frantically raising cash to keep such a thing; if it was built five years ago the planners would probably be demanding its demolition.

Dyed doves and worrisome wyverns

When it comes to the aristocracy or the gentry, on the other hand, garden eccentricity has naturally been given that much more scope, although many of the wittiest gestures could be inexpensive, as in the garden of the 1930s composer-diplomat, the eccentric fourteenth Baron Berners at Faringdon, Oxfordshire.

The first hint of his rather gentle eccentricity lay at the boundaries of the estate, where regularly spaced notices stated: 'Anyone throwing stones at this notice will be prosecuted.' At the entrance of Faringdon House itself one of Lord Berners' rather odd notices survives – one about removing hats – and then, of course, there was the peculiar warning in his marvellous tower (see Chapter 11).

At the house, one of the wittiest ideas of the late baron may still be seen, kept up by the present owners: a small flock of doves dipped in food dye making an extraordinary sight as they flutter around. These and many other of his foibles, such as dogs running around with jewelled necklaces, are also recreated in the Lord Merlin character, based on Berners, in Nancy Mitford's 1954 novel *The Pursuit of Love*. Berners, who had mechanical goldfish swimming round in coloured water bowls, kept a small piano in the back of his Rolls-Royce.

One visitor, Salvador Dalí, had a grand piano put in a shallow pond, placed chocolate eclairs on all the ebony keys and asked Berners to play for some surreal entertainment, and on another occasion Penelope Betjeman brought her horse into the drawing room for tea and cake. Berners' companion, Robert 'Mad Boy' Heber-Percy, lived at Faringdon after Berners died in 1950.

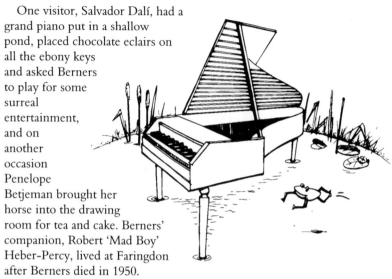

The gardens – not now open to the public – also hold diverse, more durable testaments to his ideas. What appears to be a castle turns out to be Oxfordshire's only crenellated swimming pool. The changing room has a floor made of pennies set in cement and stained-glass windows; two fearsome wyverns sit at the shallow end. (Wyvern trivia: there was a Vauxhall Wyvern car in the 1950s and every Vauxhall car badge still includes one).

Nearby, outside the orangery, sits a bizarre half-submerged statue of General Havelock. It suits the spot perfectly. He looks as though he might be relieving himself, apt for the hero who relieved Lucknow during the Indian Mutiny.

The problems with surreal gardening

One very modern gardener whom Baron Berners would surely have understood is surreal gardener Ivan Hicks, who has created a Garden of the Mind at **Stansted Park** near Rowland's Castle, Hampshire.

Mr Hicks's surreal credentials are almost unreal. His previous employer at nearby West Dean Gardens was the late millionaire eccentric Edward James, who was a good chum of Salvador Dalí and who appears in Magritte paintings. Do you know the one showing the back of a man sitting looking into a dressing-table mirror, yet in the mirror we see his back again? That's Edward James, and an oblique commentary on this strange man who built a fantasy town – like Stanley Norbury (above) being put in charge of Milton Keynes – in the Mexican jungle, and then deliberately let the jungle regrow over the gaudy Gaudiesque creations. James, who died in 1984, often took Hicks to Mexico for advice on plants and in particular trees, his speciality.

James shared a penchant for absurd notices with Baron Berners. When someone put up signs saying 'Beware of the adders' at his Monkton House gardens, James thought the dangers trivial compared to those of gardeners working on the trees and had Ls added to all the 'adders'.

Mr Hicks' Garden of the Mind at Stansted Park (admission, absurdly, £2.01, or whatever you like for children), although not yet mature, has a child-like

fantasy to it – half secret walled garden, half art gallery and temple to *objets trouvés*. 'There is a secret theme running throughout the garden, but it's also a gallery where I can try things out,' he says. 'Having said that, I don't force things. I like gardens overrun by nature. There are some beautiful silver thistles, which give a newish garden height and impact quickly. They determine where they will go by seeding themselves.' Spirals, circles and cylinders cleverly made with living trees abound. A bottomless chair sits amid a circle of aspens. 'It's the anti-stress chamber. The aspens tremble at the slightest thing, so you don't have to.' Personally, I found the seatless metal chair inside actually a little conducive to increased stress: bring a cushion.

A cylinder lawnmower sits awry, tall shoots growing through the rusting cylinder of blades. A lawn has concentric circles of mown and unkempt grass around a small hill. The natural feel of the garden is achieved by weaving in familiar fast-growing plants – teasels, foxgloves, grasses – with the more ambitious arboricultural architecture. A splendid bridge is being made of living oak, to mark the millennium, with a living river flowing underneath. Mr Hicks' son may be grown up before it supports an adult, however. Another circle of cypresses, *Columnaris glauca*, is growing into what will be a perfect living rotunda like a miniature Greek temple with pillars and dome. Nearby laburnums grow through legs of shop mannequins. A hoop of willow frames a face as visitors pass. Another cylinder of leyland cypresses has a gothic pointed door, a window and, inside, a first floor with a ladder. Eventually it will be a tower with many floors and windows.

'There are elements of Narnia, of *Alice In Wonderland*, of magic and fantasy,' Mr Hicks says. In a way his ideas go back to an experience I shared, growing up in south London at the same time. 'We used to play in bomb sites. Secret, abandoned places you could create fantasies in, with strange reminders of the houses that were there just 20 years before. Walled-in cellars all overgrown. They had the innocence of the Garden of Eden yet had been created out of terrible violence – and 20 years later they had all gone.' Something of the magic of those secret gardens of fantasy, walled off from the outside world, has been recreated in today's Sussex.

STRANGE TOPIARY

The Drunken Garden is part of Groombridge Place's formal gardens, with the old dairy adjacent containing the desk where local author Sir Arthur Conan-Doyle created tales such as this, from *The Valley Of Fear* (1895):

'Dr Watson took a stroll in the curious old-world garden which flanked the house. Rows of very ancient trees, cut into strange designs, girded it round. Inside was a beautiful stretch of lawn ... in that deeply peaceful atmosphere one could forget or remember only as some fantastic nightmare that darkened study with the sprawling, bloodstained figure upon the floor ... As I strolled around it, ... a strange incident occurred ...'

Enchanted, or downright devious?

Ivan Hicks' ideas have been adopted on a grand and, one must admit, more commercial scale at **Groombridge Place**, a perfectly preserved moated house on the Kent–Sussex border at Groombridge near Tunbridge Wells. But the Enchanted Forest which owner Andrew de Candole has encouraged Hicks to create is not just another theme park. Many of the features were not mature when I visited.

Near the house there is a maze growing in golden and green yew, which when head height will better conceal a peculiar secret about its layout that I sense is part of some pattern or puzzle the devious Hicks is setting up. In the Enchanted Forest itself there are the things families seem to love – adventure walkways in a double spiral, with pigs and deer running free round about – but Hicks is in the detail even here, with a face carved in a tree suddenly jumping out at you, for example.

Further into the forest are things that are pure Hicks – a Serpents' Lair and a Mystic Pool, whimsical construction of *objets trouvés* around the original woodland landscape that have fairytale layers of detail repaying a close and then closer look. There are Hicksian favourites which recall his Sussex base, such as a ring of trembling aspens on an island in a small lake which will soon be bent over to make a classical temple.

As Groombridge Place's gardening curator Clifford James said: 'These are living places which Ivan has to maintain. It is not something gardening staff could fix because his vision is what drives it all. There is a subtlety which avoids being theme parky. Where we do a little of that for the children, it is very much tongue-in-cheek.' Strolling through the Enchanted Forest, which is carpeted with wild garlic and bluebells in early spring, you could come across a Peruvian pipe player sitting in a natural amphitheatre with log seats all around, or a Romany caravan with a gipsy woman all ready to chat or tell your fortune, with chickens and pigs running around the fire. It is not a garden, nor a theatre, nor a fairground pleasure park, nor a natural environment, but a curious blend of all of them.

In terms of formal gardens, Groombridge Place is also deservedly well known. The ancient topiary and various views of the house were made famous in Peter Greenaway's 1983 film *The Draughtsman's Contract*, where each of the drawings of the house was exchanged for certain favours from the lady of the manor. Mr Hicks settled for more usual terms of employment.

NEITHER UNHINGED NOR UNHENGED

Henge-building stuff did not come to an end with the druids and the Stone Age. Some of the modern henges are whimsical constructions made of lift doors, or to mark a casanova's conquests, but others are of regular stone erected for less controversial reasons. Take professional gardener Len Ede of Petersfield, Hampshire. Perfectly normal, he lives in a quiet suburban bungalow in a typical cul-de-sac. He and his wife Joyce love Stonehenge, to which they regularly make the 80-mile trip. And so, when he wanted to pay tribute to his wife, to whom he'd been married for getting on 40 years, there was only one thing he could do (having built plenty of pergolas and a wall with his own motto inscribed): he built her a one-twelfth-sized Stonehenge right in the front garden, which it dominates.

'There's just something special about Stonehenge,' says Mr Ede. 'I built it for my god, and that's my wife. Other families have got gnomes and such things in their gardens but I thought she deserved something different.' The last time I looked, Len had covered the Petersfield Stonehenge with his own millennium dome, perhaps celebrating the fact that, 5,000 years apart, the British love making great but incomprehensible monuments.

The Edes are not alone in imitating the prehistoric puzzle. On the edge of Ilton Moor, there stands, amid forestry, the little-known Yorkshire Stonehenge, the **Druids' Temple**. This imitation Stonehenge was put up by eccentric early 19th-century author William Danby, probably to alleviate local unemployment. In Westleton, Suffolk, a private garden had redundant art deco lift doors arranged in a Stonehenge and in Padstow, Cornish eccentric and arch druid Ed Prynne has arranged a circle of massive megaliths near his bungalow. He told a reporter that there was one for each woman in his life. So that's what the druids were up to ... (See also *Britain's Most Magical Standing Stones*, page 182.)

TRAVEL INFORMATION

Druids' Temple, Yorkshire
Road On the edge of Ilton Moor, about 1½ miles southwest of the village of Healey and east of Leighton Reservoir. Healey is southwest of A6108 midway between Leyburn and Ripon, which is just off A1.
Tourist information ☎ 01969 623069.

Gnome Reserve, West Putford, near Bideford, Devon
Road From M5 end at Exeter, A30 and A377 to Barnstaple, A39 to Bideford, then A386, A388 towards Holsworthy south. West Putford is about 3 miles to right (north) from Venngreen.
Tourist information ☎ 01237 477676.

Groombridge Place, Kent; ☎ 01892 863999; web: www.groombridge.co.uk
An interesting moated 17th-century manor with maze, tea rooms, boat rides, and Hicks' Enchanted Forest.
Road 4 miles southwest of Tunbridge Wells on B2110. From London and M25 use A21 Hastings–Tunbridge Wells (not Tonbridge).
Rail/bus Tunbridge Wells is on the London Charing Cross–Hastings line, then either bus 291 direct or walk to Tunbridge Wells West station (at Sainsbury's car park), take steam-operated Spa Valley Railway (check if running, ☎ 01892 537715) to Groombridge, then walk downhill straight through village. Total walking: 45 min.
Tourist information ☎ 01892 515675.

Meikleour Hedge, Perthshire
Road On A93 about 10 miles north of Perth towards Blairgowrie.
Rail/bus Nearest station Perth. Bus to Blairgowrie.
Tourist information ☎ 01738 627958.

Stansted Park, near Rowlands Castle, Hampshire; ☎ 01705 412265
A classical stately home with a large estate and gardens, including Hicks' Garden of the Mind.
Road From A3 London–Portsmouth or A27 coast road, follow brown signs.
Rail Rowlands Castle on the London–Portsmouth line (get a stopping train), then a pleasant 2-mile bike ride or walk, or taxi. No buses.
Tourist information ☎ 01705 480024.

The other gardens mentioned are private.

A PLACE FOR ECCENTRICS

ATLANTIC OCEAN

Orkney Islands

Thurso

Isle of Lewis

Outer Hebrides

Isle of Skye

Inner Hebrides

Island of Mull

Islay

Arran

Inverness

Glenfinnan Viaduct

Aberdeen

North Sea

Tealing Dovecote, Angus

North Lodge, Arbroath

Castle, Military Dog Cemetery & Dovecote, Deacon Brodie's Tavern, Edinburgh

Phantassie Doocot, Lothian

Glasgow

Newcastle upon Tyne

Carlisle

Transporter Bridge, Middlesbrough

Isle of Man

N

Irish Sea

Anglesey

Holyhead

Temple Newsam Dovecote, Leeds

York

Kingston-upon-Hull

Bradford

Grimsby

Manchester

Liverpool

Sheffield

Anderton Boat Lift

Asbourne pub

Stoke-on-Trent

Pontcysyllte Aqueduct

Fantasy Village, Portmeirion

Derby

Nottingham

Cardigan Bay

Wolverhampton

Birmingham

Norwich

Fantasy Village, Thorpeness

Foxton Locks

Coventry

Tardebigge Locks

Rendlesham Hall Lodges, Suffolk

Cambridge

Ipswich

0   100km
0   60 miles

Fishguard

Wilmington Dovecote

Monnow Bridge Lock-up, Monmouth

Wheatley Lock-up

Shenley Lock-up

Oxford

Hammersmith Bridge & Monument Pangbourne Lock-up

Victoria Gate Lodge, Hyde Park, London

Swansea

Cardiff

Stag Lodge, Wimbledon

Bristol Channel

Clifton Suspension Bridge, Bristol

Dover

Lingfield Lock-up

Balcombe Viaduct

Brighton

Southampton

Transportation Bridge, Wool

Exeter

Isle of Wight

Portsmouth

Lanhydrock Lodge, Bodmin

Swanage Lock-up

Penzance

English Channel

A Place for Eccentrics

SIGNS OF SERIOUS ECCENTRICITY

Villagers of tiny Bedlam, North Yorkshire, are not exactly delighted with the name signs that have been erected there, causing one wag to add 'Twinned with L'Unacy'. No doubt they fear too many sightseers will cause, well, Bedlam.

But the novelty will wear off. Inhabitants of Nasty and Ugley, near neighbours across the Hertfordshire–Essex border, have long since got over jokes about the Nasty Boys' Choir or the Ugley Women's Institute, and if people can live in Pratts Bottom, Kent, or on Muck, Hebrides, or take jokes about what goes on at Cuckold's Cross, Hertfordshire, Over Wallop, Hampshire, Crackpot, Yorkshire or Hell Corner, Berkshire, then mere Bedlam can take it on the chin.

In fact, as with the Bedlam mental asylum once sited where the Imperial War Museum now stands, its name probably comes from Bethlehem. Like the hospital, they could always compromise with Bethlem.

Geographical confusion in some parts of Britain is more common than in Paris, Texas. We have five Californias, near Falkirk in Scotland, in Derbyshire, Norfolk, Suffolk and near Baldock in Hertfordshire; three Gibraltars, near Bedford, part of Mablethorpe, Lincolnshire, or near Woodbridge, Suffolk; two New Yorks in Lincolnshire and Tyne and Wear; a New Zealand in Derbyshire, a Quebec in County Durham, a Rhodesia in Nottinghamshire and a Palestine, near Andover, Hampshire (in the latter one travels down Mount Carmel to Zion). The former Australian penal colony of Botany Bay seems oddly popular with at least three villages, in Avon, Kent, and Middlesex, and there are countless farms named after it. Little France in Lothian; Normandy in Surrey, America in Cambridgeshire ... the list of places that aren't what they say is almost endless. If you find these puzzling, there's Conundrum in Lothian.

Seasonal offerings may be found at Good Easter in Essex; Easter Bush in Lothian; Cold Christmas in Essex; Christmas Common in Oxfordshire; and Christmaspie in Surrey. The only place with punctuation is Westward Ho! in Devon; the only one composed of initials is the hamlet of CB in Yorkshire; and the only one, well, of its kind, is Rest And Be Thankful, on the A83 between Arrochar and Inveraray in Argyll.

West Country places have a pleasing insanity which even P G Wodehouse couldn't have made up. Why is Toller Fratrum next to Toller Porcorum in Dorset? What goes on at nearby Ryme Intrinsica? Or at Ab Lench in Worcestershire, Praze-an-Beeble in Cornwall or Zeal Monachorum in Devon?

The Welsh have a happy habit of running words together in a way that even the Germans might find strange. Taken to an extreme, this gives Britain's longest railway station name sign at

Llanfairpwllgwngyllgogerychwyrndrobwllllantysiliogogogoch,

on the line to Holyhead in Anglesey. It may usually be seen with tourists being photographed alongside, and is often shortened to Llanfair PG. But it has a real meaning: 'St Mary's Church in the hollow of the white hazel near a rapid whirlpool and the church of St Tysilio near the red cave'. Welsh readers would already know that.

Other places are staggeringly unusual because of their sheer commonness, if that makes any sense. If you include double-barrelled names or those prefixed or suffixed by South or Common or whatever, Newtown has 75; Middleton, 35; Milton, 46; Norton, 40; Upton, 33; Broughton, 23; Sutton, 52; Weston, 41; and Preston, 28.

Places that shouldn't be there at all include Nowhere in Kent; five Nomanslands in Cornwall, Devon, Hampshire, Hertfordshire and Wiltshire; Noplace in County Durham, two No Man's Heaths in Cheshire and Warwickshire; an Innominate Tarn, Cumbria; and Inaccessible Pinnacle in Skye. Nonsuch in Ewell, Surrey really isn't there; it was the site of the great Tudor palace which is, sadly, gone.

THE WORLD'S ODDEST PUBS
The politically correct pub sign

The attempt not so long ago of a Derbyshire County Council 'equality officer' to ban the ancient if rather long pub sign **The Green Man and Black's Head Royal Hotel** in Ashbourne, in the Peak District, because it was 'racist', is by no means unique. It was evident that the humourless Martian embassy had not complained about the Green Man part from the inclusion of a crass, unsubtle leaflet about 'gollies'. What so offended the witless bureaucrat was the fact that a black person's head was depicted at all.

More understandably, schoolgirls had the sign of the Labour In Vain pub in Yarnfield, Staffordshire, repainted because it showed women scrubbing a small black boy. But many other signs have fallen victim to the easily offended. The Silent Woman in Oxfordshire has gone, although there are at least two Silent Womans in Slaithwaite, Huddersfield and Cold Harbour,

Dorset, and in the same county there is a Quiet Woman at Halstock (while the Wicked Lady at Nomansland near St Albans, Hertfordshire, is, of course, politically correct enough). Certain Yorkshire pubs such as the Blue Pig have offended Muslims. Harry Walshaw, chairman of the Inn Signs Society, said at the time: 'I think Live and Let Live is a good sign to follow – there are a few of those in the Home Counties, and I am delighted to say there are several more Labour in Vains.' For downright political incorrectness, at least one Nag's Head has had the equine pub sign replaced by a scolding woman.

Pubs were required to have a sign from 1751, although many are much older. Some are not what they seem. The Flying Machine near Cheltenham has a picture of the Gloster Gladiator aircraft on one sign, but on another the real source – a famous stagecoach of an earlier era. Another two-sided sign is **Deacon Brodie's Tavern** on the Royal Mile in Edinburgh which commemorates the man who was the inspiration for Dr Jekyll and Mr Hyde: one side shows the respectable daytime businessman and the other the night villain. He was hanged, appropriately, on a gallows of his own design.

The latter instrument was that referred to by most pubs named The Last Drop, which lay near execution sites, rather than the name referring to beer, as people today assume. The origin of other names is much harder to guess at: there are several pubs called The Case is Altered in Middlesex, for instance. Despite attempts to link these to court cases, the most likely source is that the local regiment was quartered in the Casa Alta in the Peninsular War early in the 19th century. Some names tell a sad story. The Never Turn Back at Caister, Norfolk, recalls lifeboat coxswain James Haylett, who was asked at an inquest why his men went bravely on into a storm and were lost. 'Caister men never turn back,' he declared.

Lastly there are plenty of pubs that locals refuse to call by their official names. A pub in Sunderland is still known as the Post Office by the regulars of one bar, although it has had four official names over the other door on another street. Printers in Fleet Street were notorious for renaming pubs and wouldn't have had a clue where The White Swan was. But if you asked for The Mucky Duck ...

The long and the short of pub names

Whoever selected the truly bizarre name I Am the Only Running Footman as the name for a pub in London, W1, was giving Ashbourne's The Green Man and Black's Head Royal Hotel a run for their money in terms of length. Running footmen used to precede the grand carriages of the great, to harry people out of the way, proclaim their masters and open gates. By the early 19th century, the fourth Marquess of Queensberry was the only noble still employing one, commemorated on the pub sign.

Much longer yet – but not quite qualifying as a pub name – is the title of a bar in the Gainsborough House Hotel, Kidderminster, Worcestershire. When locals were told it was to be renamed after one of the eponymous painter's pictures, the Blue Boy Bar might have been a reasonable guess. In fact, it is called The Rocky Valley with Two Women and a Child, a Shepherd and Sheep with a Distant Village and Mountains Bar.

Folksy sayings give rise to peculiar pub names, such as the Help Me Through the World at Bury, Lancashire. Charles Hindley in his book *Tavern Anecdotes and Sayings* suggests that this was once a common name and that the sign would have shown a man struggling through a globe, the idea being that life was tough but the pub would help you get through it.

Similar phrases include the Live and Let Live at Hexton, near Hitchin, Hertfordshire, and elsewhere – the sign usually shows a dog watching a plump duck waddling past. The Who'd Have Thought It? at Milton Combe, Plymouth; Egerton or Rochester, Kent and Wokingham, Berkshire, sometimes refers to the landlord's surprise at being granted a licence for the pub by the court, as shown on some of the pub signs. There is a Hit or Miss at Stamford, Lincolnshire, and The Same Yet in Prestwich, near Manchester – the latter presumably a misunderstanding of the landlord's instructions on how to paint the pub sign.

Another licensing mix-up is to blame for the Letter B at Whittlesey near Peterborough, Cambridgeshire. The justices had a list – A, B, C, D – to choose from at as yet unnamed houses, and the Letter B stuck. The punning sign shows a lad with his arm around a reluctant lass, the image being 'Let her be'.

Some pubs fall naturally into pairs. The story of the naked noblewoman who rode through Coventry is recalled by the Lady Godiva in that city, as is the boy who broke the ban on looking upon her fair body, with the Peeping Tom in Coventry and at Burton Green, Warwickshire.

Some themes lend themselves to sets of pubs. The new town at Harlow, Essex, presented a great opportunity: all the pubs are named after moths or butterflies but the signs show punning pictures of other meanings: the Red Admiral, the Purple Emperor, the Shark, the Small Copper and the Painted Lady give plenty of scope for fun. The last, however, was renamed the boring Jean Harlow in an unimaginative move which spoiled the set.

The *Guinness Book of Records* used to record the X, at Westcott, near Cullompton, Devon, as the shortest name, until it was boringly renamed the Merrie Harriers in 1983. The letter X was once used by excisemen to record the strength of ale – the letters XXXXX branded on barrels of Gales' winterbrew still suggest extreme strength, the 6X brew from Devizes, Wiltshire, does likewise, and the XXXX of an Australian brewery gives scope to advertising copywriters' imagination. The XL pub of Garstang, Lancashire, is probably a pun on a beer name and the word 'excel'.

Smuggling is featured in a surprising number of pub names and signs. The Revenue, at Devonport, Plymouth, shows customs men on a cliff watching for smugglers, and other coastal pubs include the Smugglers' Den, Morecambe, the Smugglers' Barn, Newport, Isle of Wight, the Moonlighters, Pegwell, Kent, or the Rum Runners, Southampton. The Slippery Sam at Petham, near Canterbury, was named after a smuggler. The Moonraker, at Swindon and elsewhere, could refer obliquely to smuggling. The original

Moonrakers, as opposed to any Moonraker pubs named after the James Bond film, were said to be village idiots who thought the full moon reflected in the village pond was a big cheese and tried to rake it out. The better explanation is that some smugglers were caught in the

act of retrieving contraband from the bottom of the village pond. They only pretended to be village idiots, the real simpletons being the revenue men who swallowed the story.

More unlikely still is the name of a pub at Copnor, Portsmouth, following in the Jolly Sailor, Jolly Farmer, Jolly Fisherman tradition. This one is the barely credible Jolly Taxpayer, a name probably not uninfluenced by the sizeable tax office nearby, housing many thirsty Inland Revenue staff.

The pub with no name

'You want the pub with no name,' we were told, and given directions from Selborne, Hampshire, to the next-but-one village.

But the pub wasn't in the centre of that tiny hamlet, Colemore, nor was there any sign of it or to it. Over the years we travelled the various lanes leading to and from the hamlet until we had covered every possible approach, but of the Pub With No Name there was no sign. Once, on a foggy winter's night after visiting several other pubs, we were driven there, and an excellent pub it was too. But in daylight it had vanished again.

Intriguingly, on the nearby main road there is a sign, or rather a post set in an empty field with an empty oblong metal frame where a sign once swung. Its absence is no temporary affair – 80 years ago, Edward Thomas – the poet who lived at nearby Steep and was killed at the battle of Arras – wrote about the Pub With No Name:

> 'The post and empty frame I knew.
> Without them I could not have guessed
> The low grey house and its one stack under trees
> Was not a hermitage but a public house.'

As in 1914, the Pub With No Name still lurks under a copse of beech, well hidden from both the main road and the side road, not very near its empty sign and not even marked at its own gate. Only a rutted, potholed farm track leads unpromisingly away from the lane.

When we did find it, we were served No Name bitter and found the pub does have a name, as mentioned in Thomas's poem *Up in the Wind*. But the proper moniker is the Pub With No Name. Let the signboard stay at the bottom of the pond where it had been thrown, the poem says, long before 1914.

Curiously, the long aversion to having a proper pub name isn't at all unusual. There is the House Without a Name at Colchester and another at Bolton. There used to be a What's in a Name at Cambridge, recalling Shakespeare's line which continues … 'that which we call a rose/Would by any other name smell as sweet'. There is a Nobody Inn, London N1, and another at Doddiscombsleigh, near Exeter, Devon, continuing a long line of corny inn jokes, the No Place at Plymouth and Gosport, and Nowhere, also at Plymouth. Dunkling and Wright in their excellent book *A Dictionary of Pub Names* say that the brewery explained this last by saying that a man, asked where he had been all day, could truthfully say Nowhere … If that didn't work he could be in the Doghouse, Kennington, London.

ECCENTRIC ENGINEERING
Awesome aqueducts and crazy canals

Floating a boatload of goods down a river to save carrying them must have made sense from early times, but in the past few centuries engineers have carried the concept to absurd heights.

Fancy, for example, cruising 120ft *above* the River Dee near Llangollen, your hand trailing off the edge of the boat over the sheer drop as you cruise along for more than 1,000ft. That this is possible on the superb **Pontcysyllte Aqueduct** is due to the brilliant engineer Thomas Telford, who completed the iron trough-on-stone arches marvel as early as 1805. It has a towpath and railing on one side, but on the other just plunges away.

Further along the same Shropshire Union Canal can be found another great aqueduct at Chirk, 710ft long, over the River Ceiriog. A railway viaduct runs parallel to this one.

What about a section of canal, 234ft long, up in the air, that can swing sideways through 90° complete with water, a boat floating on it, and, if you will, a bargee sitting on the roof smoking his pipe? This sounds like an idea that wouldn't hold water, but can be seen at the Barton Swing Aqueduct at Barton-on-Irwell, west of Manchester. Opened in 1894, it replaced an earlier stone aqueduct on the aptly named Bridgewater Canal to allow ships to pass beneath on the then new Manchester Ship Canal. The swing section moves slowly, as it weighs 1,500 tons when full of water.

Swinging a canal sideways is impressive enough, but upwards would be a fine trick. This was actually accomplished twice: first, in an inclined plane or ramp for a section of canal carrying boats at **Foxton**, on the Grand Union Canal not far from Leicester. Its remains can be seen alongside the Foxton Staircase, an impressive flight of ten locks off the Foxton–Gumley road. A canal staircase is where a set of locks are joined so that the top gate of one is the bottom gate of the next, whereas a flight of locks is just a set of locks which are close but separate.

But the real thing in terms of lifting a boat can be seen in another ingenious contraption which is being restored to full working order – the **Anderton Boat Lift**, 2½ miles northwest of Northwich, Cheshire. The extraordinary-looking device can lift two canal boats at a time, in a pair of enormous caissons full of water, from the River Weaver up to the Trent and Mersey Canal. It looks as though it shouldn't work – but it has, since 1875.

Raising canal boats the traditional way is taken to extremes on the Worcester and Birmingham Canal, which lifts boats 425ft from the River Severn to Birmingham. The 58 locks include 30 non-stop at **Tardebigge**, the world's greatest narrowboat flight of locks. The not-so-long-ago derelict Kennet and Avon Canal has a splendid flight of 29 locks at Caen Hill near Devizes, Wiltshire, and the Caledonian Canal near Fort William, in the Scottish highlands, has another set known as Neptune's staircase which will get you from the sea to Loch Ness.

Canal builders sometimes plunged their watery tunnels as deep as coal mines. At Worsley Delph on the Bridgewater Canal is the basin which was the centre of an extraordinary network of canals built underground to link the many coal mines of the area. Forty miles of canals on two different levels, linked to the collieries, were in use until about 100 years ago, the heavy boats being worked through the tunnels entirely by human effort.

'Legging' boats – using your feet on the tunnel roof and sides while lying on your back on the boat – was commonplace on the canal system, even on Britain's longest Standedge Tunnel on the Huddersfield Narrow Canal between Oldham and Huddersfield in Yorkshire. At 5,415 yards long, it is also the highest canal tunnel, at around 640ft above sea level, and besides being worked mostly by narrowboat people's sturdy legs, had certain odd features. It opens out into large natural caverns at points – little suspected by walkers on the Pennine Way long-distance footpath above – and the Leeds–Manchester railway tunnel was built just above it, linked by sloping ventilation shafts. So in the days of steam the already eerie interior would suddenly be filled with smoke, steam, the distant thunder of wheels and ghostly whistles.

Standedge is being restored in an ambitious £31 million project to reopen the route through the Pennines.

Brunel's scheme for suckers and a bit of a blow

One of the great Victorian engineer Isambard Kingdom Brunel's more crackpot schemes – and he had plenty – was the idea of sucking trains down tubes by pumping out the air ahead of them, rather in the way that messages and money used to whizz round offices and department stores in canisters shoved into hissing pipes.

To do this full scale might have been expensive but Brunel hit upon the idea of a piston being sucked along a pipe between the railway lines, and this pulling the train. To the rather obvious difficulty that air would leak in along the slot where the piston was connected to the train, Brunel countered with the idea of a greased leather flap. Pumping stations would be spaced along the track, and the carriages, with no need for a locomotive, would be sucked along.

Amazingly, Brunel persuaded the South Devon Railway to adopt this 'Atmospheric Railway' for the steeply graded route between Newton Abbot and Plymouth, thought to be too much for the steam engines of the 1840s. Even more astonishingly, it occasionally worked, and in 1847 a train of 28 tons reached 68mph, a very high speed for the day. More often, though, the system failed to work at all.

Several of the pumping stations survive to bear witness to this weird venture, including one at Starcross where there's an Atmospheric Railway pub with a grumpy picture of Brunel. A century and a half down the line, the verdict is: the whole idea sucks.

Another crackpot scheme that was built against all common sense involved blowing rather than sucking trains: George Bennie's 1930s railplane, a cigar-shaped carriage with aircraft propellers fore and aft was supposed to run suspended from an impossibly complicated gantry above existing railway lines.

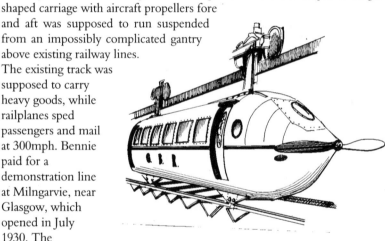

The existing track was supposed to carry heavy goods, while railplanes sped passengers and mail at 300mph. Bennie paid for a demonstration line at Milngarvie, near Glasgow, which opened in July 1930. The machine never reached anything like the predicted speeds, despite the great noise of thrashing the air, and World War II put paid to Bennie's dreams.

The ugly 'pterodactyls' on Tees

That roads can swing, lift, plunge into hills and across valleys is not so surprising, but a highway bridge high across a river where the road deck is missing except for one small section? Such a contraption is the **Middlesbrough Transporter Bridge**, still in use and indeed floodlit since the Cleveland community decided that if you must have a huge steel device dominating your town, you might as well make a virtue of necessity. The road section moves back and forth with cars and people on it, using an unlikely system of wires and trolleys running on a huge gantry.

The aim of transporter bridges is to cross a river without obstructing shipping, although the intermittent nature of the road traffic makes it more like a ferry service on wires than a regular bridge. There were others –

including a large one at Newport, south Wales – but the Middlesbrough one is still part of the road system. The Newport bridge has been restored and trips can be enjoyed across the River Usk.

Elegant the Middlesbrough bridge isn't to most eyes, being likened by one writer to 'the fossilised skeletons of a couple of long-legged prehistoric pterodactyls, heads bent aggressively across the Tees'. Yet it has survived a collision with a steamer – 'the bridge was moving, honest, Skipper' – and a German bomb on the car deck, to remain a useful commuting route across the Tees.

Transportation bridges, on the other hand, abound in Dorset. There are a number of bridges in the county, such as at Wool or Sturminster Newton, where cast-iron signs still threaten anyone defacing or damaging them with transportation – to Australia, that is. This might seem to offer a bargain trip to Bondi Beach, but transportation was actually to a penal colony where life was short and brutish. Return tickets were not available.

Haunted bridges, a dead horse, suicides and a virgin viaduct

Britain having virtually invented inventions – there's a village called New Invention in Staffordshire – the landscape is littered with fascinating railway relics, many of them disused, as nearby traffic jams testify. The most dramatic of these are the great viaducts, such as at Meldon, Devon; Chappel, Suffolk (7 million bricks); Welwyn or Digswell, Hertfordshire (100ft high, 13 million bricks); Conisbrough, Yorkshire; Lockwood, Huddersfield; and Harringworth, Northamptonshire, the longest in the British countryside at 1,275 yards and God knows how many million bricks.

Trackworkers insist that the seventh pier of the spooky Cynghordy Viaduct in Dyfed, between Llandovery and Builth Road, is haunted. One of the children of the contractor Richard Hattersley was killed there during construction. Another allegedly haunted viaduct which contains a macabre secret is the horseshoe curved **Glenfinnan Viaduct** on the Mallaig Extension of the beautiful West Highland Line. The viaduct was a radical experiment by 'Concrete Bob' McAlpine but during construction in 1900, the story goes, a horse and cart fell through planks into one of the hollow piers. So as you round the curve at the foot of impossibly beautiful mountains, there is a dead horse, head downwards, sealed beneath you.

Some viaducts have less ghastly secrets, such as the disused Cornish Treffry Viaduct between Luxulyan and St Blazey. Some 650ft of massive granite arches, complete with the coat of arms of Joseph Treffry who built it in 1839, the viaduct once carried a horse tramway, bringing china clay across the valley to a canal for shipment. But concealed within it is an aqueduct intended to power a

Balcombe Viaduct

copper mine nearby, through which runs water made milky by china clay.

The 'Virgin Viaduct' at Tadcaster, was built for trains which really never came. Britain's most elegant viaduct, however, is surely that crossing the Ouse at **Balcombe** in West Sussex. Built in 1840 for the London and Brighton Railway, the 92ft-high brick arches are crowned by a stone balustrade and – a touch of genius – each end is flanked by a pair of Italianate pavilions. The Ouse viaduct has a secret splendour invisible from trains – its pierced brick arches give an extraordinary cathedral-like vista to the walker in the valley beneath.

Mention elegance and bridge in the same breath and many will recall that the great Isambard Kingdom Brunel threw the truly dramatic 720ft span **Clifton Suspension Bridge** across the Avon Gorge in Bristol. Actually, it was not quite that straightforward. Brunel did win a competition to design it at the age of only 24, the young upstart competing against the great Thomas Telford among others. Work began in 1836 but was dogged by financial problems. Others had to finish it in 1864, five years after Brunel's death.

Notorious for suicides, the bridge bears notices from the Samaritans begging people to desist. A macabre detail is that, as the bridge stands at 287ft above a very tidal river, many have plunged through the water deep into the mud beneath. On the other hand, in 1885 one despairing lovelorn lady, Sarah Henley, wearing a hooped crinoline, was saved by the parachute-like billowing of her undergarments and picked up by a rowing boat.

If, after this, you can still bear to contemplate crossing the Clifton Bridge, you might like to consider halfway across that the chains still holding it up after all these years were not new but were secondhand from Brunel's old Hungerford Bridge across the Thames in London, demolished in 1861 to make way for a railway bridge into Charing Cross.

One bridge Brunel did live to see – but only just – is the remarkable **Royal Albert Bridge** at Saltash. The quixotic engineer faced two contradictory demands in leaping the Tamar estuary between Devon and Cornwall. First there was a probably excessive requirement from the Admiralty for a 100ft clearance above high water for warships, and secondly the Cornwall Railway demanded that he make it as cheap as possible. The result, for only £225,000 and as daringly unorthodox as ever, was two enormous wrought-iron tubes with the world's only railway suspension bridge hung beneath. Somehow the whole 733ft long bridge was erected at this great height by floating it out at high tide then building enormous stone piers beneath, as it was jacked up in time for Prince Albert to open it in 1859.

Brunel was by then dying, and had to be drawn over the bridge on a special flat truck with a bed on it – gaining much the best view. In the end, it was his memorial, not Albert's, for Brunel's name is proudly borne in huge letters on the Devon side. His bridge totally dominates the small town of Saltash and has not been diminished one jot by the modern road bridge alongside. Could it be, then, that bridge builders are given a kind of immortality denied those who must just pay the ferryman across the River Styx of the underworld?

The answer can be found in Hammersmith parish church, beneath the thundering A4 flyover in west London. A memorial tablet on the wall to W Tierney Clark, who died in 1852, bears a detailed picture of Hammersmith Suspension Bridge and the fine words: 'The great suspension bridge at Pesth in Hungary, those at Hammersmith and Shoreham, and many other works

HAMMERSMITH BRIDGE

Oddly, for all its frilly ornaments, the elegant Hammersmith Suspension Bridge in west London has three times come within an ace of being blown up. In the 1930s an IRA bomb was fizzing and spluttering when a passer-by threw it in the river; a wartime Nazi bomb fell in the river near the bridge; and then enough IRA Semtex explosive – the largest such bomb yet planted in Britain – to blow shreds of the bridge all over west London failed to detonate properly in 1996. A few months later an IRA man was shot dead in a hideout a few hundred yards away. Then, in 1998, it was controversially closed for repairs that seemed unlikely to take place as the well-to-do neighbours preferred it closed to open and was equally controversially reopened late in 1999. In the unlikely event that it is still there when you read this, it's well worth a visit. There are some pleasant pubs along the north side.

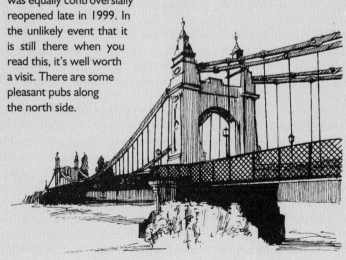

attest to his talent, perseverance and skill and are lasting monuments to his fame.' Yet a close look at the bridge on his tomb shows that it is not the current elegant **Hammersmith suspension bridge**, clearly dated in its arches 1887, but an earlier one which it replaced. As far as the throng crossing that road every morning and night is concerned, W Tierney Clark's fame is all but extinguished – so much water under the bridge.

GATEWAY TO ECCENTRICITY

There has always been an unwritten law, when it comes to British country houses, that no matter how grand, dull, conformist or pretentious the big house of the village was, the lodges could be a tad more wacky. Hundreds of houses had – or 'boasted' as oily estate agents would now say – octagonal, hexagonal or round lodges, with a central finial on the roof like the handle of the lid of a giant butter dish or sugar bowl. Sometimes the chimney pokes out of the middle. The reason for this odd shape was the same as in many similar tollhouses: to give a better view of all comers from all directions.

Lanhydrock

Lodges often make a point of being over-the-top. **Lanhydrock**, overlooking the River Fowey near Bodmin, Cornwall, has one dotted with obelisks and, as the travel writer Eric Newby said, could well have been the abode of the Red Queen in *Alice in Wonderland*.

Many a peculiar lodge has long lost the house to which it was the entrance. **Rendlesham Hall**, northeast of Woodbridge, Suffolk, has been demolished, but its somewhat eccentric lodges remain scattered round the estate. One, Ivy Lodge, is a sham ruin, a gothic arch linking what appear to be the ruined bases of massive towers that in fact never existed, clad in suitable greenery; while the other, a mile or so to the south-west, is an appealing gothic octagon where the flying buttresses unite to form a central chimney.

One of the most gorgeous gatehouses in the kingdom, **Tixall Gatehouse** near Stafford, is Elizabethan confection at its most charming. The arch through this three-storey pile, which looks more like a sizeable railway station than a mere lodge to another disappeared house, is decorated by armed warriors on the outside and voluptuous ladies on the inside. The gatehouse clock in one of the turrets vaguely strikes the hour, but has no face or hands. As the Landmark Trust which owns the gatehouse says, 'Precise time here seems unimportant, even vulgar'. The Trust bought the Elizabethan ruin without roof, floors or windows, when it was being used as a cattle shelter, for £300 in 1968 and restored it splendidly so people can stay there (see *How to Stay Eccentric*, page 225).

Another Landmark-owned lodge you can use as a holiday home, Lynch Lodge at Alwalton near Peterborough, Cambridgeshire, not only lost its original house but was dismantled and moved to another one, then proceeded to lose the 10-mile driveway it had acquired, so it is now definitely a gateway to nothing. But Lynch Lodge, with its stylish gable, is an elegant thing as befits its previous owners, the poet Dryden's family, whose home at Chesterton was demolished in 1807. The lodge was then taken to pieces and reassembled here by the Fitzwilliam family.

Stag Lodge

London has a smattering of loopy lodges, many isolated as the sea of banal building has swamped the rural estates they once served. The over-the-top **Stag Lodge**, Wimbledon, was built in 1801 complete with giant lead stag on the roof, as a gateway for nearby Spencer House. Scrap-metal thieves take note: the valuable lead stag was replaced in 1987 with a plastic replica.

The Royal Parks of central London feature many a charming example (such as Duck Island Cottage, St James's Park, built for birdkeeping in 1840) or a massively ugly one (Hyde Park Corner Lodge, built in 1827 by the 'Iron Duke' as a lodge for Apsley House). However, there is something most odd about the neatly tucked away **Victoria Gate Lodge** in Hyde Park. The garden is filled with row upon row of neat little gravestones – they are the graves of 300 pets, a habit started with the Duchess of Cambridge's dog in 1880 until the mini cemetery was full in 1903. The lodge could be described as a gateway to a doggy underworld.

A Scottish lodge with a doggy secret is the private home of **North Lodge**, at Arbirlot Road West, Arbroath. This is another isolated survivor set amidst modern buildings, and was formerly a gateway to Hospital Field, a richly carved house now completely separated from it by the main Westway road. North Lodge has a dog carved on the reverse side, but just why is a puzzle. The Lodge's owners, Kevin and Sally Milne, say: 'It is believed the dog is Maddie, a hero of a Walter Scott novel, but we want to investigate further.' Here the archway has been imaginatively filled in to make a generous living space. (For a splendid full-blown Scottish canine cemetery, complete with named gravestones, look over the battlements of **Edinburgh Castle** near St Margaret's Chapel.)

DOVECOTES, PIGEON DUNG AND GUNPOWDER

Dovecotes, like lodges, give the eccentric landowner a chance for a little architectural whimsy, without being as useless as a folly. The fact that there are societies devoted to their preservation is not all that surprising, but how many dovecotes there are surely is.

The Yorkshire Dovecote Society lists more than 200 in that county alone, and it is likely the country once boasted 25,000 when they were a vital source of fresh meat in the winter. Alan Whitworth, a historian of Slieghts, near Whitby, North Yorkshire, and an enthusiastic founder member of the society, says: 'The dovecote is the Cinderella of vernacular architecture. They are functional yet so diverse they can be weird and wonderful, even grandiose. There would be 80–90 good dovecotes in Yorkshire.' Some are huge dove cities, such as one at **Temple Newsam** near Leeds which housed 1,200 pairs of birds in a five-storey structure. The hundreds of nesting holes – one for each pair – in the 18th-century dovecote were rediscovered when partitions put up to make the dovecote into a cottage in the 1920s were stripped away. Now it is run by Leeds council and can be seen by visitors to the adjacent rare breeds centre. A more modern and more modest dovecote, fully occupied, stands nearby.

Alan Whitworth adds:

> 'They were a vital source of fresh meat in the days when all livestock
> except breeding pairs had to be slaughtered for the winter. It wasn't until
> the root vegetables arrived in the Agricultural Revolution that this
> became unnecessary. But the dovecotes were a valued source of fertiliser
> and of guano – pigeon droppings – which was a vital ingredient of
> gunpowder, and which was therefore the property of the king. There
> were some villages which had one dovecote for every two houses.'

In Scotland the importance of dovecotes can hardly be overestimated. Fife alone had 360 housing 36,000 birds as late as the 18th century. They were a severe nuisance to nearby farmers and King James VI of Scotland passed a law which said: 'No person should build a pigeon house who had not land around it or within two miles which yielded ten chalders of victuals.'

Historic Scotland has the care of two splendid isolated dovecotes besides those many attached to castles and great houses. One circular 'beehive' style dovecote is, helpfully, in Dovecot Road, Corstorphine in **Edinburgh**, and the other, the elegant gabled 16th-century **Tealing Dovecot**, is near Dundee in Angus. For its admission price (nothing), it includes an Iron Age earth house. National Trust for Scotland also has several dovecotes in its care, including the curious-sounding **Phantassie Doocot** at Preston Mill in Lothian. It's a 16th-century lodging for 500 discerning doves and an extremely strange beehive-shaped building.

Dovecotes were not solely a northern phenomenon – they were once even more common further south. Residents of **Worcester** have two splendid dovecotes on their doorstep, one at Hawford 3 miles north of the city, east of A449, and at Wichenford, 5 miles northwest, north of B4204. Both are, appropriately for the area, timber-framed in black-and-white style, and both are opened by the National Trust from Easter to October. In the same county at Hill Croome, 3 miles east of Upton on Severn, a possibly unique cruck-framed 15th-century dovecote stands next to the church.

There is a truly splendid round tiered dovecote with cruciform arrow slits at Bemerton Farm in Wiltshire, solidly built to the instructions of a homesick Russian countess. Another vast dovecote at tiny **Willington**, near Bedford, is lined with boxes for 1,500 birds. A Cornish dovecote in National Trust hands is the medieval one at the remarkable **Cotehele House** at St Dominick near Saltash, Cornwall (✆ 01579 350434).

What looks like Britain's daftest dovecote is in fact an extraordinary henhouse at Vauxhall Farm on the Tong estate on the Shropshire/Staffordshire border. The pyramid dubbed the Egyptian Aviary stands about 20ft high and was inscribed with decidedly odd exhortations to the chickens, most now eroded past legibility, such as 'Scratch before you eat', 'better come out of the way love', 'live and let live' and 'teach your granny'. It is part of a collection of peculiar buildings erected by Victorian eccentric George Durant in the 1840s, including another pyramid for pigs and a pulpit from which he could harangue passers-by.

THESE PEOPLE SHOULD BE LOCKED UP
Where to find Britain's local clinks

Town drunks, loose women, village idiots and petty criminals used to be thrown into village lock-ups. Today, more respectable types are drawn to the remaining miniature prisons, and they have set up the Village Lock-up Association to preserve those containers of erstwhile unhappiness which have happily survived.

Shenley

There's a prettily located one beside the pond at **Shenley**, near St Albans, Hertfordshire, inscribed (as many were) with an admonishing message: in this case 'Be sober, be vigilant'.

At **Wheatley**, near Oxford, a rare pyramid lock-up survives (see Chapter 5). In picturesque Pangbourne, Berkshire, on the Thames near Reading, there's a pleasing pointed-roof red-brick one which looks as though it has been lopped off a French chateau. The word 'Vigilante' is carried on the weather vane, and its massive oak door has heavy bolts. On the outside – of course. Though visible over a garden fence, the lock-up is not accessible because it's now just a garden tool shed for the house once owned by Kenneth Grahame, author of *The Wind In The Willows*. Perhaps Mr Toad could have been locked up in such a place after his motoring misbehaviour.

Not far away from **Pangbourne**, at Aldermaston, another lock-up survives behind the Hind's Head pub. It has been padlocked since its last drunken occupant burnt himself to death, his cries unheard, in the 1860s.

Swanage, in Dorset, has a splendid, suitably inscribed survivor near the town hall ('erected for the prevention of vice and immorality'), and a

Pangbourne

pepperpot-shaped solid stone one still stands at Kingsbury Episcopi (worth a visit for the name, surely), north of Yeovil, Somerset. At Stratton, Cornwall, the lock-up seems to have gone – but its heavy door studded with hundreds of nails, including those spelling out the word CLINK, is on display on the church. By far the best view, for the inmates, was from the **Monnow** Bridge lock-up at Monmouth, Gwent. This 13th-century archway rising from one of the river bridge piers was a fortified gate, look-out and lock-up, and if it hasn't yet starred in a Robin Hood type of film, it should do. Perhaps the prettiest mini-jail is that smack in the centre of **Lingfield**, close to where Surrey, Kent and Sussex meet. It appears to have its own spire, although this was probably an old town cross to which the lock-up was added. The gnarled old tree wrapped around the Peter-Pannish structure just adds to the charm, and one feels, contemplating the pleasant surroundings, that the last occupants – poachers thrown in there in 1882 – wouldn't have been entitled to a grouse.

Lingfield

To stay in a holiday lock-up, see page 224.

ECCENTRIC VILLAGES

Britain's most famous fantasy village must be the somewhat surreal **Portmeirion** in Gwynedd, Wales, not far from Porthmadog, if only because it starred in the 1960s cult television series *The Prisoner*. It offers a range of Italianate buildings, domes, pillars, arches and statuary which would not have been so odd in Tuscany but which stand out like an orange in a coal heap against the relatively grim slate-and-chapel, teetotal, no-nonsense heritage of Welsh Wales. As Gwyn Thomas said, 'There are still parts of Wales where the only concession to gaiety is a striped shroud.'

In 1926 the brilliant young Welsh architect Clough Williams-Ellis bought a rambling house in this delightful spot at the top of Cardigan Bay. He spent the next half century building this Welsh nirvana, importing unwanted bits of architecture from around the world to create surprising vistas of a stately pleasure dome amid the rhododendron-clad grounds.

Portmeirion offers a world-class pottery, while the immediate area is riddled with great little steam trains (particularly the unforgettable Ffestiniog), somehow saved from the heyday of slate mining, and it is also near the majestic ruined Harlech Castle.

Less well known but also worth examining is **Thorpeness**, Suffolk, which was started a little earlier, in 1908, when Glencairn Stuart Ogilvie inherited an estate there and started to build an upmarket holiday village. A lake called the

Meare was created with dozens of little follies on islands and inviting creeks to explore, plus whimsical notices such as 'Beware of the Crocodiles' and 'Peter Pan's Property', but then Ogilvie was a friend of Pan's creator Sir J M Barrie.

You can still hire rowing boats on the Meare. Architecturally, Ogilvie let his penchant for pseudo-Tudory run wild in black-and-white beams, with strange towers and dovecotes here and there. His wittiest gesture must be the House in the Clouds, a glorious sham, really a water tower. Some will say today it's like Disneyland, but of course it's the other way round. Disney is a huge, clever corporation which to some extent vacuums up, blandifies and brilliantly repackages the genius and whims of original eccentrics, with its own creative spin in a simplified, synthetic form to make billions of dollars. Either you like the product or you don't but here and there in the backwaters lurk the fascinating originals, warts and all.

TRAVEL INFORMATION

Anderton Boat Lift, 2½ miles northwest of Northwich, Cheshire
Road From M6 J20, M56 west for one junction, south on A559, Anderton is signed on left.
Rail Nearest station Northwich (from London Euston, change at Stockport or Crewe and Chester).
Tourist information ☎ 01925 442180.

Balcombe Viaduct, Sussex
Rail Balcombe, from London Victoria.
Road From London M25, M23 to J10 then west on A264 and immediately take B2036 south (left) to Balcombe. Viaduct is on right (west) of lane to Haywards Heath before (north of) Borde Hill Gardens (signposted).
Tourist information ☎ 01273 292599.

Clifton Bridge, Bristol
Rail Bristol Temple Meads, from London Paddington and other centres.
Road From M4 J19 or M5 J17 follow signs for city centre then Clifton.
Tourist information ☎ 0117 926 0767.

Deacon Brodie's Tavern, Royal Mile, Edinburgh
Road From England, follow A1 to end. The Royal Mile (which confusingly is marked on maps with road names such as High Street, but with both at street level) is best tackled on foot, and leads from Holyroodhouse near Waverley station to the unmissable Edinburgh Castle at the top of the hill. By the way, if you have children or ever were one, the Museum of Childhood on the way up is well done and free.
Rail From London King's Cross to Edinburgh Waverley, and from many other centres.
Tourist information ☎ 0131 473 3800.

Edinburgh Dovecot
Road Off A8 between the city centre and the bypass.
Rail South Gyle station, two stops from Edinburgh Waverley.
Tourist information ☎ 0131 473 3800.

Foxton staircase, Leicestershire
Road From M1 J20, take A4304 east towards Market Harborough, turn left (north) at Lubenham to Foxton, then take lane to Gumley and access towpath from humpback bridge. Involves some walking.
Tourist information ✆ 01536 410266.

Glenfinnan Viaduct, near Mallaig, West Highland Line
Stunning scenery, plus Glenfinnan Monument to Bonnie Prince Charlie's Jacobites.
Rail Glenfinnan station, on Glasgow–Mallaig line. Because of the horseshoe curve, you can see the viaduct well from the train.
Road On A830 to Mallaig from Fort William, reached by A82 from Glasgow.
Tourist information ✆ 01687 462170.

Hammersmith Bridge and Monument, London W6
Road Just south of A4 flyover, continuation of M4.
Tube/bus District, Piccadilly and Metropolitan lines, or Hammersmith bus station.

Lanhydrock Lodge, Bodmin, Cornwall; ✆ 01208 73320
Road Signed off A38 Exeter (M5)–Bodmin road near Bodmin.
Rail/bus Bodmin Parkway on main London Paddington and other centres to Penzance line.
Tourist information ✆ 01208 76616.

Lingfield Lock-up, Surrey
Road Just north of East Grinstead, reached from London and M25 J6 via A22.
Rail/bus Lingfield station, London Victoria–East Grinstead line.
Tourist information ✆ 01342 410121.

Longest pub name, Ashbourne, Derbyshire
Road From M1 J24 or J25, enter Derby, go round ring road and leave on A52 for 13 miles to Ashbourne.
Rail/bus Nearest station Derby (London St Pancras), then bus 107.
Tourist information ✆ 01335 343666.

Middlesbrough Transporter Bridge
Rail Middlesbrough (from London Kings Cross, change at Darlington).
Road From A1(M) near Darlington, A66(M) and A66 round Darlington.
Tourist information ✆ 01642 245432.

Monnow Bridge Lock-up and Watchtower, Monmouth, Gwent
Road From M5 J8, west on M50, then A40.
Rail/bus Newport, Hereford or Abergavenny, then bus. Times and route numbers vary.
Tourist information ✆ 01600 713899.

North Lodge, Arbroath, Angus
See Fraser Mausoleum, page 106. North Lodge is in Westway on the left.

Pangbourne Lock-up, Berkshire
Road From M4 J12, go southwest a mile to Theale, then left (north) to Pangbourne on A340. The lock-up is up the hill to the left as you enter village, but remember it is a private house (in garden on right).
Rail From London Paddington to Pangbourne.
Tourist information ✆ 0118 9566226.

Phantassie Doocot, Preston Mill, East Linton, Lothian; ☎ 01620 860426
Road Off A1 at East Linton, 23 miles east of Edinburgh.
Tourist information ☎ 0131 473 3800.

Pontcysyllte Aqueduct, Llangollen
Rail Nearest stations Ruabon or Chirk.
Road From M6 J10A, M54 then A5.
Tourist information ☎ 01978 860828.

Portmeirion, Gwynedd, at northeast corner of Wales' beautiful, sandy Cardigan Bay;
☎ 01766 770228
Road From M6 J20, use M56 and M53 to Chester, A55 along north Wales coast to
Bangor then A487 to Porthmadog.
Rail Porthmadog, reached by superb scenic coastal branch line from Machynlleth, and
thus from central England and London Euston. Or from North Coast line via branch to
Blaenau Ffestiniog and then narrow gauge steam railway through hills.
Tourist information ☎ 01766 512981.

Rendlesham Hall Lodges, Suffolk (private homes)
Road On A1152 Woodbridge–Tunstall road, the first northeast of Eyke, and the second
1¹/₂ miles further.
Rail/bus From London Liverpool St to Woodbridge (change at Ipswich), then hourly 81
bus from nearby Turban Centre.
Tourist information ☎ 01394 382240.

Royal Albert Bridge, Saltash, Cornwall
Rail Saltash from London Paddington.
Road Next to A38 bridge into Cornwall, from Plymouth. Parking nearby.
Tourist information ☎ 01752 266030.

Shenley Lock-up, Hertfordshire
Road Shenley is 3 miles from M25 J22 via B556 and B5376.
Rail/bus Nearest station Radlett (London Thameslink or St Pancras), then about a mile
walk up to Shenley or cab.
Tourist information ☎ 01727 864511.

Stag Lodge, Wimbledon, London SW19 (private home)
Road South towards Wimbledon from A3 London–Portsmouth at Tibbet's Corner
roundabout, Putney (don't take A3 underpass). Take Church Rd left at Wimbledon
village, then St Mary's Rd right.
Rail/tube Turn right walking from Wimbledon station (London Waterloo mainline or
District Line), up Wimbledon Hill Rd, turn fifth right into Woodside and first left into St
Mary's Rd.

Swanage Lock-up, Dorset
Seaside town in interesting Isle of Purbeck (typically, not an island).
Road From London/M25, take M3 to end, M27 and A31 west to Winterbourne Zelston,
go south on B3075 through Wareham. Or stop at Norden and use steam railway.
Rail/bus Nearest station Wareham on London Waterloo–Weymouth line, then bus 142,
143, 144. Through trains coming soon.
Tourist information ☎ 01929 422885. web: swanage.com

Tardebigge flight of locks, Worcestershire
Road From M5 J5, take A38 northwards to Bromsgrove, then A448 right (east) towards Redditch and canal crosses under road after about 2 miles. Locks to southwest. Best seen from minor roads or from towpath.
Rail Bromsgrove, from Birmingham New Street.
Tourist information ✆ 01527 831809.

Tealing Dovecot, Angus
Road Off the Forfar A90 road, about 2 miles out of Dundee.
Rail/bus Nearest station Dundee (London King's Cross–Aberdeen line), then bus 20a.
Tourist information ✆ 01382 527527.

Temple Newsam Dovecote and Rare Breeds Centre, Leeds, West Yorkshire
Road From M1 J46 take A63 towards Leeds.
Rail/bus Leeds, from London King's Cross and other centres, then 27 bus direct on Sun or 83 bus weekdays with ³/₄-mile walk.
Tourist information ✆ 0113 242 5242.

Thorpeness, near Aldeburgh, Suffolk
Road From London/M25, A12 to Friday Street beyond Woodbridge, right on A1094 to Aldeburgh, then coast road north 1¹/₂ miles.
Rail/bus Nearest station Saxmundham, then bus 81 (or catch same bus from Ipswich bus station).
Tourist information ✆ 01728 453637.

Tixall Gatehouse, near Stafford, across the Staffordshire and Worcester Canal from Shugborough (see Landmark Trust, page 225)

Transportation bridges, Dorset. Several locations including **Wool**
Rail Wool, from London Waterloo and other centres.
Road From M3 south end, go west on M27, then A31, A348 along back of Poole, to Wareham on A351, then A352 towards Dorchester. Turn right before level crossing.
Tourist information: ✆ 01929 552740

Victoria Gate Lodge, Hyde Park, London W1
Road Off Bayswater Rd.
Rail/bus Nearest tube Lancaster Gate (Central Line) and many buses.

Wheatley Lock-up, near Oxford
Road Off A40 London–Oxford road 3 miles before Oxford.
Rail/bus On London–Oxford coach routes. Nearest railway station: Oxford, then local bus.
Tourist information ✆ 01865 726871.

Willington Dovecote, near Bedford; ✆ 01234 838278. Open through the National Trust only by appointment.
Road Off A603 Bedford–Sandy (for A1) road.
Rail/bus Nearest stations Bedford and Sandy, from London St Pancras or King's Cross respectively
Tourist information ✆ 01234 215226.

Monumentally Eccentric

OBSCURE OBSOLETE OBELISKS

Obelisks are wonderfully useless things. Typically tall, tapering four-sided pillars finished with a pyramid, they were set up to make a point, mark something, or recall an event or an individual. As these have been totally forgotten in the case of thousands of obelisks tucked away here and there around Britain, it follows that the pillars are mostly useless – except to be hunted down by the incurably curious.

Forgotten stones and tales of heroes

However, not all wayside monuments deserve their obscurity. Many dusty, worn-down memorials are worth a second look because they mark something that really changed the world.

'Iron Mad' John Wilkinson was one of the 18th century's great ironfounders and an outspoken enthusiast for the metal which he knew had a far greater future than his contemporaries could comprehend. He was scoffed at for claiming that iron would make a fine boat and defied derision to launch the first one on the River Winster, watched by crowds who expected it to sink like a stone. Of course it didn't, and all the world's ships are descended from that heroic vision.

At **Lindale**, near Grange-over-Sands, Cumbria, can be seen Wilkinson's obelisk. It is made of iron, of course.

At Wadesmill in Hertfordshire, forgotten beside a thundering road, there is a monument to an inspiration which led to a worldwide crusade, several wars, including to a large extent the American Civil War, and to freedom for millions of oppressed people.

It was here, as a small obelisk states, that **Thomas Clarkson** (1760–1846) decided to devote the remainder of his life to abolishing slavery. Seeing a horse flogged up the long dusty hill may have provided the impetus, but this was the spot. William Wilberforce, who schoolchildren have ever since been taught was the driving force behind the abolition of slavery, was in fact a latecomer. There's another more elaborate monument at Clarkson's birthplace, at Wisbech, Cambridgeshire.

The Alleluia Monument near Mold, six miles from Flint, commemorates the defeat of the heathen picts by early Christians shouting Alleluia. It is an 18th-century obelisk set in a field a mile to the west of the village. (If you like obscure monuments, nearby, on Moel Fammau, five miles to the west of

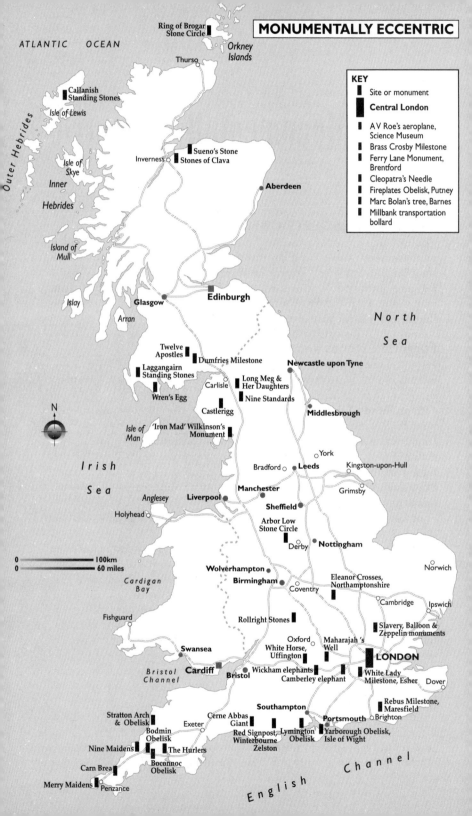

MONUMENTALLY ECCENTRIC

ATLANTIC OCEAN

Ring of Brogar Stone Circle

Orkney Islands

Thurso

KEY

▌ Site or monument

█ **Central London**

▌ A V Roe's aeroplane, Science Museum

▌ Brass Crosby Milestone

▌ Ferry Lane Monument, Brentford

▌ Cleopatra's Needle

▌ Fireplates Obelisk, Putney

▌ Marc Bolan's tree, Barnes

▌ Millbank transportation bollard

Callanish Standing Stones

Isle of Lewis

Outer Hebrides

Isle of Skye

Inner Hebrides

Sueno's Stone

Inverness Stones of Clava

Aberdeen

Island of Mull

Islay Arran

Glasgow **Edinburgh**

Irish Sea

Twelve Apostles

Dumfries Milestone

Laggangairn Standing Stones

Wren's Egg

Newcastle upon Tyne

Long Meg & Her Daughters

Carlisle Nine Standards

Castlerigg

Isle of Man

'Iron Mad' Wilkinson's Monument

Middlesbrough

York

Bradford **Leeds** Kingston-upon-Hull

Anglesey

Liverpool **Manchester**

Holyhead **Sheffield** Grimsby

Arbor Low Stone Circle

Derby **Nottingham**

North Sea

N

0 ——— 100km
0 ——— 60 miles

Cardigan Bay

Fishguard

Wolverhampton
Birmingham
Coventry

Eleanor Crosses, Northamptonshire

Cambridge Ipswich

Norwich

Rollright Stones

Slavery, Balloon & Zeppelin monuments

Swansea

Cardiff **Bristol**

Oxford Maharajah's Well

White Horse, Uffington

LONDON

Wickham elephants
Camberley elephant

White Lady Milestone, Esher

Dover

Bristol Channel

Southampton

Rebus Milestone, Maresfield

Stratton Arch & Obelisk

Cerne Abbas Giant

Exeter

Bodmin Obelisk

Red Signpost, Winterbourne Zelston

Portsmouth Brighton

Lymington Obelisk

Yarborough Obelisk, Isle of Wight

Nine Maidens

The Hurlers

Carn Brea Boconnoc Obelisk

Merry Maidens Penzance

English Channel

Mold, can be found the remains of a mega-obelisk built for George III's jubilee. Its base has walls 12ft thick and it stood atop a hill 1,820ft high. If you like the idea of Christians beating heathens, read about Leith Hill Tower in Chapter 11.)

Miles away in Sutherland, another violent turn in history is marked by the Wolf Monument. On the side of the road from Golspie to Helmsdale, south of the bottom of Glen Loth, the stone placed by the Duke of Portland in 1924 records that at this spot the last wolf in the county was slain in 1700. The last wolf on the British mainland was killed in 1743. Wildlife nuts are now considering reintroducing the beasts. Over *their* dead bodies, I hope

For a poignant Welsh wolf story, go to Beddgelert in Snowdonia, walk a short way along the banks of the Afon (River) Glaslyn, and look for a mound of stones. This is the grave of Prince Llywelyn's faithful dog Gelert. Llywelyn returned from hunting one day, having left his beloved and faithful hound Gelert to guard his infant son in his cradle. He found the cradle upturned, the boy gone and the dog's mouth covered with gore. In his fury, he unsheathed his sword and cut off Gelert's head with one huge blow. Then he discovered a dead wolf nearby, which Gelert had fought to the death to protect the child, who was asleep unharmed under the cradle.

London's simply capital obelisks and their stories

London has its fair share of redundant yet curious obelisks. For example, in 1851 it was ringed by hundreds of Coal Dues obelisks and markers of four different designs in 1851 to mark a point – you can't avoid the word – on every road, railway or canal 20 miles from the general post office in St Martin's-le-Grand. It's all the fault of the Great Fire of London in 1666, after which the City of London Corporation was empowered to levy tax on coal or wine brought within a certain distance of London to pay for rebuilding.

In 1851, because of the sprawl of London, an act laid down the 20-mile radius still marked with four types of pillar, post or obelisk, all bearing the City arms or at least the crusader shield, red cross on white with a dagger. To complicate matters, some of them were moved slightly in 1861 to coincide with the boundary of the new Metropolitan Police area, so posts such as that on Watling Street, Radlett, still have a function today. It marks where the shire Mr Plods take over from the Old Bill of the Met, often, as here, nowhere near the actual county boundary.

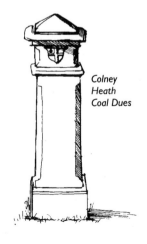

Colney
Heath
Coal Dues

More impressive are the 14ft stone Coal Dues obelisks such as the one alongside the London–Norwich main line at Chadwell Heath on the boundary of Barking and Havering boroughs; or that beside the main line at Watford, which refers on its inscription to the Coal and Wine Duties Act of 1861 (which must have updated earlier laws) and which demanded 11*d* (4½ pence in today's coin, but then a week's pay for some) for every ton of coal which rolled past southwards.

Like most taxes dreamed up for a specific purpose, the Coal Dues carried on long after the original point of the obelisks was forgotten, and were finally abolished in 1889, although we have the heritage of splendid Wren churches such as St Paul's to thank them for.

Even the dullest London suburbs are riddled with obelisks, if you know where to look, to testify to the great dramas that once happened there. A misty Sunday morning in Barnet doesn't sound too dramatic, but an obelisk at nearby Monken Hadley tells of the desperate struggle of April 14 1471, when the Earl of Warwick's army during the Wars of the Roses attacked under the cover of mist and drove Edward IV's men right back into Barnet town centre. A swift cavalry counterattack had the Lancastrians retreating, with Warwick caught on foot and slain close to where the obelisk stands. Some 1,500 men died in a battle that helped end the Wars of the Roses.

More than 200 years later a very different rebellion was crushed in 1715 and the Earl of Derwentwater was executed for taking part. An obelisk to him stands incongruously in the suburbia of Churchfield Road East, Acton.

Nearby quiet Brentford seems just as anxious to stress its blood-soaked history. In **Ferry Lane** by the Thames there's a pillar recalling how Cassivellaunus and his men repelled Julius Caesar and his centurions who were trying to ford the river at this point in 54BC; *plus* another battle fought by King Edmund 'Ironsides' against the raping and pillaging Danes in 1016; *and* commemorating the Civil War Battle of Brentford in 1642. At the time of writing Ferry Lane is being redeveloped, so the monument has been moved. See page 187.

Two London obelisks have odd royal connotations. **Cleopatra's Needle**, on the Thames Embankment near to Embankment tube, had nothing to do with Queen Cleopatra, but is a fascinating 15th-century BC relic which survived being moved by the Romans in 14BC – just after that first battle of

Cleopatra's Needle

Brentford. It was taken to England in 1878 in a sort of submarine and was nearly sunk in a storm, only to be covered in pollution and be damaged by German bombs after it arrived. Its twin was erected in Central Park, New York, in 1881.

Much more obscure is an obelisk lurking in the woods near **Tibbet's Corner** on A3 near Putney. It tells of the time when David Hartley invited the king and

queen to breakfast in 1774 and while they were eating upstairs tried to burn the house down – for which he was richly rewarded. He was voted the then fortune of £2,500 in cash by a grateful parliament and awarded the freedom of the City of London by the Corporation.

The royals, George III and Queen Charlotte, had agreed to Hartley's experiment because he wanted to demonstrate his fireplates which, he claimed, made a fireproof floor. To the great relief of courtiers, he was proved right. George III was yet to become completely mad, but if the fireplates had failed, Britain might have been even more grateful. The American colonies might not have been lost in the following nine years with a more reasonable monarch on the throne. Come to think of it, maybe the Americans should build Mr Hartley an obelisk too.

A Cornish point to be made

Good obelisk country is where you have hills to put them on, rock to build them with, money to pay for them and derring-do deeds to commemorate. Cornwall qualifies on all four counts, if in variable quantity.

A noble 123ft obelisk was erected at **Boconnoc**, near Lostwithiel, in 1771 by Lord Camelford in memory of his uncle, surpassed at **Bodmin** by a 144ft granite specimen in 1856 in memory of Walter Raleigh Gilbert, lieutenant-general of the Bengal Army. An arch and obelisk at **Stratton** commemorate the 1643 Civil War battle where, it is recorded: 'Ye army of ye rebells under ye command of ye Earl of Stamford receiv'd a signall overthrou by ye valour of Sr Bevill Granville and ye Cornish Army.' The good news is that ye obelisk has not been overthroun yet.

At **Carn Brea**, a spectacular viewpoint a little southwest of Carnbrea village, itself a little southwest of Redruth, a 90ft column erected by a grateful Cornwall in 1836 celebrates not much happening in the Peninsular War – being the Spanish peninsula, not the Cornish one. Lesser in stature but a greater storyteller is a 12ft-high obelisk atop an isolated tomb in the middle of a field at Botusfleming near Saltash. A long-winded inscription explains that it is the grave of Dr William Martyn of Plymouth who died in 1762. After saying what a good chap he was, it goes on:

'He lived and died a Catholic Christian, in the true and not depraved Popish sense of the word, and had no susperstitious veneration for Church or Churchyard ground, and willing by his example to lessen the unreasonable esteem which some poor men and women through prejudice of education often show for it in frequently parting with the earning of many a hard day's work.'

As well as possibly causing the first repetitive strain injury in a stonemason making the inscription, Dr Martyn must have spent a good deal more than the cost of a regular churchyard grave. But he had a point to be made with his obelisk, and even reserved the field and monument in perpetuity, so no future vicar could remove him to a hated churchyard. (There is no public right of way.) He was ahead of his time, and the Victorian bulging churchyard crisis eventually led to huge commercial cemeteries around London, of which he would have approved (see Chapter 5), and the eccentric concept of cremation, for which he expressed no burning desire.

For a Cornish obelisk lodge, see page 160.

When MPs were heroes

Travellers from the Isle of Wight (itself home to an insanely large and superbly sited obelisk to the not very interesting **Earl of Yarborough** on beautiful Bembridge Down), are greeted by another well-sited obelisk across the harbour from **Lymington**, Hampshire – a remarkably fine one it is too, looking as if it were built in 1980, not in 1840. It is up a road near the ferry terminal called, helpfully, Monument Lane. Perhaps its stonework is still superb because, as stated on the base, 'this monument was erected by Adelaide the Queen Dowager and their Royal Highnesses the Duchess of Gloucester and Princess Augusta'.

It was built in memory of Admiral Sir Harry Burrard Neale, who died in

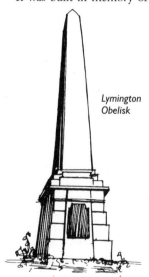

Lymington
Obelisk

February 1840 aged 75, and details his achievements at sinking or capturing 20 enemy men o' war and also keeping the crew of HMS *San Fiorenzo* loyal during what is euphemistically described on the monument as 'the critical position of the Fleet at the Nore in 1797'. I suspect they meant the worst mutiny the Royal Navy has ever seen, but such things were best not mentioned in front of Royal Highnesses. Sir Harry was Lymington's MP for 40 years, and the monument details the war hero's charity at great length. 'He delivered the poor and fatherless and him who had none to help him and caused the widow's heart to sing for joy ... His daily walk with God exemplifying the grace of his Christian charity, above all in the largeness of his charity and the beauty of his humility.'

Not much like today's MPs, then.

MILESTONES IN ECCENTRICITY

Milestones may be apparently less eccentric than obelisks – at least they have a purpose. But those which don't tell you where they are measuring to – or give completely wrong or irrelevant distances – must be considered a little odd.

Many a traveller on A22 between London and Eastbourne has been puzzled by milestones, such as that besides a pub in **Maresfield**, that show a mileage plus a ribbon tied in a bow and some bells hanging from it. The design may have been a rebus – a visual pun – spelling out the Bow Bells, the spot in the City of London to which mileages were traditionally measured; or it may simply have been making allowance for the mass illiteracy that also meant most pub or shop signs were objects – such as a boot for a shoemaker – or pictures, such as a White Horse for a pub.

The **Brass Crosby Milestone** that is neither brass nor tells accurate mileages from where it is, despite distances shown on it being detailed down to the last foot, can be found in St George's Road, London SE1 right outside the Imperial War Museum.

It is named after the lord mayor of London, Brass Crosby, who became a national hero in 1771 when he refused parliament's order to jail a printer who dared to report their proceedings in the press. Brass Crosby was thrown into the Tower but public outcry assured his release, and he eventually won his campaign for the free reporting of parliament. The milestone – more of an obelisk in size – was set up in St George's Circus as a memorial to him, but removed during rebuilding in 1905 to its present site, making the rather precise measurements on it singularly useless.

The present spot may have been chosen because during Crosby's life the War Museum was the original Bedlam lunatic asylum (a corruption of Bethlehem giving its name), and Crosby was appointed president of the asylum in 1772, helping the process of reform. So when people say parliamentary debates sound 'like Bedlam' on the radio, they are paying tribute to two different milestones, so to speak, of British life where Brass Crosby went the extra mile.

To complicate matters further, the parishioners around St George's Circus built a replica of the Crosby milestone, not near the original site, but at **Brookwood Cemetery** in Surrey where in the 19th-century parishioners started to be buried. Now that one has fallen down, but at least it doesn't bear wrong distances to anywhere.

The White Lady of Esher in Surrey is one of the most ridiculously over-the-top large milestones in the country and can be found outside the Café Rouge at the junction of Portsmouth Road and Station Road. It was set up by the Duke of Newcastle not so much to help the general traveller on the

Portsmouth Road but to mark his estate. He was fed up with travellers from London missing the turning and ending up in Guildford.

Some milestones dating from the horse and carriage age are odd because they give odd distances. One at Dumfries, fixed to the side of the Midsteeple in the pedestrianised town centre, from where one might contemplate a day's ride to Castle Douglas or Carlisle, in fact gives the distance to Huntingdon, a town of little global import – not until local MP John Major became prime minister, and, arguably, even after that – in Cambridgeshire, hundreds of miles away.

Another at Craven Arms, Shropshire, shows off somewhat esoteric mileages to 36 places, such as 233 to Newcastle. Maybe these were not craven nonsense but forerunners of those tourist signposts at places such as Land's End or the South Pole giving distances to world capitals in thousands of miles. But, even so, why Huntingdon?

Other milestones could double up as something else – the combined monument, parish pump and milestone at Ampthill, Bedfordshire, being the Swiss army knife of the genre.

CONVICTS AND MARTYRS

Australian tourists might pause, ponder and perhaps shudder if they knew the meaning of a couple of wayside monuments, one in pretty Dorset countryside and one near a London tourist honeypot.

On A31 Dorchester–Wimborne road, about eight miles from Wimborne at Winterbourne Zelston, is a **red signpost**, and many passers-by have little idea why authorities paint this one fingerpost in the county red year after year. The answer lies down the lane to Bloxworth, where, some 100 yards from the signpost, Botany Bay Farm lies on the right. A now ruined prison-like barn with narrow window slits was used to house prisoners condemned at Dorchester Assizes to transportation to the Botany Bay penal colony in Australia.

The ragged prisoners were force-marched the 70-odd miles from Dorchester to the prison fleet at Portsmouth and this barn, 14 miles from Dorchester, was the first stop. Prisoners were shackled for the night to the massive central post. It was the first night of suffering of many to come, but life was short for many transportees. Better accommodation can be had nowadays a few hundred yards up the A31 at the Botany Bay Inne.

Nearby at Tolpuddle, a few miles further down the road to Dorchester, can be seen the memorials to the most famous six ever sentenced to transportation – the Tolpuddle martyrs. These six were transported for seven years in 1834 for the crime of forming a prototype trade union to combat poverty and a cut in wages after a bad harvest. This was at a time when children in rural Britain could still die of hunger during famines. The six, led by George Loveless, met under the Martyrs' Oak, as it is now known, outside the church, and the memorial cottages at the west end of Tolpuddle also mark their sacrifice. At the other end of the village a small Methodist chapel dedicated to their memory bears their names carved on its entrance, plus a moving passage from George Loveless's defence: 'We have injured no man's reputation, character, person or property. We were uniting together to preserve ourselves, our wives and our children from utter degradation and starvation.'

What they achieved, by the national outrage that followed their sentence, was the eventual ending of such degradation and starvation for millions of working people in many countries by the growth of trade unionism.

The other place Aussies might pause to recall those bleak days is right outside the Tate Gallery on **Millbank**, on the Thames in London. A squat bollard marks the spot where thousands of prisoners clanking their chains passed 'Down Under' in a special tunnel under the road from Millbank Prison – where the gallery built by the sugar magnate now stands – to barges, which carried them downriver to ships waiting to take them to the other side of the world. This sad traffic ended in 1867. (For more on transportation, see page 157.)

Dorset, famed more for bloody, ruthless 'justice' down the centuries than for today's cream teas and scones, also has excellent statues in Dorchester by Dame Elisabeth Frink of the Dorset Martyrs. But these martyrs are Catholics, who were burnt and hanged for their faith during the post-Reformation years.

SHRINES BY THE WAYSIDE

When the funeral of Diana, Princess of Wales, in 1997 followed a route through north London up the M1 to Northampton, many were surprised by the crowds and flowers that lined every available bridge. But these were soon all gone, with surprisingly few permanent monuments, unlike the tributes to a dead queen who passed this way, in the opposite direction, 600 years previously.

The grieving Edward I, whose beloved queen Eleanor died at Harby in Nottinghamshire, didn't just order one monument but a whole set of **Eleanor Crosses**, intricate Gothic free-standing spires, to be erected at every spot where the funeral cortège stopped for a night. Only three of the original dozen elegant and richly carved spires survive – at Geddington and Hardingstone, near Northampton, and at Waltham Cross, Hertfordshire. The latter place is named after its Eleanor Cross, as is London's Charing Cross. But the soaring spire outside the station of that name is in fact a 19th-century reproduction of a long lost original.

One of London's oddest memorials is a tree in Barnes. It is the one pop star **Marc Bolan** hit in his Mini in 1976, causing his early death. Unlike, say, Jimi Hendrix who died not far away, he didn't become a much bigger star after his death than before, but the flowers, photographs and loving messages tied *daily* to his tree make this London's most enduring unofficial memorial and are quite extraordinary. The effect is a little spoilt by the crash barrier in front of the tree, but given its history, I suppose that's understandable.

There is no footpath on that side of this fast and narrow road, so view from the opposite side unless you wish to join Mr Bolan, formerly of T-Rex, prematurely. Bolan was taken to Golders Green crematorium in northwest London, last venue of many a British star of stage and screen, where he was joined by Keith Moon of The Who only two years later.

CRANKS, PIONEERS AND HEROES OF THE SKIES

Today air travel is a huge, safe and well-organised industry. Yet within living memory, flying was a seemingly impossible dream pursued by hare-brained eccentrics flying – and crashing – dangerous fragile kite-like creations of wood and canvas.

The adventures, tragedies and insanities of Britain's aeronautical eccentrics and adventurers can be traced through the landscape even today, thanks to various monuments. Many of these, including the earliest, are in Hertfordshire.

The first balloon flight in the country ended in 1784 at **Standon Green End**, in a field west of the main road about three miles north of Ware, Hertfordshire. A marker stone surrounded by railings carries a brass plaque engraved with a picture of a balloon and declaring:

> 'Let Posterity Know and Knowing Be Astonished That on the 15th
> Day of September 1784, Vincent Lunardi of Lucca in Tuscany, the
> First Aerial Traveller In Britain Mounting From The Artillery
> Ground in London and Traversing the Regions of the Air for 2 hours
> and 15 minutes In this Spot Revisited the Earth ...'

Lunardi's cat accompanied him on this flight. Whether it found its way home after landing is not recorded but, coincidentally, there are still some Italian names in the area, if not Italian cats. The monument is on private land and the farmer's permission must be sought to visit it.

Not far from this spot of ballooning pilgrimage is another monument, to what happened when the Germans developed the idea more than a century later. During World War I, zeppelins attacked the area – Hertford was blitzed mercilessly in October 1915 with great loss of life and property. Men, women and children died, seemingly defenceless against the merciless monster in the skies. German magazines gleefully published illustrations of British towns and docks burning beneath the great airships, which hovered out of range of gunners.

But airships filled with explosive hydrogen proved spectacularly vulnerable to new-fangled aircraft firing incendiary bullets, and in September 1916 the first zeppelin to be shot down over England fell in flames at Cuffley near Hertford after being attacked by Lt William Leefe Robinson of the Royal Flying Corps. A month later another was shot down nearby at Potters Bar. Leefe Robinson became an instant national hero. He was awarded the Victoria Cross and a fine monument to him was built at **Cuffley**, while a pub called the Leefe Robinson at Harrow Weald, Middlesex also recalls the feat. But the aviator himself, captured on the Western Front, died soon after returning from prison camp at the end of the war.

LLANFAIRPWLLGWYNGYLLGOGERYCHWYRNDROBWLLLLANTYSILIOGOGOGOCH

ST MARYS CHURCH IN THE HOLLOW OF THE WHITE HAZEL NEAR TO THE RAPID WHIRLPOOL OF LLANTYSILIO OF THE RED CAVE

BIDDENDEN

Previous page The Pineapple in Stirlingshire has a seamless stone blend from classical architecture to rampant fruit (AL)

Top Attempts to say this Anglesey place name leave spluttering tourists preferring 'Llanfair PG' (PA)

Above left Siamese twin sisters are remembered in Biddenden's village sign (BL)

Above middle Time stands still at Portmeirion, Wales' fantasy village (PA)

Top right Oxford's wonderful gargoyles are rude, cheeky, holy, bawdy, folksy and, in some cases, brand new (PA)

Above right A stone dog lurks at the rear of North Lodge, Arbroath. (BL)

Left This red signpost in Dorset showed illiterate guards where to chain up their charges for the night (BL)

Fixed-wing aviation was growing up fast but Leefe Robinson's courage was remarkable because Britain's first, faltering, powered flight took place less than ten years before.

The first powered flight in Britain took place on October 16 1908, at Cove Common in Hampshire. The aircraft was British Army No 1 and the pilot the American 'Colonel' Sam Cody, whose flamboyant aviator's garb of white coat and stetson made him the darling of the British public. Cody was attached to the Army's Balloon School at Aldershot and, having demonstrated the art of pulling military observers up into the air by use of chains of kites, he was trying unsuccessfully to demonstrate to British brass hats that aircraft could be used in war.

The secretary of war decided Cody was an American crank and would have to carry on on his own while the Army attended to serious business such as mounted cavalry. Cody, a hugely popular former cowboy, soldiered on with his own money until his point was proved that military aviation really had a future – and a future that Britain, with war looming, must not ignore.

Cody was killed in an air crash at Farnborough in 1913. His official memorial is a tree to which he had tethered his machine for tests in May 1908 before that first powered flight. It is in fact a replica of the tree in, appropriately for the industry, aluminium. His real memorial is the vast Royal Aircraft Establishment which sprang up at the common at Farnborough, and the biennial airshows at which all the world's latest aircraft soar over Cody's grave, proving that he was right all along.

A few months later the first all-British powered flight took place on July 23 1909, when a wooden-frame, paper-wrapped triplane contraption powered by a JAP 9hp motorbike engine took to the air at Walthamstow Marshes in East London. Its pilot, Alliott Verdon Roe, was regarded as a dangerous crank and was dissuaded from using various other sites around the country, but on that day he flew 850ft at an altitude of 10ft and a speed of 25mph, despite Leyton Borough Council's attempts to ban him. A blue plaque marks the spot, fixed on a railway arch where the line crosses the River Lea off Lea Bridge Road, Walthamstow, London E10.

More accessible is the aircraft itself, hanging in the **Science Museum**, South Kensington, like an impossibly fragile kite, with a Cody 1912 biplane and many other pioneering aircraft. A V Roe went on to found the Avro aircraft factory at Wembley, which made winning aircraft for both world wars, including the dambusting Avro Lancaster bombers. Incidentally, he started painting his name on a shed he rented at Brooklands, Surrey, before moving to Wembley, but failed to leave enough room for the final E – hence Avro.

A year later, on July 13 1910, the Honourable Charles Stewart Rolls (1877–1910), aged 32, co-founder of Rolls-Royce, was the first Briton to be killed flying a plane, not long after making the first return crossing of the English Channel. The crash happened in front of a horrified crowd at a Bournemouth competition for the 'alighting prize' by which early aviators attempted to follow a course and land within a 100ft bullseye. Rolls was a little eccentric, and dubbed by his fellow aviator Tommy Sopwith 'the meanest man I know' for his habit of sleeping under his car to avoid having to pay hotel bills.

Back in Hertfordshire, some brave early military flyers are also commemorated by a pillar at the spot where they crashed in 1912, between Willian and Great Wymondley in the north of the same county (Great Wymondley being the little hamlet near the much greater one of Little Wymondley, of course).

Parachuting, surprisingly perhaps, is about a century older than powered flight so the courage of its pioneers was all the greater, but there are few monuments to their heroic balloon-based experiments. In 1802, André-Jacques Garnerin made the first parachute descent in Britain, having started the new sport in Paris in 1797. He ascended beneath his balloon from Grosvenor Square, jumped out and landed near the site of today's Marylebone station, to the amazement of onlookers.

Thirty-five years later, Robert Cocking, the first Briton to make a successful parachute jump, failed to make the first successful landing. His inverted cone chute collapsed and trailed him to his death in a Kentish field. The first totally successful British parachutist was John Hampton, a year after Cocking's death, but it was nearly a century later before the air force fell for the idea.

What is definitely not an aeronautical monument is the forest of obelisks in west London's Brompton Cemetery, which I once tried to convince a credulous drunken tourist was a defence against zeppelins. 'Don't touch them, or rusty giant springs will hurl them skywards,' I said as we saw in the New Year at this unlikely venue. But any World War I zeppelin bombing victims buried in the cemetery were probably blown to pieces again in World War II in 1941. A visit to the Earl's Court end of the cemetery will show many a tomb bearing shrapnel damage, and several tell how they were rebuilt when a stick of Luftwaffe bombs violently raised the dead.

UNLIKELY JUMBOS

Elephants, we are told, are getting pretty damn rare. But some of the world's oddest are not roaming the African plains but are lurking forgotten in three locations not far from prosaic old Reading, Berkshire. And I'm not referring to Elephant and Castle pubs, which are relatively common – indeed there is one within this triangle of eccentric beasts – but real oddities: elephants that you'll never forget.

The first, at Stoke Row, near Nettlebed in Oxfordshire across the Thames from Reading, has its origins in a casual conversation in 1850s India and a boy being clipped round the head by a Stoke Row 'tigress'. The magnificent **Maharajah's Well** in this English village is the most unlikely thing you could expect in the sleepy Chilterns back roads. A 23ft-high bright gilded dome covers the winding machinery, which is surmounted by a cast-iron elephant, and underneath is a well dug entirely by hand, which at 368ft deep is deeper than St Paul's Cathedral is high.

The after-dinner conversation between the Maharajah of Benares and the Lieutenant-Governor of the North Western Provinces, Mr Edward Reade, turned on how Mr Reade's native Chilterns suffered from the same water shortages that troubled the maharajah's people and recalled how an urchin had been beaten (by a woman known as a tigress) for taking an unauthorised drink in hot weather, such was the bother of getting clean water in these remote English villages. Washing days were sometimes indefinitely postponed.

Maharajah's Well

Hence the maharajah's generous offer to build such a splendid well, which served villagers for 70 years until piped water arrived. The well yielded some 700 gallons daily. It cost the then vast sum of £353 13s and 7d, the machinery and elephant £39 10s 0d and the warden's cottage – a pleasing octagonal building with a central chimney like a biscuit jar – just £74 14s 6d.

It started a small craze for wealthy Indians to construct wells and drinking fountains throughout England, and many lie covered and rusting in churchyards while others adorn London's Royal Parks. But none of the others is adorned, so far as I know, by an elephant.

Incidentally, Mr Reade had already built a well for Indian villagers and the Oxfordshire locals have raised money for similar projects in recent years.

The second odd elephant in the region is also connected with water supply, or trunk sewerage perhaps, but is more prosaic. To the south of Reading, near **Camberley**, Surrey, an elephant made from proprietary concrete pipe sections stands patiently beside A30, forlornly advertising a pipe works.

(Incidentally, watch out for a 35ft-high lion if you are stalking through this elephantine triangle. The cast-iron lion at Forbury Gardens, Reading, is a monument to a massacred local regiment.)

The third site for surprising elephants in the area is at the quite extraordinary **Wickham church**, set in a lonely hamlet about seven miles west of Newbury. The church of St Swithun's contains a small herd of eight which adorn the hammerbeam ends in the north aisle, an odd addition to this jumble of architectural styles. These range from Roman stonework in the Saxon tower to Victorian high gothic of the highest quality in the interior. Apparently, when William Nicholson was restoring the church in 1845, he wanted to put angels on the beam ends, but while at the Paris Exhibition he

instead fell in love with four papier-mâché elephants in full processional dress, originally brightly coloured although now faded. He ordered four more and the result would have made the Maharajah of Benares feel most at home, but may not have been Berkshire villagers' exact concept of angels.

As for the origin of Elephant and Castle pub names, no one can remember what it was, although there is a whole district and a tube station thus named in south London. The most credible explanation is that it referred to the Infanta de Castilla, a Spanish princess who was a royal bride. It seems credible after a few pints, anyway.

BRITAIN'S TEN MOST MAGICAL (AND LEAST KNOWN) STANDING STONES

Every tourist comes to Britain having heard of Stonehenge, and quickly finds out that Avebury (see page 116) not so far away offers another great circle of stones. But both of these, impressive though they are, have their once mystical setting spoiled by cars, roads, gift shops and, yes, tourists. Luckily Britain is host to many, many more standing stones and stone circles where the only other visitor apart from you may well be a curly horned sheep. There, alone in spectacular landscape or humble farmland, you may contemplate the mysteries behind it all and the strange legends attached to these special places.

The Hurlers, Cornwall
On the east edge of Bodmin Moor, near Minions, off B3254. This supposedly represents a group of men throwing a ball on the Sabbath who were petrified for their sacrilege. Also in Cornwall are the **Nine Maidens**, south of A39 between Wadebridge and St Columb Major, before reaching B3274, and the **Merry Maidens**, a perfect circle of maidens turned to stone for, you guessed, dancing on Sunday. These are south of B3315, 4 miles southeast of Penzance. You can even visit them on Sundays, if you're not too petrified. There seems to be confusion about the legend for the Nine Maidens, which are one of several rings of stones thus named in Cornwall even when the number clearly isn't nine. But the Merry Maidens legend is secure and long-lived. There are two more stones, granite pillars called the Pipers, nearby which were devils which played a tune on a summer Sabbath evening to trick the maidens into dancing. A bolt of lightning came down and petrified the lot. Aubrey Burl, the learned scholar of

CURIOSITIES IN CHALK

The cutting of **white horses** on hillsides – leucipottomy – may not be regarded by the British as eccentric, but it surely is, as each one takes a whole bunch of people about two weeks to carve and needs to be maintained to stop it grassing over.

The best, oldest (probably Bronze Age) and most famous is the one at Uffington, Oxfordshire, and when you consider that you need steep, grass-covered chalk hills, plus people with rather odd priorities, it's not surprising that there are 12 in the south of England. There is a herd of eight in Wiltshire, and one of these is brand new, that at Devizes, carved in 1999.

Little-known outriders are at Kilburn, North Yorkshire, and, I'm told, at Strichen, Aberdeenshire. Non-equine contenders include the particularly curious Long Man of Wilmington, Sussex (south of the A276 just west of Eastbourne), a lion at Whipsnade, Bedfordshire, and odd regimental badges around Salisbury Plain; but the best of these has to be the **Cerne Giant**, Dorset. The huge figure of prehistoric origins carries a massive club but is more memorable for his whopping great sexual organ. I'm surprised the Victorians didn't have it dug up. (By the 20th century, many of the Piddles in nearby place names had long been changed to Puddles by prim and prudish Dorset folk, but in less self-consciously genteel villages the Piddle part remains unashamed.)

Back to the giant. The legend locally is that if a barren woman sleeps on the said organ for the night, she'll be pregnant before the year's end. If it is true, then the giant doesn't seem responsible, because the delightful countryside around Cerne Abbas doesn't feature lots of yokel offspring walking around holding huge implements. On May Day the Wessex Morris Men dance on the Cerne Giant at 07.00, then dance through the village beating the ground to 'awaken the spring', ending in the square at 09.00. But then May Day is a good day for West Country fertility dances generally (see page 12).

The outline is best viewed after the local girl guides or whoever have whitewashed the lines, as it can get a bit grey at times. In the beautiful village, by the way, they sell delicious Dorset Knobs, which are good with butter.

The names of the nearby villages are equally eccentric: the nearest are Up Cerne, Minterne Parva, Piddletrenthide, Nether Cerne, Minterne Magna, Up Sydling. You couldn't make them up. I'm just glad they didn't put the giant 6 miles northeast, at Droop.

such stones (see *Further Reading*, page 235), records that locals said that two stones dislodged in the mid-19th century returned of their volition, and that when an attempt was made to plough the field in World War I, the horse dropped dead as the first furrow was started. These are typical of the legends of Celtic stones and the supposed dangers of disturbing them.

Tourist information (Bodmin) ☎ 01208 76616; *(Penzance)* ☎ 01736 362207

The Twelve Apostles, Dumfries

A couple of miles north of Dumfries on A76, turn left at Holywood following B729 towards Dunscore for 400 yards. Roadside car parking, waymark and a stile over the dyke. A rather special spot, but that name: someone couldn't count to twelve, or has nicked a stone, and how did the Bronze Age people know the twelve Apostles were going to exist thousands of years later? So what were these stones, put here with such huge effort, really for?

Tourist information ☎ 01387 253862.

Stones of Clava, Inverness-shire

Near Culloden Battlefield, off B851 which turns northeast from A9 a couple of miles south of Inverness. These strange domed cairns surrounded by circles of standing stones are late neolithic. Nearby, **Sueno's Stone**, at Forres near A96, off the road to Findhorn, is judged the most remarkable sculptured stone in Britain and dates from about AD1,000. It is a shaft of sandstone carved with battle scenes and has been covered by glass to protect it.

Tourist information ☎ 01463 234353.

Callanish Standing Stones, Lewis, Western Isles

Beside A858, reached via ferry from Ullapool. In a wild moorland setting, 13 stones stand huddled in groups around what was probably a burial cairn, with rows of stones extending to north, south and in other directions. Atmospheric in the extreme. There is another stone circle nearby at Siadar on the north coast of Lewis, off A857.

Tourist information ☎ 01851 703088.

Nine Standards, Cumbria

On the Pennine watershed to north of B6270 between Kirkby Stephen and Keld. There is nothing more spooky than plodding across the boggy mountaintop in the mist and seeing these nine shapes taller than a man, created by God knows whom, loom up suddenly and menacingly and then disappear again in a swirl of cloud.

Tourist information ☎ 0176 8371199.

Long Meg and her Daughters, Cumbria

North of the road between Little Salkeld and Gamblesby, about 7 miles northeast of Penrith. Long Meg was a witch and the other stones her coven, but not a very powerful witch if she was petrified. For an absolutely lovely setting nearby, visit **Castlerigg Stone Circle** about 16 miles on the other side of Penrith, going west on A66 just before Keswick. To south of road near Briery. *Tourist information* ✆ 01768 867466.

Rollright Stones, Oxfordshire

West of A3400 Oxford–Stratford-upon-Avon road, helpfully between the villages of Little Rollright and Great Rollright. Unexpected, somehow, these stones lie in a less bleak setting than usual, and are full of legend. For a start there are said to be 77 stones, but they have never been counted to the same number twice. You try it. The King's Men are a ring of standing stones about 30 yards across, and were supposedly the army of the king, who is now the bent and lonely King Stone some 300 yards away. He was promised a new kingdom by a witch if he could see Long Compton from where he was. Having strained and strained, the king moved up the hill a little and was petrified, as was his army. On a hot summer's night, the stones are said to rush down to a nearby brook to drink. Nearby, the whispering knights huddle in a sinister conspiracy – unless they are remains of a massive burial barrow. *Tourist information* ✆ 01608 644379.

Wren's Egg Standing Stones, Dumfries and Galloway

One mile north of the coastal village of Monreith on A747 between Stranraer and Whithorn, on private land at Blair Buy farm. These are included if only for the charming name, but this is a good area for standing stones. About 10 miles north, **Torhouse Stone Circle** is south of B733 between Bladnoch and Clugston, 2 miles west of Wigtown and on the Southern Upland Way long-distance footpath, the **Laggangairn Standing Stones** are at Killgallioch about 5 miles' hike from Knowe on the way to Stranraer. These two are very early Christian stones. Access is difficult through forestry, although there are some signposts. *Tourist information* ✆ 01671 402431.

Ring of Brogar Stone Circle, Orkney Islands

About 5 miles northeast of Stromness. A magnificent, well-preserved ring of upright stones in a beautiful setting. In some ways this is better than Stonehenge, with no tourists and no admission charge; these islands are littered with impressive stones and magnificent chambered cairns that would be packed with visitors if nearer to greater populations. *Tourist information* ✆ 01856 850716.

Arbor Low Stone Circle, Peak District, Derbyshire

East of A515 Buxton–Ashbourne road and south of a minor road from A515 to Youlgreave. Spectacular setting at about 1,200ft high, signposted from A515, but the stones themselves are less spectacular, indeed not standing at all, having all toppled. *Tourist information* ✆ 01629 813227.

For more eccentric stone circles, see page 146.

TRAVEL INFORMATION

Note: The promised right-to-roam legislation may change freedom to wander around in England and Wales precisely at these kind of remote locations. Meanwhile, you have a perfect right to follow the established access paths.

Balloon Monument, Standon Green End, Hertfordshire
Road To east of A10 old London–Cambridge road just south of Puckeridge. Get farmer's permission.
Tourist information ↘ 01992 584322.

Boconnoc Obelisk, near Lostwithiel, Cornwall
Road From M5, A38 then A390. Obelisk is to south before Lostwithiel.
Rail Lostwithiel, from London Paddington and other centres.
Tourist information ↘ 01208 872207.

Bodmin Obelisk, Cornwall
Road A38 to Bodmin from end of M5.
Rail Bodmin Parkway, from London Paddington and other centres.
Tourist information ↘ 01208 76616.

Brass Crosby Milestone, Lambeth, London SE1
Rail Lambeth North (Bakerloo line).

Brookwood Cemetery, Surrey
See page 108.

Camberley elephant, Surrey
Road Off M3 J4, north a mile on A321, then right (east) on A30.

Carn Brea, Redruth, Cornwall
Road From end of M5, take A38, then A30.
Rail From London Paddington and other centres.
Tourist information ↘ 01326 565431.

Cerne Giant, Cerne Abbas, Dorset
Road: Off A352 Dorchester/Sherborne road. From London/M25, M3 then A303, south on A359 near Yeovil, B3148 to Sherborne.
Rail/bus: Dorchester South, from London Waterloo (or Dorchester West from Bristol and south Wales, then bus 216 from Trinity St.
Tourist information: ↘ 01305 267992.

Clarkson Monument, Hertfordshire
Road On west side of A10, old London–Cambridge road near Wadesmill.
Tourist information ↘ 01992 584322.

Cleopatra's Needle, Thames Embankment, London WC2
Tube Embankment, Northern, Bakerloo, Circle and District lines.

Eleanor Cross, Geddington, Northamptonshire
Road From M1 J19, which is also southern end of M6, take A14 to just before Kettering, then A43 northwest for about 4 miles to Geddington. Remains of cross is right (east) in village then on the left. NB if coming up M1 from south, you must leave at J15A near Northampton and follow A43 to Kettering because there is no access at J19.
Rail Kettering, from London St Pancras.
Tourist information ☏ 01536 410266

Eleanor Cross, Hardingstone, Northamptonshire
Road From M1 J15, A508 towards Northampton for about 2 miles. After crossing A45, the cross remains are on the right, across the main road from Hardingstone village.
Rail Northampton, from London Euston.
Tourist information ☏ 01604 622677.

Ferry Lane Monument, Brentford, Middlesex. Moved to outside County Court, a short walk west along main road, during redevelopment.
Road Brentford is near M4 J2.
Rail Brentford, from London Waterloo.

Fireplates obelisk, Tibbet's Corner, near Putney, London SW15
Road In woodland beside northbound sliproad off A3 signed Putney. From Tibbet's Corner roundabout (don't go through A3 underpass) take opposite exit (signed Wimbledon), then immediately left into Withycombe Rd. Park and walk back under roundabout on footpaths to woodland.
Rail/bus Putney from London Waterloo, turn left and walk up to top of Putney Hill. Bus 14 to southern terminus.

'Iron Mad' Wilkinson's Monument, Lindale, Cumbria
Road Off A590, west from M6 J36.
Rail Grange-over-Sands, from London Euston.
Tourist information ☏ 01229 587120.

Lymington Obelisk, Hampshire (near Sway and Luttrell's towers)
Road From London or M25, take M3 to J14 near end, M27 west to J1, then A337 to Lymington.
Rail Lymington is on the end of a short branch from Brockenhurst on the London Waterloo–Weymouth line.
Tourist information ☏ 01590 689000.

Maharajah's Well, Stoke Row, Oxfordshire
Road Best approach from M40 J6, B4009 southwest, B480 left, B481 right towards Reading. Stoke Row is on right after crossing A4130. Or same road from Caversham, on the north side of Reading (off M4).

Marc Bolan's tree, Queen's Ride, Barnes, London SW13
Rail Barnes station, from London Waterloo, then walk over road bridge at station and turn left back to previous bridge over the tracks.
Bus 22 from Piccadilly ends on Putney Common at other end of Queen's Ride.

Millbank transportation bollard, London SW1
Road On Millbank, outside Tate Gallery and near Vauxhall Bridge.

Rail/tube Use Vauxhall (from Waterloo mainline or Victoria Line) and cross bridge to north side of Thames, then turn right.

Rebus milestones, Sussex
Road A22 from London and M25 to Eastbourne, although some villages with old milestones have been bypassed (eg: Maresfield).
Rail Buxted on London Victoria–Uckfield line.
Tourist information ↘ 01273 483448.

Red signpost, Dorset
Road On south side of A31 Southampton–Dorchester road near Winterbourne Zelston.
Tourist information ↘ 01305 267992.

Science Museum, South Kensington, London, SW7; ↘ 020 7938 8000;
web: www.nmsi.ac.uk
Road Difficult parking, south of Albert Hall on south side of Hyde Park.
Rail South Kensington tube (Circle, District and Piccadilly lines), follow foot tunnel.

Stratton Arch and Obelisk, Cornwall
Road On A39 near Bude. From M5 J27 A361 to Barnstaple, then A39.
Tourist information ↘ 01288 354240.

White Horse, on the edge of the Vale of White Horse, Oxfordshire
Road From M4 J14 north on A338 to Wantage, east on B4057.
Foot The ridgeway long-distance path which goes east–west here takes in an iron age hill fort and standing stones within 3 miles to the west.
Tourist information ↘ 01367 242191.

Wickham elephants, Berkshire
Road Off B4000 which connects Newbury and A338 just north of M4 J14.
Tourist information (Reading) ↘ 0118 956 6266.

Yarborough Obelisk, Isle of Wight (near Bembridge Fort)
Road From London or M25 take A3 to Portsmouth, ferry to Fishbourne, then A3054 east to Ryde, A3055 south past Brading, then left on B3395. Look for second lane on right.
Rail Sandown station (from London Waterloo). Trains go on to piers either side of Solent for foot ferry (included in ticket). Then walk from Sandown along coast northwards (1 hour, steep). Well worth it.
Tourist information ↘ 01983 403886.

Zeppelin Monument, Cuffley, Hertfordshire.
Road From M25 J24, north on A1000 then right on B157 to Cuffley.
Rail Cuffley is on London King's Cross–Hertford North line.
Tourist information ↘ 01992 584322.

Towering Eccentrics

IN SEARCH OF UTTER FOLLY
Mad Jack and wagers

Few follies are as absolutely useless as their strict definition requires. Even those wonderfully peculiar buildings leased to well-to-do holidaymakers by the Landmark Trust (see page 225) have a present use, as accommodation, and often a past one, however unusual the former prisons, forts, pigsties or lighthouses might be. Ditto the follies sold through the specialist estate agency Pavilions of Splendour (22 Mount View Rd, London N4 4HX; ➤ 020 8348 1234), although recently they sold a particularly useless tower set amid a wild wood in Kent.

Occasionally, however, a delightfully dotty eccentric, with more money than sense, some would say, dots his bit of Britain with a collection of totally useless and inexplicable structures.

Such a group are **Mad Jack Fuller's follies** around Brightling, East Sussex, just down the road from Kipling's house, Bateman's. One of these, the conical steeple shape of the Sugar Loaf, rises on a hill near Wood's Corner crossroads. (You'd have to be pretty long in your sweet tooth to remember sugar loaves, although there are suitably shaped mountains named after them all over the world, but they were conical blocks of sugar sold by grocers which would keep a sweet-toothed family happy for months.) From there you can see the observatory, a domed building amid trees, and the Brightling Needle, a fine obelisk that Cleopatra would have appreciated. The other side of the village offers the Brightling Tower, which looks like a windmill sliced off at an angle, and the Rotunda Temple, a circular affair with pillars. In the village churchyard is Fuller's quite splendid pyramid (see page 86).

Mad, Honest or Jolly Jack Fuller (1757–1834) was from a family which had made its fortune landowning in the High Weald, iron founding when Sussex made the best guns for the Navy, and from slaves in Jamaica. He wasn't entirely mad, with various local philanthropic efforts – in marked contrast to his endorsement of slavery overseas – such as buying a lifeboat for Eastbourne or building a wall round the estate at Brightling to relieve unemployment. Indeed this, rather than just livening up the view, might have been his motive for building the follies.

But the Sugar Loaf is said to have arisen from a drinking session between friends of this rich young man (who was later to decline a peerage). He wagered that a certain number of church steeples could be seen from his

TOWERING ECCENTRICS

KEY

Tower

Folly, sham or gargoyle(s)

Central London

Kew Pagoda

King's Cross Lighthouse

Leinster Gardens, Bayswater

Severn Droog Castle

ATLANTIC OCEAN

Orkney Islands

Thurso

Isle of Lewis

Outer Hebrides

Inner Hebrides

Isle of Skye

Island of Mull

Inverness

Aberdeen

North Sea

Islay

Arran

Glasgow

Wallace Monument, Stirling

The Pineapple, Dunmore

Edinburgh

Rosslyn Chapel

Melrose Abbey

Newcastle upon Tyne

Carlisle

Isle of Man

N

Culloden Tower, Richmond

Middlesbrough

follies, Brightling

Red Devil, York

St Mary's, Beverley

Irish Sea

Bradford

Leeds

Kingston-upon-Hull

Grimsby

Anglesey

Manchester

Wentworth Woodhouse follies

Holyhead

Liverpool

Sheffield

Lincoln Imp

Riber Castle, Matlock

Mow Cop, mock ruin

Derby

Nottingham

0   100km

0   60 miles

Wolverhampton

Birmingham

Triangular Lodge, Rushton

Norwich

Cardigan Bay

Coventry

Cambridge

Tattingstone Wonder

Fishguard

Broadway Tower

Gothic Temple, Stowe

Ipswich

Nelson's Tower, Llanarthney

Oxford gargoyles

Ayot St Lawrence

West Wycombe cottages

Swansea

Baron Berners' Folly, Faringdon

Reading

LONDON

Bristol Channel

Cardiff Castle

Bristol

Beckford's Tower

Leith Hill Tower

May's Folly, Hadlow

Dover

Massey's Folly, Farringdon

Mad Jack Fuller's

Crewkerne Minster gargoyles

Southampton

Sway Tower

Luttrell's Tower, Eaglehurst

Royal Pavilion, Brighton

Haldon Belvedere, Exeter

Barwick Park follies

Portsmouth

Peter's Tower, Lympstone

I of Wight

Penzance

English Channel

home, Brightling Place. Sobering up in the morning, he found he was wrong by one – Dallington spire was not in sight. So he had an imitation one immediately raised on the horizon instead.

A wager led to the building of another fine folly in a patch of Yorkshire littered with magnificent and eccentric buildings – the **Wentworth Woodhouse** estate, around the quite astonishingly enormous great house, or rather pair of houses, one with a 600ft Palladian façade – that better deserve the name palaces.

In 1780 the second Marquess of Rockingham (twice prime minister) bet that he could drive a coach and horses through the eye of a needle. The

needle-like pyramid the Needle's Eye has a suitably shaped opening in it through which he was able, just, to drive his carriage.

The estate, northwest of Rotherham, also offers a domed and vaulted bear pit, a fine obelisk to Lady Montagu who, an inscription says, introduced smallpox inoculation in 1720, a large mock castle, a rotunda, another obelisk, the second marquess's seriously over-the-top three-storey mausoleum at Nether Haugh, and the extraordinary Hoober Strand tower (see page 205).

The house, now a grade I listed building, somehow avoided the fate of many other similar huge edifices which were demolished and sold for rubble in the face of 20th-century death duties, designed to grind down the super-rich, and crippling maintenance costs. Wentworth Woodhouse became surrounded by mining, the house became a teacher training college for a while, and was acquired by a reclusive millionaire Wensley Haydon-Baillie in 1986 whose fortune, like so many others, evaporated somewhat in the 1990s. At the time of writing this forgotten gem, which could be South Yorkshire's pride and joy, was for sale, its future use uncertain.

The park and follies have never been public property, but despite the appearance in recent years of unfriendly and controversial Keep Out signs, you can use an Ordnance Survey map and find your way about the land quite legally on the marked footpaths and bridleways.

Another Jack, a treacle eater

A cluster of totally pointless follies, if not without points, can be found at **Barwick Park**, Somerset, just south of Yeovil on A37 road to Dorchester. Landowner George Messiter is said to have had

Barwick Park dovecote

them put up in the early 19th century to create employment during a slump in trade.

They include a needle-sharp obelisk (on the left just before A37 crosses the railway); a thing that looks like an extended dovecote on top of arches with a ball on top; and the oddest, Jack the Treacle Eater. This a rough stone arch, built in the fashion of pretending to be a ruin, incongruously holding aloft the much finer masonry of a round tower, a conical roof and a statue of said Jack, a messenger who worked for Messiter and was, it is said, fuelled by treacle.

Like all these stories attached to follies, it is hard to know if the legend was created to explain the folly or the other way round. All the Barwick follies could have been simply eye-catchers, to improve the long views from the house. If they are true follies, it would be folly indeed to try to find much of a purpose for them.

Folly de grandeur

Even royalty are not immune from creating follies – in fact they can make them bigger and better than most. I'm not talking about Prince Charles's in fact rather sane model village at Poundbury, next to Dorchester, but to two majestic creations which, although well known to most Brits, must get a mention.

One is the splendid pagoda at **Kew Gardens**, which soars storey after storey like a backdrop for the *Mikado*. It was an unlikely birthday present for a princess, but I can't quite imagine the scene. Could they wrap it up? Did the podgy spoilt brat refuse to climb it? Who are the humourless mandarins who stop visitors from climbing it today?

The other is the **Royal Pavilion** in Brighton, created by the Prince Regent who became George IV in 1820. As Prince of Wales, he carried on an affair with a divorcee here, and the ensuing fuss made the recent sad tale of the 1990s Princess of Wales seem a re-run of history. (In fact the whole story was even sorrier, as you can find by checking the tomb of two tradesmen killed at the spurned Queen Caroline's funeral. They are at the parish church at Hammersmith, west London, under A4 flyover.)

Be that as it may, the prince's love life in Brighton set the racy reputation which the former quiet fishing port of Brighthelmstone has enjoyed ever since as the dirty weekend capital of Britain. Whether the countless Mr and Mrs Smiths checking into the resort's hotels in the mid-20th century took any notice, John Nash's extravagant Royal Pavilion is thoroughly and incurably eccentric, and much more enduring than any outrage at whatever that particular Prince of Wales got up to.

BRITAIN'S TOP TEN (PLUS) TOWERS (MOSTLY WITH VERY TALL STORIES)

1 **Wallace Monument**, Causewayhead, Stirling

Spectacularly sited atop Abbey Craig, this 220ft tower bursts from the trees like a romantic rocket blasting into science fiction orbit.

Hollywood couldn't do it better, although the film *Braveheart* lit the boosters under interest in Wallace, numbers of visitors to the tower trebled, and a tacky – to some tastes – sculpture of Mel Gibson (well, it looks like him) was installed at the shop. Ignore it if you don't like it, but the views from the superb tower are exceptional. Don't rush through Stirling itself, it's worth a closer look.

Road M9 from Edinburgh to J10.

Rail Stirling, from Glasgow or Edinburgh.

Tourist information ☎ 01786 475019.

Wallace Monument

2 **Sway Tower**, Hampshire

Near the New Forest village of Sway, Sway Tower is aptly named, for it was built to prove it wouldn't, but nearly did. Judge A T T Peterson, retired from the Calcutta High Court, wanted to prove the efficacy of Portland cement concrete blocks without reinforcement. He persuaded local workmen to assemble the blocks like a giant Lego kit into the slim 218ft high tower entirely without scaffolding, so they had to be well paid.

Built in Indian-Gothic style between 1876 and 1879, and accompanied by another smaller tower nearby, the main tower has a hexagonal turret taking a spiral staircase up 330 steps, and 11 rooms. On top is a Mogul-style lantern for the view, but the judge was refused permission for a light, the Admiralty decreeing that it would confuse shipping looking for the Needles lighthouse, only six miles away.

In fact, building such a slender tower of unreinforced concrete was stretching a point, and it has since been reinforced. Nearby are various concrete lodges and walls, none of them now remarkable, as is always the case with truly pioneering endeavours. In other words, the judge was right about the coming age of concrete.

Road From south end of M3 from London/M25, continue to west end of M27, take A337 south to Brockenhurst, then B3055 to Sway.
Rail Sway, from London Waterloo.
Tourist information ☎ 01590 689000.

Faringdon, Oxfordshire

This Faringdon has the fascinating folly of Lord Berners, the last true folly built by, perhaps, one of the last eccentrics. But why does Farringdon, Hampshire, also have one, not to mention a mystery one at Farringdon, London? See below, page 199.

May's Folly, Hadlow, Kent

An extraordinary flight of fancy soaring heavenwards like a French cathedral or Bruges Town Hall from open countryside in storey after neo-gothic storey, it is improbable that it has survived nearly two centuries.

The story goes locally that Squire May built the thing either to see the sea, in which case he would have been disappointed, or that he had an unfaithful wife, and that the 170ft tower was to give her the feeling that wherever she went in Kent, he was watching her. The truth isn't known, but Walter Barton May (1783–1853) inherited not only stacks of money (twice) but also his father's love of grandiose building – his father had built Hadlow Castle, a fabulous neo-gothic pile. To save on running costs and sell the scrap building materials, the castle was demolished in that widespread fashion of the 1930-1950s, completely incomprehensible only 20 years later, of pulling down entire, beautiful stately homes. Today it would have been converted into bijou apartments or been sold for millions – with its sumptuous interiors it would have rivalled Knebworth House, Hertfordshire, for frequent use as a neo-gothic film-set.

The tower, some stables and outbuildings and lodges are today still private homes and other houses have filled gaps in the grounds. (There was a fad in the early 19th century to build towers apeing a recently described and pictured octagonal tower in Portugal; at Fonthill Abbey in Wiltshire the eccentric bisexual playboy mad party-giver William Beckford built a 300ft similar tower in 1812; he was aiming for 450ft, but it collapsed in 1825, an earlier one having collapsed too. His habit of plying his workmen

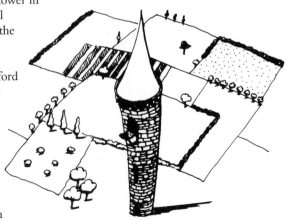

with alcohol and making them work round the clock probably didn't help. Their habit of not using foundations definitely didn't. Beckford had earlier built a seven-mile, 12ft high wall round his estate. In 1825 – he had sold Fonthill for a fortune three years before it collapsed – he also built an eerie, octagonal 154ft high lookout tower at Lansdown Hill, Bath, near his new home. Beckford and his attendant, the exceedingly smelly dwarf Porro, are buried here.)

Suspicious Squire May did better and his 1838 effort has just about survived near on two centuries; it is true that his wife left him at about the time the tower was started. Whether the obsession with piling stone upon stone caused the marriage break-up or was caused by it will never be clear, but Squire May left his mark on Kent. But whether this soaring tower will continue to dominate this part of Kent is doubtful, as in 1994 emergency repairs to the crumbling tower included dismantling the lantern and certain gables and parapets to lessen the weight. The search was on in 1998 for a million pounds to repair the structure. You may think if the National Lottery can fund endless ugly follies elsewhere, why not repair this splendidly barmy one?

Little Berkhamsted, not far from Hertford, has a tower called Streatton's Folly with a story that is in some ways similar. This, too, is actually someone's home rather than being part of the heritage industry, so must be viewed from the road. The story is that a rich and canny merchant built it so high that he could see the Thames near Tilbury. Through his telescope he could identify which ships had come from where and, armed with this intelligence, would saddle a fast horse and ride into London to take advantage of merchants not quite so up-to-date.

May's Folly
Road From London/M25, A21 to Tonbridge (not Tunbridge Wells), then A26 north east about 4 miles.
Rail/bus London Charing Cross or Victoria to Tonbridge, then bus 7.
Tourist information ↘ 01732 770929.

Beckford's Tower, Bath
Road From M4 J18, Bath is 10 miles south on A46. Beckford's Tower is on the northern fringes of Bath, up a steep hill west of Charlcombe.
Rail From London Paddington to Bath.
Tourist information ↘ 01225 477101.

Streatton's Folly

Peters Tower, Lympstone, Devon
This tower, vaguely based on St Mark's in Venice, appropriately stands right on the water's edge in the wide Exe estuary south of Exeter. The

clocktower is a memorial to Mary Jane Peters, built by her grieving husband William Peters in 1885, and has been carefully restored after being given to the Landmark Trust (see page 224), so you can holiday in it, at a price, but not visit.

Road From M5 J30 near Exeter, a few miles south on A376.
Rail On Exmouth branch line from Exeter.
Tourist information ↘ 01392 265700.

Cardiff Castle, Cardiff; ↘ 029 2087 8100
For a completely over-the-top clocktower, with ingenious and extraordinary decorations, don't miss the one at Cardiff Castle. You may not be able to stay the night there, but the whole castle offers romantic eccentricity and flamboyant architectural detail on a grand and sometimes amazing scale, thanks to the flamboyantly rich third Marquess of Bute and his eccentric architect William Burges.

Road M4 to Cardiff. Look for Castle St in the city centre.
Rail London Paddington and other centres to Cardiff; walk about 500 yards down Westgate St to castle.

Broadway Tower, Broadway, Worcestershire; ↘ 01386 852390
A classic folly well known because of its superb situation beside the A44 Oxford–Worcester road as it plunges over the escarpment down into the Cotswolds. Some may think it an almost too perfect tower above the almost too perfect village of Broadway, lovely, but museum-like. The tower at the top of Fish Hill is alleged to offer a view of 12 counties and was built by the sixth Earl of Coventry in 1789. It includes on its three floors exhibitions on the surrounding country park and the Pre-Raphaelite brotherhood.

This is relevant because William Morris used it as a holiday home and in 1876 wrote a letter calling for the formation of the Society for the Protection of Ancient Buildings. So the now overblown and top-heavy heritage industry, then of course much needed, started here. Ironically, Broadway Tower isn't in the grip of one of those great bureaucracies, but is privately owned yet open to the public. A little-known relative of Broadway Tower is the **Dunstall Castle Folly** off A4104 near Upton upon Severn. This was another eye-catcher for the once-vast Croome estate and is a mock-Norman castle ruin, built as a ruined arch with towers.

Road On Oxford–Worcester A44 (connecting there with M5 J7).
Rail/taxi Moreton-in-Marsh (London Paddington–Worcester line) then taxi.
Tourist information ↘ 01386 852937.

Culloden Tower, Richmond, Yorkshire
It is odd to see something so handsome commemorating something so bloody as the battle of 1746, but the tower was started in that year by the MP for Richmond, John Yorke, to mark the defeat of the last serious challenge to Hanoverian rule, when Bonnie Prince Charlie's rebel army had

reached much further south than this. Whether the ruthless suppression that followed the battle, or the centuries of greatness Britain united was to enjoy, mattered more to Scots, or indeed the English, is still being hotly debated.

The octagonal shaft rises like a pillar from parkland in this gem of a town. Perched above the tumbling waters of the River Swale, the tower offers the highest standards of gothic and classical carving on different levels, and as a Landmark Trust property, is available for holiday lets (see page 224). The dramatic Hoober Strand (see page 205) was built to commemorate the same battle.

Road Off A1 south of Darlington.

Rail/coach/bus Darlington, from London King's Cross (or National Express coach) then bus 27 or 28.

Tourist information ➘ 01748 850252; web: www.richmond.org

Leith Hill Tower, near Coldharbour, Surrey; ➘ 01306 711774

The views from here are quite extraordinary, but as this 18th-century tower is atop the highest point in the southeast, with its top 1,029ft above sea level, this is logical. Even so, when I realised on a crystal clear day that everywhere I had previously visited that week – the Docklands of London, Crowborough, Sussex, the sea at Shoreham, and the South Downs near Petersfield, Hampshire, were all visible – I gripped the battlements in astonishment. The height lets you see through the gap in the South Downs to Shoreham, and you look down on Gatwick as if from a plane.

There is a steep but pleasant half-mile walk to the tower from the car park through woods. You wouldn't imagine that a desperate battle in AD851 here, involving perhaps 30,000 men, saw the heathen Danes who had burnt London wiped out by the Christian army of Ethlelwulf, Alfred the Great's father. Blood flowed and severed heads and limbs fell thick on the hillside, say the chronicles, but don't let it spoil your picnic.

The tower was built by local eccentric Richard Hull in 1766 as a 'Prospect House' and he was buried at the foot of the tower at his request in 1772. It has since been alternately vandalised and restored. It is National Trust owned (the Trust also owns Hull's nearby home at Leith Hill Place), with a tea and cake bar in the base of the tower, smack over Hull's bones. As for Alfred the Great, another great tower for views in the care of the National Trust is the 160ft King Alfred's Tower on the Stourhead estate, Warminster, Wiltshire; ➘ 01747 841152.

Road Difficult to find. You need the east–west A25, an old route parallel and south of the M25 and connecting with radial routes from London/M25 such as A24 at Dorking or A23 at Redhill; or approach via A247 from A3 north of Guildford. At Abinger Hammer on A25, turn south on B2126, then left (east) to Abinger and right (south) from that village, and look for signs.

Rail Only 2 (steep) miles from Ockley on the London Waterloo–Horsham (via Dorking) line, for energetic walkers or mountain bikers.

Tourist information ➘ 01483 444333.

The Pineapple, Dunmore, Stirlingshire

Absolutely extraordinary, eccentric and brilliant creation, a two-storey summer house built for the fourth Earl of Dunmore. The seamless stone blend from classical architecture to rampant fruit is magic, on a par with the fur coats turning to fir trees in *The Lion, the Witch and the Wardrobe*. It is also an elaborate joke.

The fourth Earl of Dunmore was governor of Virginia where sailors used to stick a pineapple on a gatepost to announce their return home. Lord Dunmore's attitude, on being forced home in 1777, was that as governor he would have the biggest pineapple of the lot to mark his own reluctant return. It is now owned by the National Trust for Scotland, and leased to Landmark Trust (see page 224). At the time it was built, pineapples were still unknown to most people in Britain. The first fruit in Britain was grown at Dorney, Buckinghamshire, in 1665, which is why there is a Pineapple pub there.

Road Dunmore (National Trust for Scotland) is off A905 east of Stirling. From M9 J7, use M876 spur to north, then A905 northwest towards Stirling.

Rail/bus Stirling, then bus 75 and ask to be dropped off at turning.

Tourist information ❧ 01786 475019.

Luttrell's Tower, Eaglehurst, near Southampton

A well-situated and pretty – you could say refined if you did not know what was round the corner – Georgian folly, right on the edge of the Solent near the corner of Southampton Water, with views down both approaches and across to Newport on the Isle of Wight. There are particularly good views of the container ships, ferries and cruise liners coming out of bustling Southampton, plus the giant tankers turning in front of the tower heading for the huge Fawley refinery and power station just around the corner, but out of view. If you love Georgian architecture *and* modern shipping, this is Nirvana, with a grand oriel window (a bay window projecting upstairs) overlooking the maritime view.

It was built for Temple Luttrell, who died in 1803. He was an MP and a smuggler, which probably explains why a tunnel leads from the basement directly to the beach. It's now run by the Landmark Trust, so if you're well off you can use it as a holiday home (see page 224). But everyone may see it by driving to Calshot, where to the left there's a good castle, one of many guarding the Solent. Walk instead half a mile to the right along the pebbly beach and you'll see the folly at the top of a ridiculously over-the-top staircase and its ruined boathouse on the beach.

Road A326 from M27 J2, and then B3053 (in fact straight on) down the west side of Southampton Water, along the edge of the New Forest, as far as one can go to Calshot.

Rail/bus Southampton from London Waterloo and other centres, then bus X9 to Calshot beach.

Tourist information ❧ 01703 221106.

TRUE FOLLIES COME IN THREES

The last great private folly to be built in Britain, before the Disneyesque commercial fibreglass fakery of theme parks took over in their plastic parodies, was the **Faringdon folly** in Oxfordshire. Built by the truly eccentric composer-diplomat, the fourteenth Baron Berners, the tower sits atop a landmark hill crowned with Scotch pines and beeches just outside the town, and makes a fine sight approaching from Berkshire or the Wiltshire Downs. The 100ft-square brick tower's bulk is concealed by trees, leaving the octagonal neo-gothic top poking out with its eight pinnacles and flagstaff.

The folly has generated as much controversy and legend in its short life as many of its much older brethren. The notion of building it received much publicity at the time and the local council voted against it, without the benefit of details, purely on hearsay about Lord Berners' supposed plans to use the folly as a lighthouse, probing the rural darkness with a great beam, and to install a powerful siren on top. A public inquiry ensued, which gave Fleet Street diary writers the chance to record this exchange between the architect and crusty old Admiral Clifton Brown, who objected that the tower would spoil his views:

> *Architect*: 'But you could not see the tower from your garden without a telescope!'

> *Admiral*: 'Sir, it is always my custom to look at the view through a telescope.'

As for legend, if there are some inaccuracies about the tower they were not exactly weeded out by the late Robert Heber-Percy, who died in 1987 having donated the folly to the community in 1983. He told how Lord Berners had given him the tower as a 21st birthday present and how annoying this was, as he had requested a horse. He also recounted how Lord Berners wanted, once dead, to be stuffed and mounted in the belvedere room at the top of the tower, eternally playing cheerful tunes on an automatic grand piano. Heber-Percy went on to say that he 'funked it' because of the impossibility of getting a grand piano up the narrow wooden stairs that cling to the tower's plunging and otherwise blank interior.

The trust which now opens the tower to the public tries to bring down to earth some of the tall stories attached to the tower. It corrects books which claim a 140ft height and insists on a mere 100ft. It denies that you can see six counties from the top and lists a mere five. It denies the claim – made about many a folly from Dorset to Sussex – that it was built to alleviate dire unemployment at the time. Only one extra man was taken on the estate staff. It even points out that Mr Heber-Percy was born in 1911, so it would have been a late 21st birthday present.

However, some elements of the story remain unchallenged. First, the hill was called Folly Hill long before the tower was built. Secondly, the fine trees were planted by Poet Laureate Henry James Pye in the late 18th century. (He built Faringdon House and wrote a poem at Eaglehurst, which also boasts a fine tower. He was such a lousy poet that the rhyme *Four And Twenty*

Blackbirds originated as a lampoon of his corny style.) Thirdly, the bones of Cromwellian soldiers *were* unearthed while the tower was being built – Parliamentary forces laid siege to an earlier Faringdon House. Fourthly, the eccentric notices plastered by Lord Berners about his estate did include one at the top of the tower stating: 'Members of the public committing suicide from this tower do so at their own risk.' And finally, in another war – World War II – the tower was employed as an observation post, soon thankfully returning to the uselessness which qualifies it as a true folly.

Even if you know the other Farringdon – near Alton, Hampshire – you may not know there's a jolly good folly there too, as it's tucked away in the village centre off the main roads. A tiny, sleepy village with thatched cottages, Farringdon had an eccentric vicar in the Revd T H Massey from 1857 to 1919 (his grave may be seen outside the church door). He decided Farringdon needed a town hall on a scale which would have suited a city like Winchester or made a substantial part of a small university or a railway station for a grand spa town (when the railway did arrive at the other end of the village, Farringdon Halt was a few measly planks beside a single line and has long since closed).

Massey's Folly

The resulting pile of castellated towers, red brick and decorative terracotta panels can still be seen, although the Revd Massey tore down several towers which displeased him. When he wasn't building follies, he was either alienating his flock by his offensive preaching, so that he was left with a congregation of two, or buying up houses to prevent Methodists, whom he detested, living in Farringdon.

If you now expect another piece of architectural eccentricity in Britain's third Farringdon, between Fleet Street and King's Cross in London, I won't disappoint you. Walk the full length of Farringdon Road north to King's Cross, and where Gray's Inn Road and Pentonville Road converge (we're on the blue corner of the Monopoly board) what is known as the **King's Cross Lighthouse** sits atop the otherwise very plain four-storey buildings.

Some claim it was once a fairground helter-skelter tower but it would have to have been, impossibly and improbably, moved up there. Inspections of the interior, say Camden council, show that it can't have been a clocktower or a camera obscura. Obscurer are its origins indeed, and maybe it was a totally useless architectural flourish, a genuine third Farringdon folly.

THE TRIANGULAR ANGLE

Not long ago, one of Britain's most astonishing yet little-known buildings reached the 400th anniversary of its completion. Far more than an intriguing folly, Sir Thomas Tresham's Triangular Lodge tells a story of religious oppression, torture and courage through its mathematical puzzles and secret codes in stonework. Surprisingly, it is neither unique in Britain in being triangular, nor in putting a passionate story into our architectural heritage.

A brilliant puzzle in stone

There is something mystical or magical about the figure three, trefoils, or tridents – the image crops up in theology from the ancient Greeks to Shiva, star of the Hindu pantheon – as well as the more obvious Holy Trinity of Christian worship.

Few can have taken this latter more seriously than the late 16th-century English Catholics who defied persecution by the Protestant authorities. Of these Sir Thomas Tresham, whose coat of arms included the trefoil, immortalised his passionate faith in stone.

Sir Thomas's **Triangular Lodge** at Rushton, Northamptonshire, is a brilliant and astonishingly well-preserved folly, a mathematical essay in stone to the Trinity, and was built between 1593 and 1595.

The pleasure of this triangular building starts with looking at the apparently square elevation, then walking round to see the knife-edge 60° corners, the floor plan being an equilateral triangle, with each side exactly one-third of 100ft long. There are three three-by-three gables on each side, each crowned by three-sided pinnacles rising through stone triangles.

The mathematical conceit goes on and on: there are three floors with three windows on each, all decorated with triangles, trefoils, or other emblems. On a frieze running round the 33ft-long sides is an inscription with 33 letters on each side, and there are three sets of three gargoyles. Each face is dedicated to one of the Holy Trinity and the inscription varies accordingly.

Inside, each floor has one large hexagonal room, leaving three tiny triangular ones, one of which accommodates the stairs. It is a magical construction, with the odd patches of light from triangles, diamonds and cruciform slits thrown on to the geometric walls. Any hint of humourless mathematical severity is relieved by flamboyant and crazily detailed motifs on the roof gables and pinnacles.

The iron fastening rods running through the building are finished with a large black 15 on one face and a 93 on another – both divisible by three, of course, but together giving the start date of the building – with TT for Thomas Tresham on the third.

'Some brilliant details of the mathematical puzzle have gone unsolved until this century,' said English Heritage's custodian at the time of my visit, John Froment.

'For example, what appear to be dates in the triangular gables. On the north face, the face of God, so to speak, the dates are 1641 and 1626, clearly in the future at the time of construction. Subtracting the start date, 1593, however, gives the supposed dates of the deaths of Jesus and the Virgin Mary – AD33 and AD48.'

Triangular Lodge

Similarly, the numbers on another pair, 3898 and 3509, are the BC dates of the Great Flood and the call of Abraham. What about the puzzling code – 5555 – above the door? John Froment adds: 'Some have read this as 3333, which caused puzzlement. If you add Bede's calculation of the date of Creation – 3962BC – and the start date of the Lodge, 1593, you have 5555.' The sum of two creations, one vast, one small.

Other details are yet more cryptic. The waterspouts are each marked with one initial – these were realised centuries later to form an acronym, the first letters of a key part of the Latin mass, then banned on pain of huge fines and imprisonment, both of which Tresham endured for his faith.

Still more architectural puns, perhaps, remain unsolved. Over the door, one inscription seems clear enough – *Tres Testimonium Dant*, meaning 'these three bear witness'. English Heritage's booklet on the Lodge, pointing out that Tres was Tresham's wife's pet name for him, suggests the inscription also means 'Tresham bears witness'. This would, however, be bending Latin grammar – the equivalent of saying 'Tresham bear witness' in English – more than such a fastidious man could bear, despite his wit.

(If I told you that directions to John Froment's nearby house included third street on the left, then third door on the right, and that the street name begins Tre-, you might think I was taking a serious work too trivially. It must be merely coincidence.)

It has also been debated by scholars whether Tresham's obsession with numbers was purely religious, or as some sensationalists or idle theorists have suggested, a cover for black magic.

It is true that some ten miles away lies the shell of Lyveden House, sadly unfinished before Tresham's death in 1605. There, several other numbers are explored, chiefly the figure five. The cruciform building ends in walls with bay windows, each starting 5ft from the corner, going out 5ft, along 5ft, in 5ft, and 5ft to the next corner, making five fives. The ground plan is of four squares in the wings and a central one, making five. The top frieze has quotations from the Latin Bible carved at one letter per foot, worked out so that each side starts and finishes with the five letter words 'Jesus' and 'Maria'; and, over the main door, each word has five letters.

Black magic? Far from it: Sir Thomas was a deeply religious man with a brilliant mind, who enjoyed a contrived conceit as much as the metaphysical poets of the era. Perhaps he knew that Cromwell's commissioners, half a century later, would smash down anything overtly Catholic, as they did with many a beautiful medieval stained-glass window or church statue.

In any case, the detail on this delightful lodge is as sturdy a survivor of bitter religious division in this country as that curiously long-lived children's playground song that goes 'Do the hokey cokey...' – a satire on the Catholic Latin mass *Hoc est enim corpus meum hoc est corpus meum*, the Latin words which the priest said over the bread in the Mass which mean 'This is my body'. 'And you turn around' refers to the action of the priest after consecrating the bread and wine: because the altar was against the east wall of the church, he had his back to the people, so he had to turn around to show the consecrated bread to them. The same ridicule gives us the phrase hocus-pocus. Both remnants in our culture bear witness, as does Tresham's tremendous lodge, to desperate divisions.

Swashbuckling at Severndroog

Religious piety was not the inspiration for another triangular tower with a tale to tell which overlooks the homes of thousands of Londoners; it came about after a swashbuckling fight against pirates in the exotic east.

Severndroog Castle in Castlewood Park off Shooters Hill, near Blackheath in southeast London, was built in 1784 for the widow of Sir William James as a tribute to the heroic attack led by Sir William, with four ships and thousands of men, on the original Severndroog Castle, a nest of pirates on the Malabar coast of India. That castle was taken in 1755.

With turrets at the corners rather than sharp angles, the tower is 46ft higher than St Paul's, so it is worth a visit for the splendid view. Early on the tower was used for surveying, and later, in the 19th century, ladies and gentlemen would meet there to dance quadrilles to a military band. Today the ground floor houses a tearoom, so you may have your own version of these genteel picnics.

Madras memories

Oddly, at least two other triangular towers sport an Indian connection. The superbly sited **Haldon Belvedere**, 800ft up on the hills near Exeter, was built in 1788 by former governor of Madras Sir Robert Palk, then MP for Ashburton, as a memorial to his friend General Stringer Lawrence, father of the Indian Army.

The romantic folly on a wooded Devon hilltop, fully restored at a cost of £450,000, was leased to the Devon Historic Buildings Trust in 1994. The tower had been bought by a Mrs Annie Dale for £650 in 1933, and her son Edward, who bequeathed it indirectly to the trust, lived there until his death in 1994.

Equally well-sited is **Nelson's Tower** (also known as Paxton's Tower) at Llanarthney, Carmarthenshire, built by the Master of Calcutta Mint, Sir William Paxton, after the battle of Trafalgar in 1805. Again turreted on the corners, and now in the care of the National Trust, this tower has three doors. Over each is an inscription praising the 'invincible commander, Viscount Nelson, in commemoration of deeds before the walls of Copenhagen, and on the shores of Spain...'. One side is in English, one in Welsh and one in Latin. You cannot stay in the tower, but you can in Tower Hill Lodge which has a superb view of it, through the Landmark Trust (see page 224). From the tower itself, the view is described as one of the best in Britain.

Yet more triangles

Not all triangular towers are massive. In Cornwall there is an unusual triangular tower with dished sides at Cotehele House, Calstock, standing some 60ft high complete with sham windows. This is a straightforward folly.

More massive by far is the impressive, lighthouse-like **Hoober Strand**, a truncated pyramid with rounded corners, part of Britain's most marvellous and imaginative group of follies at Wentworth Woodhouse in Yorkshire (see page 191). Hoober Strand, topped by a lantern and railing, contains an elegant spiral staircase, and was built in 1748, ostensibly as a tribute to George II subduing 'a most unnatural rebellion in Britain'.

Sadly, one of the few 20th-century triangular towers, a striking art deco triangular tower at Lee-on-the-Solent, is no more. This prospect tower, which had an excellent view across the Isle of Wight from a platform at the top, has been demolished by a community which seems to have had all the flair and imagination of an amoeba on valium, having also filled in its seafront lido, lost its pier and cut off its railway branch line in its seeming desperation to return to prim, suburban, deserved obscurity. No doubt they will say they were victims of bigger forces, but did they fight hard enough?

Lastly, a truly exotic triangular building, the **Gothic Temple at Stowe**, Buckinghamshire, is another which fans of eccentric buildings can also enjoy as a holiday home, through the Landmark Trust (see page 224).

Stowe – the great house itself has been occupied by Stowe public school since 1923 – is where Lord Cobham had Capability Brown create elegant landscaping in the mid-18th century. This was adorned by dozens of follies and architectural oddities.

James Gibbs designed the Temple, built in 1741, which is formed on a triangular plan with hexagonal turrets adjoining each corner. All the rooms are circular, with the main triangle housing a large circle on the ground floor and a circular gallery on the first floor, giving a spacious view of the domed and gorgeously painted heraldic ceiling.

Two of the side hexagons contain small circular rooms on each level – bedrooms, kitchen, bathroom – and the third a circular staircase which leads to a hexagonal belvedere at roof level, giving a splendid view over the landscape now managed by the National Trust.

ALL A SHAM

Towns in Western films called Vulture Gulch or Carcass Creek, where the bank, sheriff's office and saloon are merely one plank thick frontages, turn out to be heirs to a barmy British tradition: the sham. Sham castles, sham churches, sham ruins and even sham smart townhouses are to be found around the country, although you would, naturally, miss them at first glance. Some are frontages put up to maintain discreet appearances, some are fantasy follies to make a picturesque view, and some are infamous disguises to make the banal or scatological appear more fragrant.

West Wycombe in Buckinghamshire (see page 99), which has so many eccentric features, includes in West Wycombe Park a pair of cottages disguised as St Crispin's Chapel and set behind the lake to improve the view from the great house. That the cottages are somewhat small adds to the false perspective, although they do therefore look most odd from Chapel Lane, which they front on the High Wycombe side. Chapel Lane is on the left on the main A40 from High Wycombe before you reach West Wycombe.

Aristocrats have often been high-handed in their attempts to create views for the fashionable parks around their homes. At **Ayot St Lawrence** near Hatfield in Hertfordshire – the same village where playwright George Bernard Shaw spent his declining years in a revolving summerhouse, still to be seen – there's an apparently large Palladian church, with a splendid white pillared front neatly facing Ayot House. Behind this somewhat two-dimensional façade, however, there's a much smaller and undecorated plain brick church holding the larger frontage up. The white rendering of the façade, it should be noted, ends just where it goes out of sight of the great house. White or not, the sham church has been persistently associated – even in the second half of the 20th century – with black magic ever since it was built.

This church, Sir Lionel Lyte's whim, also meant the demolition of the ancient parish church set more conveniently – for other people – in the village, but its destruction was not complete. An equally fashionable 'Gothic' ruin was desired – and is even repaired, as a ruin of course.

This flippant whim of an arrogant all-powerful aristo was far from unusual. Not far away at Tring, Sir Robert Whittingham had the entire thriving village of Pendley flattened in the 15th century to improve his view.

Neither is vandalising a church that rare. At **Mount Edgcumbe**, near Plymouth, there's a splendidly convincing ruin stuffed with medieval stonework, gargoyles and window tracery, but it's not in the least medieval. The whole thing is a folly, put up as a purpose-built ruin in the 18th century with the stones taken from churches the Mount Edgcumbe family owned at Stonehouse, across the water.

Ruins built as such, as romantic eye-catchers, are almost as common as muck, if a little misleading. **Mow Cop** in Staffordshire, that splendid natural outcrop, is topped by a totally fake ruin, for example. It wouldn't get planning permission nowadays, but would anything imaginative? Ditto **Riber Castle** overlooking Matlock in Derbyshire, which is about as medieval as a Victorian public toilet. Actually Riber really is in danger of becoming a real ruin, not a sham ruin, so while one can walk through great scenery to the wildlife park around it, the building itself is fenced off.

Such ruins were usually placed at a suitable viewing distance from the great house, as at Uppark, near Harting, Sussex. Uppark itself became a real ruin when it burnt down accidentally in 1990, but the National Trust simply recreated it at a cost of many ruinous millions. But the fake ruin is maintained, as a ruin, of course.

Some shams you could pass every day without noticing. If you deal with anyone who gives a London address at 23 or 24 **Leinster Gardens** – neighbours in a respectable street – you may be dealing with a con artist. The two houses appear there in the right sequence, but they are a thin sham without foundations or substance, even the windows being painted on. When the gracious wedding cake five-storey terrace was broken in 1865 for the South Kensington extension of the new-fangled underground railway, property owners demanded that instead of a yawning gap over the railway track, a

phoney frontage be erected to continue the line of the buildings. At first glance, you hardly notice the join, though from the back – it is between Bayswater and Paddington stations – the thing looks like a film set.

Suffolk is a good county for shams, one of them being the well-known **Tattingstone Wonder**, built in 1760. A farm building masquerades as a castle with the aid of a three-sided tower grafted onto a barnlike roof, complete with buttresses and battlements, looking most imposing from one side but an obvious sham from the other. It is a quarter-mile south of Tattingstone Place, whence it was designed to be an eye-catcher.

On the other side of Alton Water reservoir from Tattingstone lies another sham. A pair of cottages has been set to catch the eye in Woolverstone Park. One end looks like a chapel with a tall, pointed, mullioned window and crenellated top, but it is a sham painted onto the end of the cottage called the Cat House. The story goes that when a cat was sitting in the window it was safe for smugglers coming from the nearby River Orwell to bring up their contraband, but now the cat is also painted on, it would seem to have lost its usefulness.

CARTOONS OF THE SKY

Why should Britain's Christian churches and ancient halls of learning be attended by grinning demons, obscene oafs and spitting monsters? I refer, of course, to gargoyles, the sometimes ghastly and grotesque effigies of horror or humour high on walls that the busy traveller will miss.

The true gargoyle, by the way, conveys water from the guttering and vomits it forth over the pavement well clear of the wall, thus avoiding the need for greatly overhanging eaves (it is these which create the dry band of pavement or 'eavesdrop', within which one might secretly listen to the conversation within the house).

So it's no coincidence that gargoyle and gargle are alike words, linked by these literally spitting images. Carvings of faces and monsters which decorate edges or corners of roofs but don't convey water are, strictly speaking, grotesques. Let's not be that pedantic.

Gargoyles of academe

Oxford is the best place for fantastic and fanciful gargoyles, and there it's no forgotten medieval art. Thus the 1960s restoration of St Edmund Hall has modern gargoyles depicting college characters of the day in somewhat cartoon fashion: the dean and his favourite Labrador dog; the bursar and his moneybags; the principal and his squash racket.

Three other colleges – Brasenose, Magdalen and New College – plus the Bodleian Library, offer some of the best ribaldry in stonemasonry, often on a good and evil theme. The 15th-century Duke Humphrey Library near the Sheldonian (itself ringed with giant heads) has a choir of angels facing a choir of demons.

New College has the Seven Virtues on the sunny south side of the Bell Tower and, perhaps more interestingly, the Seven Deadly Sins on the dark north side. The vulgar and bawdy is quite permissible at gargoyle level. At Magdalen College, which features a busty wench modelled cheekily on one of the college serving maids, a monkey squats defecating into a drainhead. This is despite a pious-looking bishop overlooking the bridge and blessing travellers. Many of the carvings serve to mock mankind, as with the grotesque pulling a face behind a serious soldier on the side of the Bodleian Library. To see for yourself in detail, take the excellent walking tour recommended in the inexpensive and excellent book *Oxford's Gargoyles and Grotesques* by John Blackwood, available in the city's bookshops.

A belief in imp possibilities

Gargoyles have been credited with bringing bad luck or good right into the modern era. Notorious in this way is the **Lincoln Imp**.

Legend says the little cross-legged grinning imp was sent to earth on the wind by the Devil to work some mischief. When Lincoln Cathedral was being built in the 11th century, the imp pushed his luck in tripping up the bishop and trying to knock over the dean, the story goes. A watchful angel turned him to stone, but he has sought to exercise his harmful influence ever since. In the mid-1990s, for example, a particularly bitter dispute among the dean and chapter hit the headlines. Who was really behind this? Who, for that matter, was responsible for the bad luck of Lincoln (nickname the Imps) in home football games?

A **Red Devil** may be seen not far away in Stonegate, an ancient street in central York, near the glorious York Minster church. It is said to be bad luck to catch his eye. It would certainly be bad luck to catch one of his two sharp horns.

Gargoyles can even be used to settle 450-year-old scores. When Magdalene College, Cambridge, redeveloped a disused wharf in the city into the Quayside centre in the 1980s, an unusual detail was specified – a particularly ugly gargoyle of a banker who had cheated the college of its endowment in 1542.

A gaggle of giggling gargoyles

Not all gargoyles are malignant by any means. **Crewkerne Minster** boasts one of the best west fronts in Somerset, but the passing visitor might miss the happy gargoyles playing musical instruments on the south side.

Melrose Abbey

That such figures of fun go back a long way is demonstrated by a gargoyle of a pig playing the bagpipes at Scotland's romantic ruined **Melrose Abbey**. This, once the richest abbey in Scotland, has much other surviving Gothic stonework of the highest order and some interesting later graves (see also Chapter 5).

For more mutant stonework of a rather curious sort, try the quite remarkable **Rosslyn Chapel** near Edinburgh. Here you will find fallen angels, a Prentice's Pillar of extraordinary detail (the apprentice who carved it in the master mason's absence was struck dead with the mason's mallet in a fit of jealousy) and inexplicable, fantastical dark carvings thought to be related to the Knights Templar. But then unnatural goings-on are still happening in the area – the nearby Roslin research institute is where Dolly the cloned sheep was created in the 1990s. You can stay in nearby Rosslyn Castle for a week or so: see page 224.

An English church with peculiar carvings not to be missed is **St Mary's, Beverley**, Yorkshire. Aside from the remarkable range of musical carvings, and more depicting 14th-century ailments, see if you can detect the bag-carrying pilgrim rabbit, said to have been an inspiration for Lewis Carroll's White Rabbit in *Alice In Wonderland*.

Lampooning the lofty

Even living royalty are sent up in gargoyles, and unlike many a former king and queen, having one's head taken off mercilessly in these cartoons of the sky is quite acceptable to the Palace. At St John the Divine, a Victorian gothic masterpiece in Vassal Road, Kennington, south London, the recent restoration of the spire features cheeky heads of the queen and Prince Charles. But then, as the church stands on land belonging to Prince Charles's Duchy of Cornwall and the spire is dedicated to the queen, leaving their heads out of the 60 new gargoyles would have been impolite. The other heads, mostly sponsored by members of the church at £25 a head, include local figures such as schoolteachers, a man killed by drug dealers, plus the young Princes William and Harry. You will, however, need a good telescope to see any details at all, as the spire is unusually high. Even the princes' crusty grandfather, the Duke of Edinburgh, was sent up in stone in an earlier 20-year restoration of Westminster Abbey's west front.

When the work at St John the Divine was finished, architect Giles Quarme – mindful perhaps of royalty's past habits of taking off heads in a different way – explained: 'This is within a great tradition of the grotesque in architecture; when you do portraits in stone you have to accentuate the features to make them stand out. The last thing we would want to do is humiliate any member of the Royal Family.' Unlike those impudent imps in Fleet Street ...

TRAVEL INFORMATION

Baron Berners' folly, Faringdon, Oxfordshire
Open: first Sun in month, April–Oct 11.00–17.00. Historic small town.
Road From M4 J15 at Swindon, A420 towards Oxford to Faringdon.
Rail/bus Swindon or Oxford (from Paddington, London) then 66 bus hourly, not Sun, sadly, but you can see the outside.
Tourist information ☎ 01367 242191.

Barwick Park follies, near Yeovil, Somerset
Road Off A37 a couple of miles before Yeovil coming from Dorchester. Look out for needle; the rest are within a mile to east and north. From London/M25, M3 to J8, then A303 to Yeovil.
Rail/bus Yeovil Junction, on London Waterloo–Exeter line; turn immediately right and then left into Two Towers Lane. Follies on right hand side, village on left.
Tourist information ☎ 01935 471279.

Crewkerne Minster, Somerset
Road From M5 J25 take A358 southwest, then A30 east.
Rail On London Waterloo–Exeter line.
Tourist information ☎ 01460 73441.

Gothic Temple, Stowe, Buckinghamshire; ☎ 01280 822850 (National Trust)
Rail/bus Milton Keynes then bus.
Road From M1 J15A, A43 south, then A413 towards Buckingham. Stowe is on the right.
Tourist information ☎ 01908 558300.

Haldon Belvedere, near Exeter, Devon
Open Sundays and Bank Holidays, April–Sept, and school summer holidays Mon–Fri 14.99–17.00. It's also hired for weddings, meetings, etc (Ian Turner, ☎ 01392 833668), and there is a holiday apartment to let (Rural Retreats, ☎ 01386 701177).
Road Signposted from A38 going towards Plymouth, look for white tower. At Dunchideock.
Tourist information ☎ 01392 265700.

King's Cross Lighthouse, King's Cross, London N1
Notorious area at night.
Road East end of Euston Rd ring road.

Rail Opposite King's Cross main line terminus from north and east, tube station on Piccadilly, Victoria, Metropolitan, Circle and Northern City branch lines.
Bus Many routes.

Leinster Gardens, Bayswater, London W2
Rail/bus Use Bayswater tube, then follow line towards Paddington on foot. Many buses pass Bayswater.

Lincoln Imp, Lincoln Cathedral
Road From A46 from A1 at Newark and also from Leicester and English Midlands.
Rail From London King's Cross.
Tourist information ↘ 01522 529828.

Mad Jack Fuller's follies, East Sussex
Around the tiny village of Brightling, south of larger village of Burwash (with Kipling's house, Batemans, and pubs).
Road From London or M25, take A21 Hastings road to Hurst Green then right on A265 to Burwash. Explore roads to Brightling to left.
Rail/bus Etchingham station, on London Charing Cross–Hastings line, is 2 miles from Burwash, then walk, 318 bus (not Sundays) or taxi.
Tourist information ↘ 01424 773721.

Massey's Folly, Farringdon, Hampshire
Sleepy picturesque backwater.
Road Off A3 at only roundabout from the London outskirts to Portsmouth, 50 miles from London. Turn north up B3006 towards Alton through Selborne (pubs, shop, tea shop and museums), then Farringdon is down narrow lanes to left.
Rail/bus Alton or Petersfield stations, from London Waterloo, then 72 bus; get off at old toll house for walk to Farringdon. Not Sundays.
Tourist information ↘ 01420 88448 (Alton).

Melrose Abbey, Borders
Road From Edinburgh, or A1 near Darlington, take A68 which passes close to Melrose.
Rail/bus Edinburgh Waverley station, from London King's Cross and many centres; then bus Lowland 62 from St Andrew's bus station, Edinburgh.
Tourist information ↘ 0131-473 3800.

Mount Edgcumbe, Cornwall
Road From M5 end at Exeter, take A38 to Plymouth, through city to Devonport for ferry to Torpoint, then follow signs.
Rail/bus Plymouth station, from London Paddington and many other centres, then walk to Royal Parade and catch bus 33 to Admiral's Hard in Stonehouse district. Then Cremyll foot ferry (a great, inexpensive ride) direct to country park.
Tourist information ↘ 01752 266030

Mow Cop, Cheshire
Road From M6J17 travel east on A534 to Congleton, then south on A34 for about 5 miles and it is on the left (east).
Rail Nearest station: Kidsgrove, from London Euston via Crewe.
Tourist information ↘ 01260 271095.

Nelson's or Paxton's Tower, Llanarthney, Carmarthenshire
Road From the end of the M4 continue towards Carmarthen. Turn right (north) on
B4310 and after about 2 miles right again on B4300 going east. The tower is on the
right after Llanarthney.
Rail Nearest stations Carmarthen (from London Paddington) or Llandeilo (Central
Wales line).
Tourist information ✆ 01558 824226.

Oxford gargoyles
Road From London/M25 or Birmingham, take M40.
Rail/bus On London Paddington–Birmingham line and also cross-country routes.
Frequent coaches from London.
Tourist information ✆ 01865 726871.

Pagoda, Kew Gardens, Surrey; ✆ 020 8940 1171
The world's leading botanic gardens, plus other follies.
Road South of Kew Bridge on the north/south circular roads and north of A316 which
links M3 to Chiswick.
Rail Kew Gardens, District Line tube and North London main line.

Red Devil, Stonegate, York
Road A64 links to A1 from north and south.
Rail From London King's Cross and other centres.
Tourist information ✆ 01904 554488.

Palladian church and ruin, Ayot St Lawrence, Hertfordshire
Tiny village also offers Shaw's Corner (home of writer) and pub.
Road Travel north on B651 from St Albans (signed from M25 and M1) through
Wheathampstead; turn right at end of village and look for signs on left.
Rail/bus St Albans City from London King's Cross Thameslink, then bus 357, then walk
approx 1 mile).
Tourist information ✆ 01727 864511.

Riber Castle, Matlock, Derbyshire
Amid great scenery.
Road From M1, go to Derby, take A6 to Matlock, then from Crown Square roundabout
take A615 to Tansley, turn right into Alders Lane and follow signs.
Rail/bus Branch line train from Derby to Matlock, then a stiff 20-min walk. Details of
route from TIC (below). Or hourly 158 bus from Matlock bus station.
Tourist information ✆ 01629 55082.

Rosslyn Chapel, Midlothian; ✆ 0131 440 2159
Road Signed off A701, south from Edinburgh a couple of miles from A720 ring road.
Rail/bus Edinburgh Waverley station, from London King's Cross and many centres; then
bus Eastern 315 from St Andrew's bus station.
Tourist information ✆ 0131 473 3800; web: www.rosslynchapel.org.uk

Royal Pavilion, Old Steine, Brighton; ✆ 01273 290900
Road From London and M25, A23.

Rail From London Victoria and other centres.
Tourist information ☎ 01273 292599.

Severndroog Castle, Castlewood Park, near Blackheath, London SE18
Rail Eltham, from Charing Cross, then walk up Well Hall Road.
Road From Rochester Way A2, turn north on Well Hall Rd, then right on A207
Shooters Hill. Park is on the right. Caution at night: this area became notorious for
unsolved racial attacks in the 1990s.

St Mary's, Beverley, Yorkshire
Road 8 miles north of Hull. From M6, M1 or A1 use M62 east to J38, then B1230.
Rail From London King's Cross, change at York or Hull.
Tourist information ☎ 01482 867430.

Tattingstone Wonder, Suffolk
Near Flatford Mill, of Constable fame (National Trust).
Road From London or M25 take A12 and look for right turn at Capel St Mary about 4
miles short of Colchester.
Road Nearest station Manningtree, then about 3-mile walk or taxi.
Tourist information ☎ 01473 258070.

Triangular Lodge, Rushton (not nearby Rushden), Northamptonshire
Road From M1 J19, A14 east to Rothwell, A6 north to Desborough then turn east
(right) for Rushton.
Rail Nearest station Kettering (London St Pancras–Nottingham line).
Tourist information ☎ 01858 821270.

Wentworth Woodhouse follies, Rotherham, Yorkshire
Ownership and use of property changing at time of writing. Use OS maps to follow
rights of way.

'I think for my part one half of the nation is mad – and the other not very sound.'

Tobias Smollett

Part Four

Practical Information

Nuts and Bolts

12

A visitor from New Zealand suggested this helpful nuts and bolts chapter mainly for first-time visitors to Britain (although it could be argued that it's the only chapter without nuts). Natives may skip it, or could read on and drop me a line with further suggestions ...

GETTING AROUND

Most places of interest in this book have travel information attached at the end of chapters if they are worth a visit as well as reading about. If rail, road or bus details are not given in particular locations, it is because they are impractical.

Self-drive and roads

The motorway system (blue signs, blue on maps, numbers such as M1 or A3(M) etc) connects many major centres with a 70mph speed limit (many Brits are as keen to add 10 per cent here as they are reluctant to do so on restaurant bills). It leaves many gaps to be covered by A roads (green signs, red or green on maps, called A9 etc). B roads and unclassified roads (white signs usually with black or blue edges, yellow or white on maps) give access, slowly, to the real Britain. The speed limit is 60mph apart from on dual carriageways, where it is 70mph, and in urban areas it is 30mph where regular street lights can be seen, unless signs say otherwise.

Motorways usually give quick access but have disadvantages:

- The M25 and other motorways near London, and those near Birmingham, can jam up spectacularly in peak hours or even during the day. Then they can become hell-on-earth as there is no chance of getting off the road. Listen to local radio when on these routes. Modern RDS car radios often have a TA button for traffic announcements. If pressed, TA will show on the display and traffic warnings from any local station will interrupt your radio or even tape listening and could save a lot of boring queuing in traffic jams. Even then you need a passenger to work out what the junction numbers mean or check them before setting off.
- August Saturdays are equally hot and hellish on the routes leading to/from main holiday areas because this is changeover day for millions of holidaymakers. Avoid routes to Exeter (M5, A30 and A38) and the West Country, or the M6 to the Lake District at these times.

- Equally, avoid leaving south coast beaches such as Bournemouth, Brighton for London at 16.00–20.00 on a hot summer Sunday, as you will queue much of the way back. Spend the evening there and travel back late in half the time.
- Motorway service areas are infrequent, sell overpriced petrol and oft-criticised food in places with the ambience, often, of third-rate airports. If you have plenty of time and are not running out of petrol, turn off for cheaper pub food, more choice, and cheaper fuel.
- The main thing you see on motorway journeys is tarmac and the backs of lorries. Often there will be a parallel A road which it superseded, or meandering empty B roads which get you into the real Britain (warts and all). If you've got plenty of time, check out the map, avoid heavily built-up areas, and take a gamble on a side route. Remember, the rolling English drunk made the rolling English road, so don't expect to get anywhere fast. If you don't want to take a gamble, get *5 Minutes Off The Motorway* (Cadogan Books, £3.99) for guidance about food and drink.

Hire cars

Major chains are in most areas and may operate a no-need-to-return-to-point-A deal. These include (with phone number and quote for weekend in smallest car at time of writing, age/licence requirement and any website):

Budget ☏ 0541 565656 (£75.01; 25; www.drivebudget.co.uk)
Avis ☏ 0870 60 60 100 (£87; 25; www.avis.com)
Europcar ☏ 0870 607 5000 (£66.11; 25; EU licences only, www.europcar.com)
Hertz ☏ 08708 448844 (£38 – a promotional rate; 25; www.hertz.com)
Kenning ☏ 0870 1 555900 (£65.75; 23; www.kenning.co.uk).

The moral is: don't settle for the first rate quoted, but phone around. Use Yellow Pages and also check local operators. These were all for similar cars, with just about everything included except petrol. Unblemished licences and some credit standing are usually required. Discounts are often given for frequent flyer or motoring organisation memberships or for just haggling a little. Bicycle and motorbike hire is less common, but growing, particularly in tourist areas. Check Yellow Pages locally or tourist information.

Rail

When I was in New Zealand I was astonished to find there was just one train a day between the two principal cities in North Island; and in America that the train from Boston to New York was slower, cheaper and less frequent than the bus. In Britain, trains on intercity routes whack along at up to 125mph and even where I write in sleepy Hampshire there are four trains in each direction an hour, with services from before dawn to midnight. Trains are expensive, however, and following privatisation, fares can be complex. Discount cards for various groups are available (see *Express coach travel*, page 221), plus a Network Card, which bizarrely works only within about 100 miles of London. Under 5s go free, under 14s at, usually, half-price. Tips:

- Don't travel in major city areas before 09.30 unless you have to as it's twice as expensive and four times as horrible (due to overcrowding). Also avoid 17.00–19.00 if possible.
- For long distances, check out bargain advance booking fares which can halve the cost but often apply to certain trains only. For instance, Brighton to Manchester (1999) prices comes down from £57 return to £33 with a week's advance booking.
- A ticket does not, strangely, represent a seat. If you've ever had to stand from Darlington to London you'll never forget to book a seat *as well* as a ticket on a long-distance run. It costs only a little more and has to be done in advance. Most people don't book a seat and retain the freedom to go on any train and return on any train (subject to ticket type restrictions). Booking seats is impossible and/or unnecessary on most local or rural branches.
- If you want a total freedom-to-roam-around-Britain railcard for a week, month or whatever and have just arrived in the country, forget it. You have to buy them from abroad for some insane reason. See your travel agent.
- Information: National Inquiries gives fares and times from anywhere to anywhere at a local call charge on ☎ 0345 484950. This works pretty well but to buy a ticket or reserve a seat you will have to phone a booking line or the train company concerned – such as GNER for London to Edinburgh. You can get numbers from the above National Inquiries. This is necessary only on long-distance runs and can also be done at any major station. On shorter or secondary routes just check the time by phone, then turn up and go. For advance information/online ticketing, try the website www.thetrainline.com
- Rail staff may quote the obvious routes and fares. Persist and find out if there is more choice. There are three operators and fares from London to Gatwick Airport, for instance, and direct trains from dozens of places to the west and north of London direct to Gatwick. If you are told to go via London, which involves tedious Tube (underground train) transfers, there may be a good cross-country train or connecting ones which could be cheaper and more interesting and relaxing, if not faster, eg: Bournemouth–Edinburgh, Portsmouth–Cardiff, Norwich–Liverpool, Brighton–Manchester are all possible direct trains, with each holding many more possibilities by changing to local lines.

Metro railways

London The London Underground, known as the Tube, is the world's biggest with more than 250 stations and had the world's first clear and still excellent route map. It is, however, almost unbearably overcrowded in rush hours and often disrupted by much-overdue reconstruction. Travel is cheaper after 09.30 and discount books of ticket (carnets) may be bought for the central Zone 1. A lot of money and time queuing can be saved over a day, week, or month by getting a Travelcard for the required zones (concentric circles, getting bigger from Zone 1) which offers the marvellous flexibility of covering the red bus network and the main line above-ground railways as well as the Tube in that area. The overground trains, omitted from the normal Tube map and forgotten by most tourists, offer far more travel possibilities in the outer suburbs and are particularly strong in south London where the Tube hardly penetrates. Find a (relatively rare) London Connections wall map in stations to show both systems, or get your own free one from mainline stations. For travel information for London bus and Tube (but not main lines), ✆ 020 7222 1234; mainline: 0345 484950.

Outside London Glasgow has an underground (look for the U sign). A few other cities such as Newcastle upon Tyne have good Metro systems and others such as Birmingham, Sheffield and Manchester have a network of suburban rail services plus a smattering of reborn tram systems (as does Croydon in South London), but nothing as comprehensive as London. All have bus networks and local rail networks. Major Metros are:

Manchester Metrolink ✆ 0161 205 2000; web: www.lrta.org/metrolink.html
Newcastle ✆ 0191 2325325; web: www.tyneandwearmetro.co.uk

Steam railways

Officially abolished in the late 1960s when the steam engines were sent to scrapyards, amazingly, 40 years on, more than 100 branch lines and steam centres have been painstakingly reopened, and on a summer weekend thousands of volunteers operate these for the sheer love of it. However, many are in the nature of an admittedly pleasant but fairly expensive theme park ride and don't actually connect anywhere with anywhere. Some of the longer ones which really take you somewhere interesting through great scenery and connect with the main line (name of connecting station given in italic plus phone number, 1999 return adult price and length of line) are:

North Yorkshire Moors Railway *Grosmont* to Pickering (✆ 01947 895359, £9.20, 18 miles).
Paignton and Dartmouth Railway Devon, *Paignton* to Kingswear (includes ferry to Dartmouth at end of trip; ✆ 01803 555872, £7, 7 miles).
Severn Valley Railway Worcestershire, from *Kidderminster* to Bridgnorth (✆ 01299 403816, £9.20, 16 miles).
Strathspey Railway Scotland, *Aviemore* to Boat of Garten (✆ 01479 810725, £5, 5 miles).
Vale of Rheidol Railway Ceredigion, narrow gauge from *Aberystwyth* to Devil's Bridge (✆ 01970 625819, £10.50, 12 miles).
Watercress Line Hampshire, *Alton* to Alresford (✆ 01962 733810, £8, 10 miles).

Steam tours There are also steam tours where old trains are allowed out on the main line for an all-day or even weekend trip. They are not cheap, particularly at the luxury end of the market (the Orient Express) but great fun, if only because the trains go at a decent speed out on the main line. Beware of joining a tour that gives you six hours exploring Yorkshire freight lines but only 20 minutes at the seaside, unless that's what you want. For details of current tours, prices and operators' phone numbers, find *Railway Magazine* in a large newsagents or a local library.

Buses

Local buses Most settlements of at least large village size in Britain can be reached by local bus, but as bus services have been privatised and split up, finding out routes and times is difficult and easiest done within the relevant area. Use directory inquiries on 192 (free from phone boxes) and ask for the bus station in the nearest town. In case of difficulties, local libraries can be amazingly helpful. Find them via 192 or in local phone books. Many county councils offer a timetable and advice service. Beware, there is also something advertised as Bus Journeycall on ➙ 0906 5500000 which I found at the time of writing to be useless and expensive. It wouldn't give connections to villages at either end of my journey and charged an outrageous pound per minute for not helping me (see below about premium rate calls under Telephones).

A website: www.showbus.co.uk/timetables.htm, fails to give total timetable access, but if your route isn't given by a series of links, then at least you should find the phone number of the operator there.

London buses London, of course, offers traditional Routemaster double deckers with fabulous views upstairs at the front on a few routes such as 9, 10, 22 and 159. For London bus information: ➙ 020 7222 1234. Economy fares: see Travelcards in *Metro railways* section, page 219.

Sightseeing buses All touristy cities such as London, Edinburgh or Oxford have circular route buses, often with an open top and commentary, which you can in many cases get on and off at will, so lasting for a day of sightseeing.

Remote areas Some remote areas are served by the imaginative Postbuses whereby some Post Office vans doing their rounds now have seats. Details from county council transport departments or local libaries. Kent, for example, has 15 routes, some operated by estate cars. Another useful bus for remote spots is the Mountain Goat bus in the Lake District. This penetrates remote valleys and is helpful in planning a walk so that, for instance, you are not forced to plan circular routes back to your car. For details ➙ 015394 45161.

Express coach travel Connects most major towns and cities. The system is better organised with phone bookings possible (advisable at busy times), and the main company is National Express (➙ 0990 808080) with Victoria coach station, London (walkable from rail/Tube station) a focal point. Coach (British for long-distance bus) travel is generally slower and less frequent than train but cheaper. It does at least operate on December 26, which trains don't. There are also bargain day return fares. Tourist Trail Passes for nationwide travel over a certain period are available from National Express bus stations or travel agents, or by phone with a credit card. There are also discount coach or rail cards, for students, young persons or lone parents, disabled people, soldiers and the over 50s. (Why don't they just make a Sucker Card for people who work for a living and charge them double?) Discount cards are usually valid for 12 months and give major discounts each time you use them, but are not good value for a short period.

A website which works out times and fares for you and allows online booking is www.nationalexpress.co.uk.

Taxis

Officially designated metered taxis (see sign on roof and council authorisation plate on back of cab) in cities are unlikely to con you. In London, just hail a black cab; in the provinces, if there is no taxi rank outside stations, look for a number in phone booths or directories. London cabbies are superbly trained in terms of getting you through the metropolis, often throw in a free lecture about what's wrong with Britain, johnnie foreigner, etc, but charge like a wounded bull if you go outside the London area. They are legally obliged to take you anywhere within the London area if they stop when vacant (the yellow word TAXI being lit on the roof) so don't take any 'I'm only going east, love' excuses. Obviously, they will not be going anywhere fast in central London during rush hours. In the unlikely event of a serious dispute take either the number the driver is obliged to wear on his lapel or the number on the white plate on the back of the cab and complain via the police, who are responsible for taxis in London only.

Minicabs

There are also minicabs – unmarked cheaper cars which you have to contact by phone (see hotels, pubs, cards in phone booths, directories etc). These may overcharge you if you don't have an idea of what it should cost, and safety is more in question in terms of the car, unaccompanied females being attacked, or just getting lost. Get a few quotes to make sure you are not being ripped off. For several people it may be the cheapest way, if not the safest.

Maps

Road directions in this book are given from the nearest motorway or major road, so a basic national road map (free with most hire cars) is a must. Better ones are published by Ordnance Survey (OS), A–Z, and the AA in large book form and can be bought in petrol stations.

For hiking, biking, climbing, etc, the OS publishes brilliant local maps on a variety of scales down to the 1:25,000 Pathfinders (£4.50) showing every fence and hedge. These cover irritatingly small areas and are being replaced by bigger Explorer maps on the same scale. The best compromise for most outdoor pursuits is the 1:50,000 scale Landranger maps, but as they are expensive (£5.25 each), be selective about which of the 204 covering the country you really need. For road touring, OS does the Travelmaster series (£4.25), one for the whole country and then eight for various regions (eg: Devon and Cornwall). OS maps can be found in bookshops, tourist-related shops and outdoor pursuit shops. OS customer information helpline: ✎ 08456 050505; web: www.ordsvy.gov.uk.

In London, if you are staying for any length of time and seeing more than the obvious monuments, a street-by-street guide such as *A–Z* or *Streetfinder*, from bookshops and big newsagents, is a must. Indexed street maps are available for most cities and towns from bookshops and garages.

For online maps of nearly every town plus all UK countryside: www.multimap.com.

Paths

England and Wales are criss-crossed with a unique network of public footpaths, bridleways (for horses, walkers and mountain bikes) and other public rights-of-way shown on OS maps. You have a perfect right to travel through farmland, glorious private estates, even people's gardens on these paths which are often also waymarked on the ground by local councils with small signs and often small arrows on fences, etc. As I once told a landowner who had put a barbed wire fence across one, they are the Queen's Highway as much as the mightiest motorway in the land and must not be obstructed. He moved the fence. Technically, you have the right to pass and repass rather than sit down and have a picnic or pitch camp.

In Scotland, the situation is less formal. In open country and the Highlands just follow any path and you should be all right, unless told otherwise by notices or stalkers (of deer, not people). At the time of writing the government is considering extending this right to roam to the rest of Britain. Further information is available from: Ramblers Association, ☎ 020 7339 8500; Scottish Ramblers: ☎ 01577 861222.

Economy tip A truly great walk such as the Coast to Coast walk across northern England (two weeks, see pocket-sized book by A Wainwright, *Westmorland Gazette*, £7.95) infuriatingly requires four expensive OS maps for just one day of 14 as you wander along the edges of the pages. Save more than £40 by buying the whole thing on two Footprint ribbon maps, showing a mile-wide band. These cost £2.95 each plus 40p p&p from Unit 87, Stirling Enterprise Park, Stirling FK67 7RP. Generally, if you are looking for somewhere that may be on one of several maps, check it out in a public library before buying.

WHERE TO STAY
Hotels

These are mostly shockingly expensive compared with American motels or French hotels (eg: £50 per person for medium standard). However, don't be afraid to haggle and don't agree the first price quoted. Hmm and ermm and say something like 'I was looking for something at a better rate' and if they're not busy they'll knock off £10 or give you breakfast for free.

Full English (or British) breakfast, by the way, is the full monty with more types of cholesterol than you've eaten for years. It's a bargain because you won't need any lunch. Remember you can ask for scrambled or boiled egg, or beans on toast, if you can't face any more fried food, but ask the night before. Continental breakfast (a roll, jam and coffee) is for supermodels, heart attack victims and wimps.

Be clear about whether you're paying by the room or per person (more usual). If you've got the time and the money, country inns and pubs can offer

HOW TO STAY ECCENTRIC

If you've ever wondered about spending a night in a brothel, or putting the children behind bars, now's your chance. Or, indeed, you could enjoy a stay in a lighthouse, an onion store or an old fort – all are on offer from the Distinctly Different group of B&Bs and hotels.

The properties have all been converted to hotel or B&B accommodation. There is a village lock-up at Farndon, near Chester (which retains its barred windows) or another at Wirksworth, Derbyshire which keeps its iron-studded doors with trapdoors for feeding and locks on the outside.

Then there are the possibilities of wild nights – weatherwise – at old lighthouses at West Usk lighthouse, St Brides Wentlloog, Gwent; Great Ormes Head, Llandudno, or Kirkcolm, near Stranraer, which last affords views across to Northern Ireland and the Mull of Kintyre.

The Boatmen's Brothel at Jackfield near Ironbridge, Shropshire, has had its cubicles converted to more respectable use while the onion store is at Wellow Mead, on Florence Nightingale's old estate at Sherfield English, Romsey, Hampshire. Or, if you feel besieged by life, you can hire a massive Victorian fort accommodating up to 30 people complete with deep cannon casemates at Polhawn Fort, Rame, Torpoint, Cornwall. All are marketed through Distinctly Different.

The Landmark Trust lets a truly remarkable range of whole properties for longer periods as holiday homes, be it a water tower at Sandringham, Norfolk, a bathhouse at Stratford upon Avon, a House of Correction near Grantham, Lincolnshire, various fantastic or grim castles or towers (many detailed in this book) and even a pigsty at Robin Hood's Bay, North

wonderful atmosphere and country house hotels offer delusions of stately living. Scotland offers a crown rating system for hotel standards, and although England and Wales have traditionally not bothered with ratings and left them to motoring organisations, etc, the tourist authorities have at last decided to introduce an official star system.

Cheaper chain hotels offer basic facilities at a room rate, but if you just need to get your head down after a long drive, who cares about the ambience? Travelodge (✆ 0800 850950) is one – see ads in national papers for frequent discount deals, which may let children stay free for two-night weekends.

Bed & breakfast

Usually cheaper than hotels (£15–30 per person), bed & breakfast (B&B) means a room in a family house. You may have to share the bathroom, you will certainly have to be out by a certain time in the morning, but you'll meet some local people. Breakfast compares with what is offered by hotels. Drink the tea, it's usually better than the coffee. Get numbers and prices through tourist information centres in the relevant area (numbers given throughout book at chapter ends).

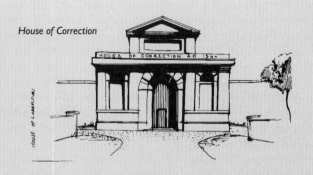

House of Correction

Yorkshire.

These properties are not cheap, particularly in high season, and the Trust's foreign purchases such as Italian villas seem to fit oddly with the whole concept, but as a major building preservation charity it has saved and restored many extraordinary gems at great expense, and as the castles, watchtowers, etc often accommodate a large number of visitors, the cost can be divided among like-minded friends. The catalogue makes a great coffee-table browser.

And don't come home complaining that a medieval castle is a bit cold in January, as one Sunday paper hack did recently.

Distinctly Different, ↘ 01225 866648.
The Landmark Trust, ↘ 01628 825925; web: www.landmarktrust.co.uk

Youth hostels

These offer basic accommodation, but not so often dormitories nowadays, at bargain prices (£7–12 typically) in often beautiful locations; good for outdoor activities, families and groups. You are expected to go out during the day. Hostels vary from almost bare log cabins in mountain areas to virtual hotels in big cities, where a room can cost as much as £22. You don't have to be young but must be a member of the England and Wales YHA, the Scottish YHA or your own country's YHA. Guest membership is £11 a year and you can join at your first hostel. The *YHA Guide*, which members receive, gives locations and helps you book ahead by phone (advisable): ↘ 01727 845047. There is a separate Scottish YHA (↘ 01786 891400) but the membership applies across the border. Web: www.yha.org.uk.

FOOD

British food has come on by leaps and bounds in the last 30 years, but that was starting from almost wartime drabness. Pubs now offer a large range of usually competitively priced if not too adventurous meals, and children's portions on request. To generalise, Britons don't choose to eat British food unless they're rich (some excellent expensive restaurants serve fish, game and regional specialities), poor (roadside or transport cafés, pronounced caffs, also called 'greasy spoons'), or in a hurry (motorway services, the Little Chef chain of pull-ins, or the traditional fish 'n' chips). Chip shop specialities to look out for include: pickled eggs, gherkins (south), mushy peas and curry sauce (north of Watford), black pudding, white pudding or haggis supper (north of Newcastle). These all taste good out of a paper wrapper in a freezing street. The chips, by the way, should be as fat as your fingers and possibly bendy and soaked in vinegar. Those thin crispy things are french fries. And if Americans want 'chips', they should ask for crisps.

Most Britons much prefer Indian, Chinese or Thai food for a treat, so much so that I have American friends who come over partly because of the excellent and cheap Indian food. Of course, if you choose a smart restaurant in a well-to-do area, it won't be so cheap.

Our weird licensing laws
It can be difficult to explain to visitors used to European cafés, why you have to leave children outside most pubs, why you can't get a drink even in big cities after leaving work at 23.00, or why the supermarkets cover up the alcohol (or just pretend it's not there) at certain times. In England and Wales, most pubs are still inflexible about allowing children into a bar unless:

- you're eating with them
- the pub has a children's licence
- there is a family room (no bar)
- the landlord ignores the law.

Opening hours are particularly inflexible on Sundays (typically 12.00–14.00, and 19.00–22.30) and you can't even buy a can of beer in a shop outside these hours. These restrictions also apply to religious public holidays (Good Friday and Christmas Day). In Scotland, as in many things, the rules are much more flexible (having been much more restrictive until recently).

TELEPHONES
In emergencies dial 999, and ask for fire, ambulance, police or coastguard – calls are free of charge. Directory enquiries is 192, free from phone boxes; if you're paying, hang on and get a second query for the same call. Always check the small print about any lines advertised offering to help you – they are obliged to state if they are a premium rate number, which often start with an 08 or 09 and frequently rip you off for doing very little. On the other hand, 0800 or 0500 numbers are free, and 0345 ones are at cheap local rates. You have to pay for local calls in Britain, and most hotels charge more on top.

Some phone numbers in Britain have just changed their codes. If you are given old London numbers starting with 0171, replace that with 020 7, and replace 0181 with 020 8. For other changes, see the local phone directory.

Eccentric Days Out

13

Travellers in various parts of Britain might prefer to miss the obvious beefeaters, theme parks and stately homes and use this book to strike out to discover the surprising, the downright peculiar or the simply rather curious (not to mention the real and the mostly free as opposed to the fake and the rip-off). Here are some suggested itineraries which, being off the beaten track, in most cases take in some of the most unspoilt countryside in Britain. These necessarily consist more of places and things than people and ceremonies, because it is not feasible to include the events in the Eccentric Year (Chapter 1), which occur at frequencies from daily up to once every 100 years. Check the relevant month there to see if something strange is happening near your route.

These itineraries are drawn up with road travel in mind, except for three London ones where you could use public transport. Many involve some effort in walking to and finding some of the sights, which are often fairly remote and hidden away. Travel details are not repeated, as they are given at the ends of the chapters after the relevant pages referred to, but you'll need a good road map (see page 222).

As this book is about being eccentric, you will no doubt diverge from the suggested route and find your own oddities. If they are fascinating, do drop me a line.

Cornwall	Cupid's Obelisk, Mount Edgcumbe (page 78), The Hurlers, Minions (page 182), Lanhydrock Lodge, Bodmin (page 160), Bodmin Obelisk, (page 173), Carn Brea, Redruth (page 173), Pilchard Museum, Newlyn (page 53).
Central Dorset and south Somerset	'Wrong' Hardy Monument, Portesham (page 99), Hardy's heart, Stinsford (page 98), Cerne Giant (page 183), Barwick Park follies, Yeovil (page 189), musical gargoyles, Crewkerne Minster (page 207).
East Dorset and Purbeck	Mappowder boy crusader (page 101), Red signpost, Winterbourne Zelston (page 176), Transportation Bridge, Wool (page 157), Swanage Lock-up (page 163).

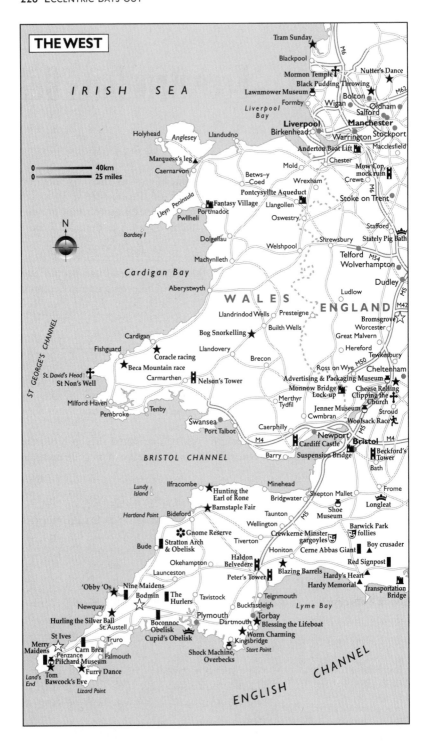

THE WEST

IRISH SEA

Tram Sunday

Blackpool

Nutter's Dance

Mormon Temple
Black Pudding Throwing
Lawnmower Museum
Bolton

Formby
Wigan
Oldham
Salford

Liverpool Bay

Holyhead
Anglesey
Llandudno

Liverpool
Manchester
Birkenhead
Warrington
Stockport

Marquess's leg
Caernarvon

Betws-y-Coed
Mold

Chester
Macclesfield

Anderton Boat Lift

Mow Cop mock ruin
Crewe

Wrexham

Stoke on Trent

Lleyn Peninsula

Fantasy Village
Portmadoc
Pwllheli

Pontcysyllte Aqueduct
Llangollen

Oswestry

Stafford

Bardsey I

Dolgellau

Welshpool
Shrewsbury

Stately Pig Bath

Machynlleth

Telford
Wolverhampton

Cardigan Bay

Dudley

Aberystwyth

WALES

Ludlow

ENGLAND

Llandrindod Wells
Presteigne

Bromsgrove
Worcester

Cardigan

Bog Snorkelling

Builth Wells

Great Malvern

Fishguard

Coracle racing

Llandovery

Brecon

Hereford

Tewkesbury

St David's Head
St Non's Well

Beca Mountain race
Carmarthen

Nelson's Tower

Ross on Wye

Cheltenham

Advertising & Packaging Museum

Milford Haven

Monnow Bridge
Lock-up

Cheese Rolling
Clipping the
Church

Pembroke
Tenby

Merthyr
Tydfil

Jenner Museum

Stroud

Swansea
Port Talbot

Caerphilly

Cwmbran

Woolsack Race

BRISTOL CHANNEL

Newport
Cardiff Castle
Suspension Bridge
Barry

Bristol
Beckford's
Tower

Bath

Lundy
Island

Ilfracombe

Minehead

Frome

Hunting the
Earl of Rone
Barnstaple Fair

Bridgwater

Shepton Mallet
Shoe
Museum

Longleat

Hartland Point

Bideford

Taunton

Wellington

Barwick Park
follies

Gnome Reserve

Crewkerne Minster
gargoyles

Boy crusader

Bude

Stratton Arch
& Obelisk

Tiverton

Honiton

Cerne Abbas Giant

Launceston

Okehampton

Haldon
Belvedere

Red Signpost

Blazing Barrels

'Obby 'Os
Nine Maidens
Bodmin

Peter's Tower

Hardy's Heart
Hardy Memorial

Transportation
Bridge

The
Hurlers

Tavistock

Teignmouth

Buckfastleigh

Lyme Bay

Newquay

Hurling the Silver Ball
St Austell

Boconnoc
Obelisk
Cupid's Obelisk

Plymouth
Dartmouth

Torbay
Blessing the Lifeboat

St Ives
Merry
Maidens
Penzance

Truro
Falmouth

Kingsbridge

Worm Charming

Carn Brea
Pilchard Museum
Furry Dance

Shock Machine,
Overbecks

Start Point

Land's
End
Tom
Bawcock's Eve

Lizard Point

ENGLISH CHANNEL

ST GEORGE'S CHANNEL

N

0   40km
0   25 miles

Gloucester/Somerset	Advertising and Packaging Museum, Gloucester or Jenner Museum, Berkeley (page 49), Clifton Bridge, Bristol (page 158), Beckford's Tower, Bath (page 195), Longleat (page 77) or Stourhead (page 197).
Isle of Wight and Hampshire	If starting on Isle of Wight: Yarborough Obelisk, Bembridge (page 174), Wireless Museum, Ryde (page 54), ferry from Yarmouth. Hampshire: Lymington Obelisk (page 174), National Motor Museum, Beaulieu (page 48), Sway Tower★ (page 193), Luttrell's Tower, Eaglehurst★ (page 198), Surreal Garden, Stansted Park (page 143), Pub With No Name, if you can find it (page 153).
Oxfordshire	Baron Berners' Folly, Faringdon (page 199), Shark House, Headington★ (page 123), Gargoyles, Oxford (page 207), Wheatley Lock-up (page 162).
Thames Valley	Pangbourne Lock-up★ (page 162), Elephant Triangle (page 180), Max Bowker's garage, Swallowfield★ (page 131).
Buckinghamshire and northwest London	West Wycombe Park, Hellfire Caves and Dashwood Mausoleum (page 100), St Mary's, Harrow-on-the-Hill (page 97), Swaminarayan Hindu Temple, Neasden (page 119). If you are using the Tube system, omit the first two (or use main line from High Wycombe, reached by bus from West Wycombe), and add Giro's Memorial Grave (page 88).
Southwest London	Stag Lodge, Wimbledon★ (page 160), Buddhapadipa Temple, Wimbledon (page 117), Fireplates Obelisk, Putney (page 173), Burton Tomb, Mortlake (page 94), Hammersmith Bridge and Monument (page 159), Leighton House (page 94). The first three are walkable with an *A–Z* type map, then walk or take a bus down Putney Hill to Putney station, take a train two stops west to Mortlake for Burton's tent, then 9A bus to the last two. Total walking about 2½ miles. Ideal for cycling, in which case don't miss, so to speak, Marc Bolan's tree (page 177).

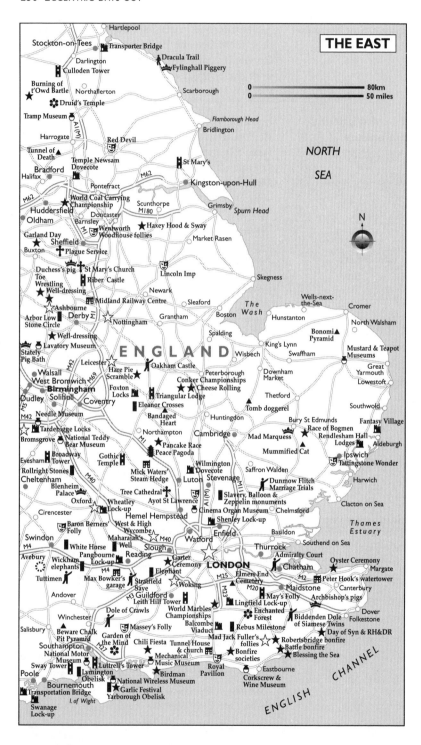

THE EAST

0 ————————————— 80km
0 ————————————— 50 miles

N

NORTH SEA

ENGLAND

The Wash

Thames Estuary

ENGLISH CHANNEL

Hartlepool
Stockton-on-Tees
Transporter Bridge
Darlington
Culloden Tower
Dracula Trail
Fylinghall Piggery
Burning of t'Owd Bartle
Northallerton
Scarborough
Druid's Temple
Tramp Museum
Flamborough Head
Bridlington
Harrogate
Red Devil
Tunnel of Death
Bradford
Temple Newsam Dovecote
St Mary's
Halifax
Pontefract
Kingston-upon-Hull
World Coal Carrying Championship
Scunthorpe
Grimsby
Spurn Head
Huddersfield
Oldham
Doncaster
Barnsley
Haxey Hood & Sway
Garland Day
Wentworth Woodhouse follies
Market Rasen
Sheffield
Plague Service
Buxton
Skegness
Duchess's pig
St Mary's Church
Lincoln Imp
Toe Wrestling
Riber Castle
Well-dressing
Newark
Ashbourne
Midland Railway Centre
Sleaford
Wells-next-the-Sea
Cromer
Arbor Low Stone Circle
Derby
Nottingham
Grantham
Boston
Hunstanton
North Walsham
Well-dressing
Spalding
Bonomi Pyramid
Lavatory Museum
King's Lynn
Wisbech
Swaffham
Mustard & Teapot Museums
Stately Pig Bath
Walsall
Leicester
Oakham Castle
Downham Market
Great Yarmouth
West Bromwich
Hare Pie Scramble
Peterborough
Lowestoft
Birmingham
Foxton Locks
Conker Championships
Cheese Rolling
Thetford
Southwold
Dudley
Solihull
Coventry
Triangular Lodge
Tomb doggerel
Needle Museum
Eleanor Crosses
Huntingdon
Bury St Edmunds
Fantasy Village
Tardebigge Locks
Bandaged Heart
Cambridge
Mad Marquess
Race of Bogmen
Rendlesham Hall Lodges
Bromsgrove
National Teddy Bear Museum
Northampton
Mummified Cat
Aldeburgh
Broadway Tower
Pancake Race
Ipswich
Evesham
Gothic Temple
Peace Pagoda
Tattingstone Wonder
Rollright Stones
Cheltenham
Mick Waters' Steam Hedge
Wilmington Dovecote
Saffron Walden
Harwich
Blenheim Palace
Luton
Stevenage
Dunmow Flitch Marriage Trials
Oxford
Tree Cathedral
Wheatley Lock-up
Ayot St Lawrence
Slavery, Balloon & Zeppelin monuments
Cirencester
Hemel Hempstead
Cinema Organ Museum
Chelmsford
Clacton on Sea
Baron Berners' Folly
West & High Wycombe
Shenley Lock-up
Basildon
Swindon
Maharajah's Well
Watford
Enfield
Southend on Sea
White Horse
Pangbourne Lock-up
Slough
Thurrock
Admiralty Court
Avebury
Reading
Garter Ceremony
LONDON
Chatham
Oyster Ceremony
Wickham elephants
Elephant
Peter Hook's watertower
Margate
Tuttimen
Max Bowker's garage
Strafield Saye
Woking
Maidstone
Canterbury
Andover
Guildford
Leith Hill Tower
Elmers End Cemetery
May's Folly
Archbishop's pigs
Winchester
Dole of Crawls
Lingfield Lock-up
Biddenden Dole of Siamese Twins
Dover
Massey's Folly
World Marbles Championships
Enchanted Forest
Folkestone
Salisbury
Beware Chalk Pit Pyramid
Garden of the Mind
Balcombe Viaduct
Rebus Milestone
Day of Syn & RH&DR
Southampton
Chili Fiesta
Mad Jack Fuller's follies
Robertsbridge bonfire
National Motor Museum
Tunnel House & church
Mechanical Music Museum
Bonfire societies
Battle bonfire
Blessing the Sea
Sway Tower
Luttrell's Tower
Royal Pavilion
Eastbourne
Poole
Lymington Obelisk
Birdman
Corkscrew & Wine Museum
Bournemouth
National Wireless Museum
Transportation Bridge
Garlic Festival
Yarborough Obelisk
I. of Wight
Swanage Lock-up

Central London Sham houses, Leinster Gardens, Bayswater (page 205), Marquess of Anglesey's Leg, National Army Museum, Chelsea (page 87), Giro's Memorial, Waterloo Place (page 88), Operating Theatre Museum (page 52), King's Cross Lighthouse (page 199), Brass Crosby Milestone, Kennington (page 175).

Surrey Brookwood Cemetery (pages 90 and 175), Shah Jehan Mosque, Woking (page 118), White Lady Milestone, Esher (page 175), Leith Hill Tower, Coldharbour (page 197).

Sussex Lingfield Lock-up (just in Surrey) (page 164), Balcombe Viaduct (page 158), Clayton Tunnel House★ and church (page 126), Rebus Milestone, Maresfield (page 175).

Kent–Sussex borders May's Folly, Hadlow★ (page 194), Enchanted Forest, Groombridge Place (page 145), Mad Jack Fuller's follies (page 189), Corkscrew Museum, Alfriston (page 50).

Hertfordshire Ayot St Lawrence (page 206), Cinema Organ Museum, St Albans (page 49), Shenley Lock-up (page 163), Zeppelin Monument, Cuffley (page 178), Streatton's Folly, Little Berkhamsted★ (page 195), Balloon Monument, Standon Green End★ (page 178) and Clarkson Monument (page 169).

Suffolk Mummified cat and Guildhall, Lavenham (page 98), Tattingstone Wonder (page 207), Rendlesham Hall Lodges★ (page 150), Thorpeness fantasy village (page 164).

Norfolk and East Anglia Bonomi Pyramid, Blickling Hall (page 86), Mustard and Teapot Museums, Norwich (page 52), Railway memorial, Ely Cathedral (page 96).

Northamptonshire Triangular Lodge, Rushton (page 201), Eleanor Cross, Geddington (page 177), bandaged heart, St Mary's Church, Woodford (page 101), Foxton staircase canal locks (page 154).

English West Midlands Tardebigge locks (page 155), Railway grave, St John's Church, Bromsgrove (page 97), Needle Museum, Redditch (page 52), Broadway Tower (page 196), Rollright Stones, near Stratford-upon-Avon (page 185).

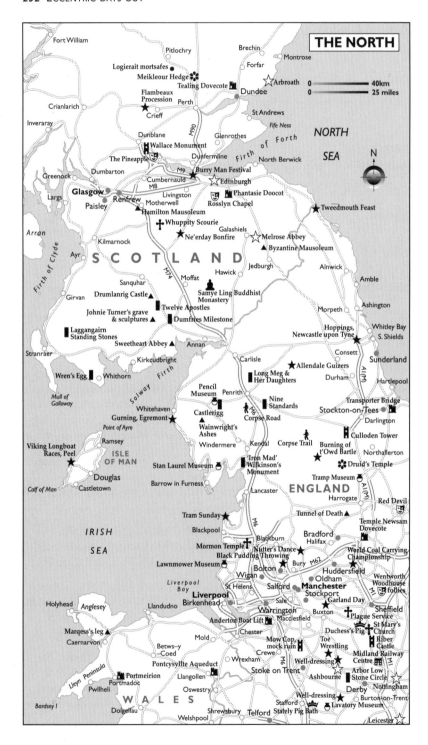

Peak District   Longest pub sign, Ashbourne (page 150), Riber
                           Castle, Matlock (page 206), Arbor Low Stone
                           Circle (page 185).

North Wales   Pontcysyllte Aqueduct, Llangollen (page 154),
                           Portmeirion fantasy village (page 164), Llanfair
                           PG and Marquess's leg, Plas Newydd, Anglesey
                           (page 87).

Cumbria   Stan Laurel Museum, Ulverston (page 51), 'Iron
                           Mad' Wilkinson's Monument, Lindale (page 169),
                           Corpse Road, Haweswater (page 93), Nine
                           Standards, near Kirby Stephen (page 184) or
                           Castlerigg Stone Circle, Keswick (page 185).

Northwest England   Preston Temple (page 118), Lawnmower
                           Museum, Southport (page 51), Anderton Boat
                           Lift, Northwich (page 155), Mow Cop (page 206).

Northeast England   Corpse Trail, Swaledale (page 93), Culloden
                           Tower, Richmond (page 195), Druids' Temple,
                           Ilton Moor (page 146), Transporter Bridge,
                           Middlesbrough (page 156), and Dracula Trail,
                           Whitby (page 94).

Scots Borders and   Melrose Abbey (page 102), Byzantine Mausoleum,
Lothian   Borders (page 104), Rosslyn Chapel (page 209),
                           Edinburgh dovecote (page 162), Deacon Brodie's
                           Tavern, Edinburgh (page 151).

Southwest Scotland   Sweetheart Abbey (page 102), Johnie Turner's
                           grave and sculptures, Glenkiln, near Dumfries
                           (page 103), Twelve Apostles, Holywood (page
                           184), Dumfries milestone (page 176).

Central Scotland to   The Pineapple, Dunmore (page 198), Wallace
Angus   Monument, Stirling (page 193); Mortsafes,
                           Logierait (page 103), Meikleour Hedge (page
                           141), Fraser Mausoleum, Arbroath (page 104).

★ Denotes private property which should be viewed from a distance from a
public road or footpath. For places of worship, see note in Chapter 6.
Inclusion in this list does not guarantee a right of access; please phone to check
seasonal opening hours, etc, if visiting attractions.

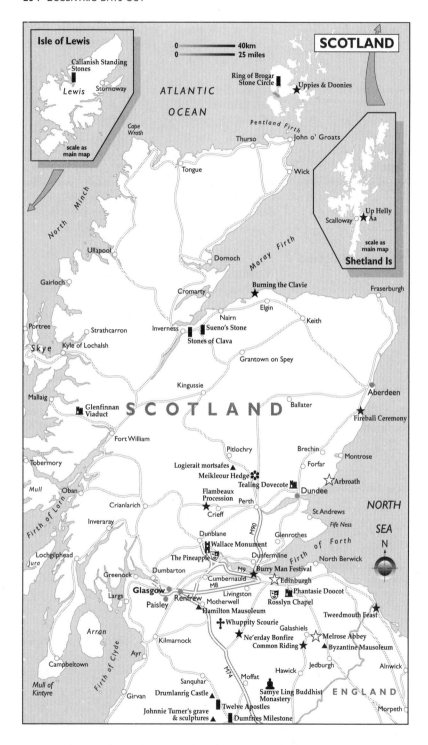

SCOTLAND

0 ————————— 40km
0 ————————— 25 miles

Isle of Lewis

Callanish Standing Stones

Lewis

Stornoway

scale as main map

ATLANTIC

OCEAN

Ring of Brogar Stone Circle

Uppies & Doonies

Pentland Firth

Cape Wrath

Thurso

John o' Groats

Tongue

Wick

Scalloway

Up Helly Aa

scale as main map

Shetland Is

North Minch

Ullapool

Dornoch

Moray Firth

Fraserburgh

Gairloch

Cromarty

Burning the Clavie

Elgin

Keith

Portree

Nairn

Sueno's Stone

Strathcarron

Inverness

Stones of Clava

Skye

Kyle of Lochalsh

Grantown on Spey

Mallaig

Kingussie

Aberdeen

Glenfinnan Viaduct

S C O T L A N D

Ballater

Fireball Ceremony

Fort William

Pitlochry

Brechin

Montrose

Tobermory

Logierait mortsafes

Forfar

Mull

Oban

Meikleour Hedge

Tealing Dovecote

Dundee

Arbroath

Flambeaux Procession

Perth

NORTH

Crianlarich

Crieff

St Andrews

Fife Ness

SEA

Inveraray

Dunblane

Glenrothes

Firth of Lorn

Wallace Monument

Firth of Forth

N

Lochgilphead

The Pineapple

Dunfermline

North Berwick

Jura

Dumbarton

Burry Man Festival

Greenock

M9

Cumbernauld

Edinburgh

Phantasie Doocot

Largs

Glasgow

M8

Livingston

Renfrew

Motherwell

Rosslyn Chapel

Paisley

Hamilton Mausoleum

Arran

Whuppity Scourie

Tweedmouth Feast

Kilmarnock

Galashiels

Ne'erday Bonfire

Melrose Abbey

Firth of Clyde

Ayr

Common Riding

Byzantine Mausoleum

Campbeltown

Hawick

Jedburgh

Alnwick

Mull of Kintyre

Sanquhar

Moffat

E N G L A N D

Girvan

Drumlanrig Castle

Samye Ling Buddhist Monastery

Morpeth

Johnnie Turner's grave & sculptures

Twelve Apostles

Dumfries Milestone

Appendix

FURTHER READING

Not all these books are in print but most are obtainable free through British libraries. Readers in Britain or overseas can buy some titles through the internet bookshops such as amazon.com, often at a considerable discount.

A272 An Ode to a Road by Pieter Boogaart, Pallas Athene, £14.95, ISBN 1-873429-29-0. A deeply eccentric ramble across the Weald of Sussex and into Hampshire by an Anglophile Dutchman who recognises a daft thing when he sees it.

A Coast to Coast Walk by A Wainwright, Michael Joseph £10.99, ISBN 0718140729. Incredibly, the whole book is hand-written. The expensive and beautifully illustrated coffee-table version is for armchair hikers and loses the flavour of the pocket version.

Eccentric Travellers by John Keay, BBC Consumer Publishing, £9.50, ISBN 0 719 53868. Marvellous yarns about dotty Brits rampaging around the world.

Something Lost Behind the Ranges by John Blashford-Snell, HarperCollins, £18, ISBN 0 00 255034 2. I will resist the temptation to say ditto. This is a sometimes funny, sometimes serious autobiography by Britain's greatest professional soldier-turned-explorer, and may need updating if he survives the trip at the time of writing.

The English Pig by Robert Malcolmson and Stephanos Mastoris, Hambledon Press, £14.95, ISBN I 85285 174 0. Yes, I know it's what hammy German officers say in third-rate war films, but this is a thorough and affectionate portrait in pork.

First Childhood and *A Distant Prospect* by Lord Berners, Phoenix Paperbacks, £6.99 each, ISBN 075380946X and 0753810166 respectively. Memoirs from the above eccentric. Not for you if you find the concept of idle rich offensive, but then they weren't idle (unlike some of today's rich) and they weren't boring (ditto).

Great Stone Circles by Aubrey Burl, Yale University Press, £19.95, ISBN 0 300 07689 4. Academic archaeology but fascinating, good pictures and is that Christian name a coincidence?

Lord Berners: the Last Eccentric by Mark Amory, Pimlico Paperback £12.50, ISBN: 0712665781.

Fiction

The Pickwick Papers by Charles Dickens. Penguin Popular Classics, £1. ISBN 0140621105. If you don't already know it, Dickens creates endless eccentrics here, and many more in his other novels.

The Pursuit of Love by Nancy Mitford (which leads to her *Love in a Cold Climate*). Published together by Modern Library at £15.95; ISBN 0679600906. A thinly disguised Lord Berners appears as Lord Merlin.

The Underground Man by Mick Jackson, Picador, £6.99, ISBN 0330349562. The novelised story of William Cavendish-Bentinck-Scott, the deeply eccentric tunnelling fifth Duke of Portland.

County Index

Asterisk★ denotes counties grouped together

Alphabetical Index